Lecture Notes in Computer Science 10228

More information about this series at http://www.springer.com/series/7408

Lin Zhang · Lei Ren
Fabrice Kordon (Eds.)

Challenges and Opportunity with Big Data

19th Monterey Workshop 2016
Beijing, China, October 8–11, 2016
Revised Selected Papers

Springer

Editors
Lin Zhang
Beihang University
Beijing
China

Lei Ren
Beihang University
Beijing
China

Fabrice Kordon
Université Pierre and Marie Curie
Paris
France

ISSN 0302-9743 ISSN 1611-3349 (electronic)
Lecture Notes in Computer Science
ISBN 978-3-319-61993-4 ISBN 978-3-319-61994-1 (eBook)
DOI 10.1007/978-3-319-61994-1

Library of Congress Control Number: 2017948644

LNCS Sublibrary: SL2 – Programming and Software Engineering

Printed on acid-free paper

This Springer imprint is published by Springer Nature
The registered company is Springer International Publishing AG
The registered company address is: Gewerbestrasse 11, 6330 Cham, Switzerland

Preface

The 2016 edition of the Monterey Workshop was the 19th in the series, initiated in 1993 and devoted to exploring the critical problems associated with cost-effective development of high-quality software systems. Monterey workshops have a rich history of bringing together both American and European scientists who share a common interest in seeing that software development research serves as a catalyst for practical advances in next-generation software-intensive systems. These workshops have been highly praised by participants for their high quality of presentations and discussions and given rise to many new collaborations that have significantly advanced the field.

The year 2016 marked the 23rd anniversary for the Monterey Workshop. For nearly a quarter of century, the Monterey Workshops have established themselves as an important international forum to foster – among academia, industry, and government agencies – the discussion and exchange of ideas, research results, and experience in developing software-intensive systems, and have significantly advanced the field. The community of the workshop participants has grown to become an influential source of ideas and innovations and its impact on the knowledge economy has been felt worldwide. The workshop in 2016 was held in Beijing, China, during October 8–11 2016.

More than 40 scholars, engineers, and students from six countries attended the workshop. Two keynote speeches were given: "Software Decay as a Big-Data Problem View Through the Architecture Lens" by Prof. Nenad Medvidovic from the University of Southern California, USA, and "Performance of Big Data on Small Nodes" by Yong Meng TEO from the National University of Singapore. In all, 27 papers were presented and extended versions of 18 selected papers are included in these proceedings, which address challenging issues in big data and artificial intelligence and their applications in different areas, such as manufacturing and transportation.

As the first Monterey Workshop held outside the United States and Europe, we would like to take this opportunity to thank the Steering Committee for their support and guidance. We also thank the authors and reviewers for their valuable efforts to make the workshop a memorable and successful event.

March 2017

Lin Zhang
Lei Ren
Fabrice Kordon

Organization

Steering Committee

Egidio Astesiano	University of Genoa, Italy
Manfred Broy	TU Munich, Germany
Fabrice Kordon	P. & M. Curie University, France
Luqi	Naval Postgraduate School, USA
Bill Roscoe	Oxford University, UK
Janos Sztipanovts	Vanderbilt University, USA

General Chairs

Lin Zhang	Beihang University, China
Fabrice Kordon	P. & M. Curie University, France

Program Chairs

Du Zhang	Macau University of Science and Technology, Macau, SAR China
Lei Ren	Beihang University, China
Liviu Iftode	Rutgers University, USA

Contents

Theoretical Underpinnings for Big Data

A Hybrid M&S Methodology for Knowledge Discovery 3
Jae Kwon Kim, Jong Sik Lee, and Kang Sun Lee

A Model-Driven Visualization System Based on DVDL 11
Yi Du, Lei Ren, Yuanchun Zhou, and Jianhui Li

A Practical Energy Modeling Method for Industrial Robots in Manufacturing. 25
Wenjun Xu, Huan Liu, Jiayi Liu, Zude Zhou, and Duc Truong Pham

An Optimization Method for User Interface Components Based on Big Data 37
Fei Lyu, Lei Ren, and Yi Du

Clustering-Based Data Aggregation and Routing for Real-Time WirelessHART Communication 43
Feng Li, Chunhui Wang, Lei Ju, and Zhiping Jia

Big Data Management

Constrained Semantic Grammar Enabled Question Answering System 55
Dongsheng Wang, Shi Wang, Weiming Wang, Jianhui Fu, and Yun Dai

Information Composition Analysis and Adaptation Access of CNC Lathes in Cloud Manufacturing Environment 66
Lei Qiu, Chao Yin, and Xiao-bin Li

Interactive Animation Editing Based on Sketch Interaction. 77
Yan Huang, Ti Zhou, Yanfeng Li, Yan Zhang, and Cuixia Ma

Manufacturing Service Reconfiguration Optimization Using Hybrid Bees Algorithm in Cloud Manufacturing 87
Wenjun Xu, Xin Zhong, Yuanyuan Zhao, Zude Zhou, Lin Zhang, and Duc Truong Pham

MyTrace: A Mobile Phone-Based Tourist Spatial-Temporal Behavior Record and Analysis System 99
Lei Dou, Haitao Qu, Xiaoqiang Bi, Yu Zhang, Chongsheng Yu, Jian Qin, Xiaoting Huang, and Xin Li

Big Data Simulation

Multi-source Information Intelligent Collection and Monitoring of CNC Machine Tools Based on Multi-agent 111
Yun Yang, Chao Yin, Xiao-bin Li, and Liang Li

Ontology Management and Ontology Reuse in Web Environment. 122
Yapeng Cui, Lihong Qiao, and Yifan Qie

Research on the Shortest Path of Two Places in Urban Based on Improved Ant Colony Algorithm 131
Yanjuan Hu, Luquan Ren, Hongwei Zhao, and Yao Wang

RUL Prediction of Bearings Based on Mixture of Gaussians Bayesian Belief Network and Support Vector Data Description 139
Qianhui Wu, Yu Feng, and Biqing Huang

Industrial Track of Big Data

Social Recommendation Terms: Probabilistic Explanation Optimization 155
Jie Liu, Lin Zhang, Victor S. Sheng, and Yuanjun Laili

Towards a Holistic Method for Business Process Analytics 168
Gianna Reggio, Maurizio Leotta, Filippo Ricca, and Egidio Astesiano

Traffic Flow Prediction with Improved SOPIO-SVR Algorithm 184
Xuejun Cheng, Lei Ren, Jin Cui, and Zhiqiang Zhang

Workshop Multi-source Information IntelliSense Method Based on IPv6 Intelligent Terminal. 198
Chao Yin, Zhengbing Pan, Xiaobin Li, and Liang Li

Author Index 209

Theoretical Underpinnings for Big Data

A Hybrid M&S Methodology for Knowledge Discovery

Jae Kwon Kim[1], Jong Sik Lee[1], and Kang Sun Lee[2(✉)]

[1] Department of Computer and Information Engineering, Inha University, Incheon, South Korea
jaekwonkorea@naver.com, jslee@inha.ac.kr
[2] Department of Computer Engineering, Myongji University, Yongin, South Korea
ksl@mju.ac.kr

Abstract. M&S (Modeling and Simulation) has been widely used as a decision supporting tool by modeling the structure and dynamics of real-world systems on a computer and simulating the models to answer various what-if questions. As simulation models become complex in their dynamics and structures, more engineers are experiencing difficulties to simulate the models with various real-world scenarios and to discover knowledge from the massive amount of simulation results within a practical time bound. In this paper, we propose a hybrid methodology where the M&S process is combined with a DM (Data Mining) process. Our methodology includes a step to inject simulation outputs to a DM process which generates a prediction model by analyzing pertaining patterns in the simulation outputs. The prediction model can be used to replace simulations, if we need to expedite the M&S-based decision making process. We have applied the proposed methodology to analyze SAM (Surface-to-air missile) and confirmed the applicability.

Keywords: Modeling and simulation · Data mining · Knowledge discovery · Simulation output analysis

1 Introduction

M&S (Modeling and Simulation) is the use of models, including emulators, prototypes, and simulators to develop data as a basis for making managerial or technical decisions [1]. As M&S has been widely used to support decision making on complex systems, more engineers are experiencing difficulties to perform massive amount of simulations and analyze simulation outputs to understand the simulated systems. The needs of discovering knowledge from the simulation outputs become imminent in order to save time and costs for M&S based decision supporting.

Data mining is the knowledge discovery process by finding correlations or patterns among datasets [2]. An efficient data mining technique might be utilized in the post-analysis phase of M&S in order to discover patterns and relations among the simulation outputs and to facilitate the knowledge discovery on the given systems.

L. Zhang et al. (Eds.): Monterey Workshop 2016, LNCS 10228, pp. 3–10, 2017.
DOI: 10.1007/978-3-319-61994-1_1

In this study, we propose a new decision supporting methodology that combines M&S with a data mining technique. We develop simulation models of real-world systems based on DEVS (Discrete Event System Specification) formalism [3], and simulate the DEVS models in various scenarios. Simulation outputs are then sent to the ANN (Artificial Neural Network) - based data mining module, where patterns and relations among the datasets are automatically learned. Based on the ANN prediction model for the simulated system, we can answer what-if questions without going through expensive simulations.

We have applied the proposed methodology in analyzing SAM in AAW. Based on the simulation outputs from SAM simulator, our ANN model successfully learned the relationships between the starting positions of the aircraft and the hit/miss result of the SAM. After the ANN data mining module created the accurate prediction model on the SAM simulator, we were able to utilize it to decision makings on the given system without going through expensive simulations.

This paper is organized as follows. Section 2 reviews the related research works and outlines the research issues. Section 3 proposes our hybrid M&S process with an emphasis on the data mining process. Section 4 illustrates the proposed methodology with an example of SAM simulator. We conclude in Sect. 5 with summary and future works to achieve.

2 Related Research

Remondino proposed two types of usages that combine DM techniques to M&S [4]. The endogenoususe is concerned with providing the agents participating in the simulation with the DM techniques in order to improve their performance. He established data mining agents in the context of a multi-agent system, making use of DM techniques to perform distributed mining. On the other hand, the exogenous application focuses on using DM techniques to analyze the data resulting from the simulation. He performed a series of simulation experiments using an agent based model of a biological phenomenon. Afterwards, he proceeded to perform a DM analysis with the obtained data to detect if there was any novel pattern.

Painter proposed a simulation model that combines data mining and knowledge-based techniques [5]. The simulation model was developed for supporting decisions on the maintenance of aircraft engines, especially to determine life-cycle cost (LCC) and operational availability. Simulation output is subjected to data mining analysis in order to understand system behavior in terms of subsystem interactions and the factors influencing life-cycle metrics. The insights obtained through this exercise are then encapsulated as policies and guidelines to make better decisions on life-cycle asset ownership.

Trepos proposed an automatic approach for mining the simulation outputs on water pollution [6]. He applied two symbolic learning techniques (i.e. ILP (inductive logic programming) and attribute-value technique) on simulation data and successfully detected spatial rules that represent surface flow and pollutant pathways from plot to plot involved in water pollution by herbicides.

As we can learn from the related research works, combining DM techniques to M&S has apparent advantages in acquiring deep knowledge on the given systems and facilitating the decision supporting process.

3 A Hybrid M&S Process

3.1 Overall Process

As shown in Fig. 1, our methodology is comprised of the following two phases:

- Phase I: The target system is represented with DEVS models. Based on the real-world scenarios, the models are simulated under various conditions. The simulation outputs are stored in the database.
- Phase II: Pre-processing is performed on the simulation outputs in order to construct proper training datasets. Then, the training datasets are handed to the data mining process where the relationships and the patterns inside the datasets can be extracted. We use ANN for the data mining process. Detailed explanations on ANN can be found in the following section.

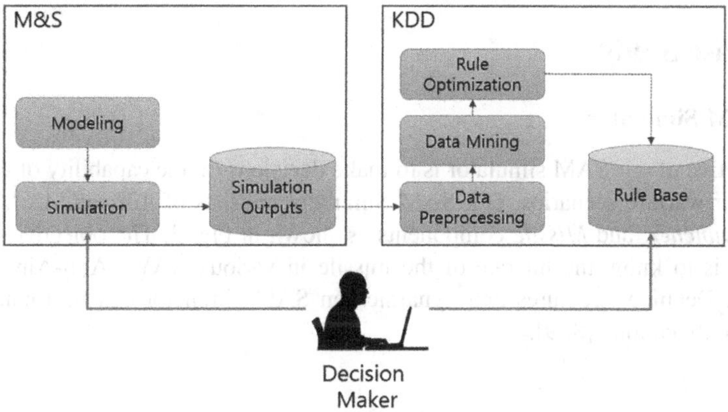

Fig. 1. A proposed method: M&S is performed with KDD process

3.2 Artificial Neural Network

A classification method typically uses univariate analysis, multivariate analysis and artificial neural networks (ANNs). While the univariate analysis is simple to conduct, it is low in accuracy and unable to analyze multi-variables. Multivariate analysis performs well in analyzing multi-variables. However, it is difficult to analyze the relationship between complex variables. ANN is trained using the backpropagation network (BPN) [7] as shown in Fig. 2. The goal and motivation for the backpropagation network

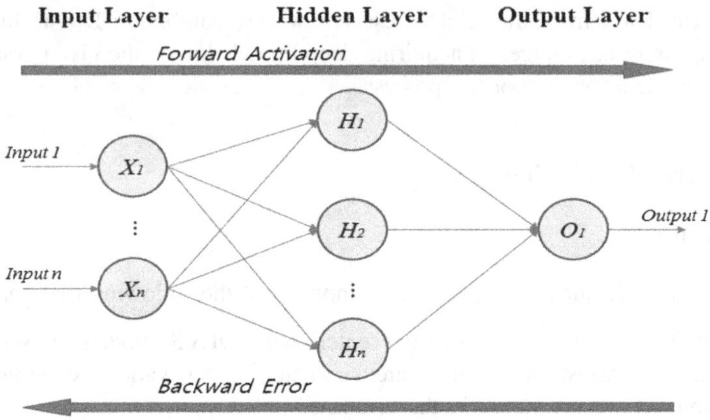

Fig. 2. Backpropagation structure

is to find a way to train a multi-layered neural network such that it can learn the appropriate internal representations to allow it to learn any arbitrary mapping of input to output.

4 A Case Study

4.1 SAM Simulator

The objective of our SAM simulator is to make decisions on the capability of the SAM in anti-war warfare scenarios. Our SAM Simulator consists of *Aircraft*, *AA (Anti-Air) Radar*, *Launcher,* and *Missile* components as shown in Fig. 3. The objective of SAM simulator is to know the hit rate of the missile in various AAW (Anti-Air Warfare) scenarios. Detailed structures and dynamics on SAM simulator can be found in our previous publications [8, 9].

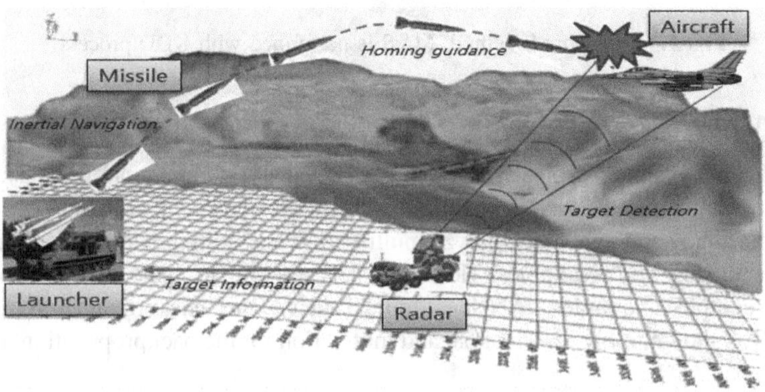

Fig. 3. SAM simulator

4.2 The Hybrid Analysis on SAM

Figure 4 sketches the overall process of analyzing SAM based on the proposed methodology. DEVS based SAM simulation model is composed of 4 atomic models and a single coupled model. Each atomic model sends the results to the internal simulation output database. The ANN data mining process is started with the simulation outputs and continued until it successfully creates a prediction model on SAM.

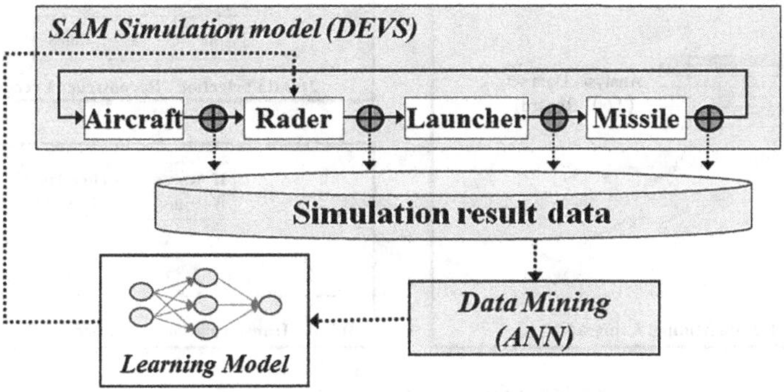

Fig. 4. The hybrid analysis on SAM

In order to analyze SAM by data mining, we should pre-process the simulation outputs in order to construct training datasets for ANN. For the SAM analysis, we extract the position of the aircraft (i.e. Xa, Ya) as the input variables of ANN and Range DR as the output variable of ANN from the raw simulation outputs.

RangeDR is a boundary to detect an aircraft from radar, as shown in Fig. 5. The goal of this prediction model is to determine whether the missile should be fired or not according to Xa and Ya, if the aircraft is found in the area for RangeDR curve. Figure 6 describes the data mining of simulation outputs.

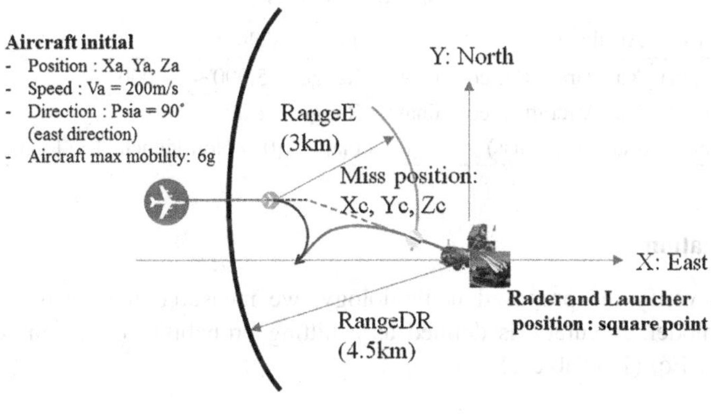

Fig. 5. Decision support section

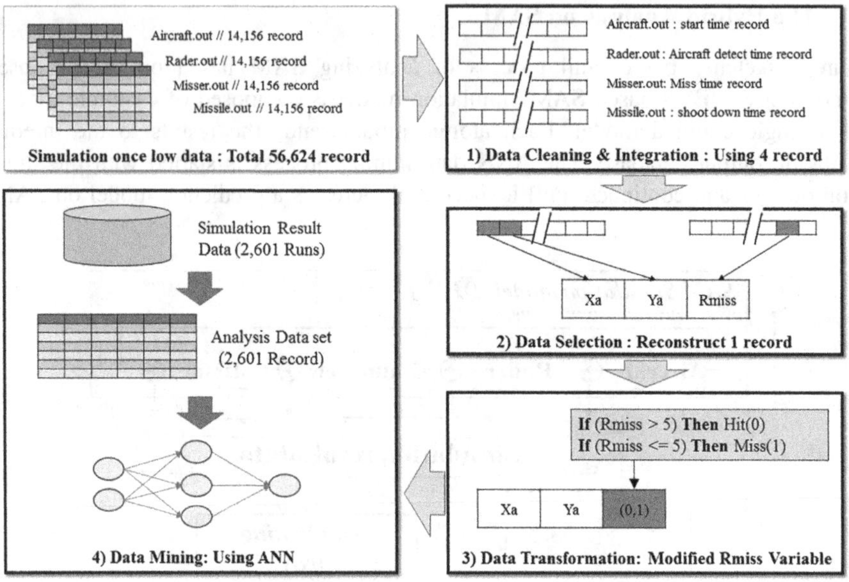

Fig. 6. ANN based data mining process

56,624 records were produced from 2,601 simulations. By going through the data cleaning, integration and selection process, we were able to construct the training datasets which were comprised of the position of the aircraft and the final distance between aircraft and the missile. In the data transformation process, the final distance was transformed to 1 if it was less than 5; if the final distance is less than 5, the missile is considered to hit the aircraft. Table 1 shows the input and output variables for ANN. The ANN model was comprised of 1 input layer, 2 hidden layers and 1 output layer, as shown in Fig. 7.

Table 1. Variables

Parameter	Attribute	Type	Value
x1 (Input)	Xa (Aircraft X-coordinate)	Range	−5,000 ~ −4,000
x2 (Input)	Ya (Aircraft Y-coordinate)	Range	−1,000 ~ −80
Output	Launch (Rmiss)	Flag	[0 = Non-launch, 1 = Launch]

4.3 Evaluation

In order to verify the proposed methodology, we measured the accuracy of ANN prediction model. Accuracy is defined as a hitting probability of the missile and is measured by Eq. (1) (Table 2).

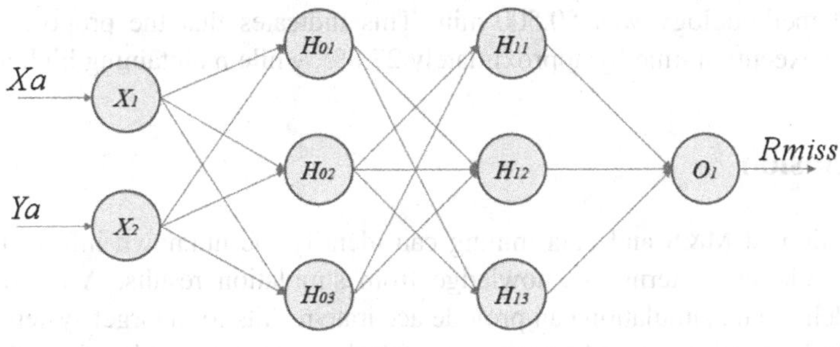

Fig. 7. ANN learning model

Table 2. Confusion matrix

Outcome of the launch test		Predict class	
		Positive	Negative
Actual class	Positive	TP (True positive)	FP (False positive)
	Negative	FN (False negative)	TN (True negative)

$$\text{Accuracy} = (\text{TP} + \text{TN})/(\text{TP} + \text{TN} + \text{FP} + \text{FN}) \quad (1)$$

The accuracy of ANN prediction model was 97.308, which was high enough to be utilized in the prediction of missile behavior.

As shown in Fig. 8, the execution time of our methodology is slightly higher than the M&S-based methodology, since it requires extra time to train ANN. Once the ANN prediction model is generated (after 1800 simulation runs), the decision making process can be done either by the ANN prediction model or by the SAM simulation. Therefore, there is an outstanding time savings after 1800 simulation runs. For 2,600 runs, the

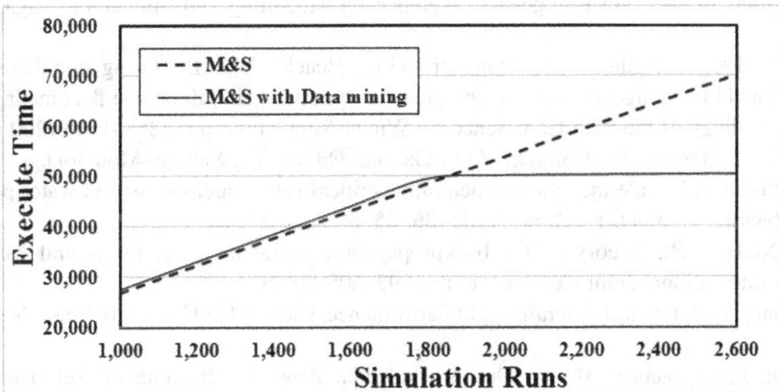

Fig. 8. Execution time: M&S vs the proposed methodology

execution time was approximately 70,000 min for M&S while the execution time of our hybrid methodology was 50,500 min. This indicates that the proposed method reduced the execution time by approximately 27.8%, while maintaining high accuracy.

5 Conclusion

A combination of M&S and data mining can identify the unknown information, and acquire the hidden patterns or knowledge from simulation results. A discrete-event based modeling and simulation can provide accurate results for a target system through mathematical specifications. Moreover, an analysis using data mining from the results of discrete simulations can further support decision making by learning new patterns.

In this paper, we proposed a hybrid methodology that combines M&S and data mining for the analysis of SAM in AAW. The proposed methodology is efficient enough to support decision makings on the SAM simulator with approximately 95% accuracy and 27% speedup. In the future, we will attempt to increase the accuracy of the prediction model and devise a more rigorous process that combines M&S and data mining.

Acknowledgement. This work was supported by Defense Acquisition Program Administration and Agency for Defense Development under the contract UD080042AD, Republic of Korea.

References

1. Taylor, S.J., Khan, A., Tolk, K.L., Morse, A., Yilmaz, L., Zander, J.: Grand challenges on the theory of modeling and simulation. In: Proceedings of the Symposium on Theory of Modeling & Simulation-DEVS Integrative M&S, p. 34 (2013)
2. Jiawei, H., Kamber, M.: Data Mining: Concepts and Techniques. The Morgan Kaufmann Series, 2nd edn., pp. 1–6. Elsevier, Amsterdam (2006)
3. Zeigler, B.P., Praehofer, H., Kim, T.G.: Theory of Modeling and Simulation: Integrating Discrete Event and Continuous Complex Dynamic Systems. Academic Press, Cambridge (2000). pp. 76–96
4. Remondino, M., Correndo, G.: Data mining applied to agent based simulation. In: Proceedings of the 19th European Conference on Modelling and Simulation, Riga, Latvia (2005)
5. Painter, M.K., Erraguntla, M., Hogg Jr., G.L., Beachkofski, B.: Using simulation, data mining, and knowledge discovery techniques for optimized aircraft engine fleet management. In: Proceedings of the 38th Conference on Winter Simulation, pp. 1253–1260 (2006)
6. Trépos, R., Masson, V., Cordier, M.O., Gascuel-Odoux, C., Salmon-Monviola, J.: Mining simulation data by rule induction to determine critical source areas of stream water pollution by herbicides. Comput. Electron. Agric. **86**, 75–88 (2012)
7. Hecht-Nielsen, R.: Theory of the backpropagation neural network. In: Neural Networks, IJCNN International Joint Conference, pp. 593–605 (1989)
8. Filippone, A.: Advanced Aircraft Flight Performance. Cambridge University Press, New York (2012)
9. Leeman, E.L.: Tactical Missile Design, 2nd edn. American Institute of Aeronautics and Astronautics, Reston (2006)

A Model-Driven Visualization System Based on DVDL

Yi Du[1(✉)], Lei Ren[2], Yuanchun Zhou[1], and Jianhui Li[1]

[1] Department of Big Data Technology and Application Development, Computer Network Information Center, Chinese Academy of Sciences, Beijing, China
duyi@cnic.cn

[2] School of Automation Science and Electrical Engineering, Beihang University, Beijing, China

Abstract. Though model-driven engineering (MDE) methodology has made significant improvements in terms of efficiency and effectiveness in many areas of software development, the same cannot be said in the development of data visualization systems. With this challenge in mind, this paper introduces DVDL, a modular and hierarchical visualization description language that take advantage of the model-based design of MDE to describe visualization development at an abstract level. This paper also presents DVIZ, a visualization system based on DVDL. With a growing popularity and demand for data visualization technology, a number of visualization tools have emerged in recent years, though few would be considered as adaptable and scalable as DVIZ. Some of its key features include the ability for users to select data source, configure properties of visual elements, publish and share result. The system also supports real-time result generation and multi-visuals interaction. Lastly, since DVIZ is web-based, it supports distribution of result across various social media.

Keywords: Visualization system · User interface description language · Model-driven development methodology · End user programming

1 Introduction

With visualization, one can discover new information and obtain deep understanding behind the vast amount of data presented to them. With an increasing need for this kind of visual communication, more is needed to be invested in development of data visualization tools. Development of visualization tools requires many steps, including data conversion, visual mapping, view conversion and more [1], which can be achieved with a model-driven approach. Model-driven engineering (MDE) is a software development methodology that focuses on creating and exploiting conceptual models to solve a specific problem. This approach, aimed to increase productivity and simplify the design process by maximizing compatibility between systems, has proven to be efficient and effective in the development of interactive application sequences. External library like Prefuse [2] and Lyra [5] are examples of visual development tools that reflects the principles of model-driven approach. Nonetheless, model-driven approach

L. Zhang et al. (Eds.): Monterey Workshop 2016, LNCS 10228, pp. 11–24, 2017.
DOI: 10.1007/978-3-319-61994-1_2

is not without some notable compromises that prevent wide adoptions in area of data visualization system development. For one, models created in the process are often too specific to be applied appropriately by most visualization system development tools. This also makes them difficult to be reused. Additionally, most visualization system development tools are difficult to use and incompatible to rescale. Given these challenges, model-driven methodology is still not popular by visualization system developers.

This paper introduces DVDL, a description language that paves the groundwork for developing visualization systems. DVDL inherits many properties from E-UIDL, an extendable user interface description language that divides the user interface into seven modules using a modular and hierarchical design. Fundamentally, DVDL is a specification language that is built on the principles of model-driven engineering. The paper also presents DVIZ, a versatile and scalable visualization system developed with DVDL description language. This system allows users to organize and import their data sources, configure properties and setting, publish and share results.

The rest of this paper is structured in five sections. The first section serves as an in-depth study of model-driven design and brief description of several visualization aid development tools currently available. Then, the second section introduces and describes DVDL and its qualities. Next, the third section focuses on the design and implementation of DVIZ visualization system and its relation to DVDL. Section 4 provides some preliminary examples of data visualization using DVIZ. Finally, the fifth section is a brief conclusion and discussion for the paper.

2 Related Works

2.1 Model-Driven Methodology and Description Language

Model-driven engineering methodology is designed to improve efficiency and productivity of a software development process by systematizing the process into different abstract models. This design has been verified in the development of interactive applications [6–8]. User interface description language, or UIDL, is a description language based on model-driven development methodology. By working with abstract models, designers and developers are able to collaborate on creating user interfaces in a standardized and synchronized manner. Some popular examples of UIDL for traditional graphic interface include UIML, XML, DSIL, XIML, UsiXML and MARIA. E-UIDL [9, 10] takes advantage of these characteristics of UIDL, and enhances them with supports for scaling and abstraction, to deliver a new model of UIDL and related tools. Some other description languages worth mentioning are VisQL and Vega. VisQL is designed by van Vijk [11] to help describe transitions and navigations of visuals. This language tackles the issue on an algorithmic level by establishing the mathematical model of the interaction process and giving an equivalent description. VisQL evolves from Polaris. Thus, it shares similar features like organizing data query, analysis and visuals, as well as supporting multiple types of visualization type, such as table, graph, map and timeline. VisQL continues to evolve over time, now supporting design and implementation of Tableau system. However, since VisQL has not been made public, we are unable to examine its scalability and other properties. Vega, on the other hand, is a new visual declarative language designed by Jeffrey Heer [12, 13] based on his experience with visualization development tools [2, 3] and systems [5]. Vega is in the format of JSON. Incorporating declarative programming concept, the language and its related tools and systems are useful for developing visuals, by dividing the visuals into several key abstract components, such as data, data transform, scales, guides, and marks. However, when it was originally conceived, Vega primarily concerns development of a single visual and thus it has difficulties when required to generate and interact with multiple visuals.

2.2 Visualization Systems

Visualization systems are applications designed to visualize data by designers and end-users. They are intuitive and easy-to-use, and do not require much effort or prior experience in order to generate a visual. Though, because of high level of abstraction, these applications are usually not as versatile in terms of data analysis. Visualization systems can be categorize into grammar-based and chart-based. Generally, grammar-based visualization systems are more versatile in term of functionalities and allows more customization by users than chart-based systems, which only require the user to select the visualization method. Though, the latter system excels in the area of affordance and is more suitable for people with little background in design. Examples of chart-based visualization systems include Many Eyes [14], which begins with the option for users to select the visualization method after importing the data. Then, it will generate the visuals based on the selected method and appropriate configurations. The system provides a compatible data model, which in theory would facilitate the addition of new visualization methods. In reality, the system performs poorly because models and association between interaction and visualization are often not properly defined. Likewise, Polaris [4] describes the visualization at the graphics level and is able to generate multi-dimensional visual from data using scatter plot. Polaris is based on Tableau, and has achieved great success among corporations. Also, another example would be ParanoramicData [15], which also supports hand and pen gestures to facilitate visual and associative analysis. However, this system can only follow few basic visualization methods and has no model supports, and thus not suitable for more complex data analysis. All of the systems mentioned do not support option to share result, with the exception of Many Eyes, and so distribution of results would be an issue.

3 DVDL

3.1 Design Features

E-UIDL [10] is a model-driven user interface description language. It incorporates modular design principles by dividing the user interface into seven modules: AFUI, CUI, ADATAMODEL, CDATAMODEL, UM2, MAPPING and RESOURCE. E-UIDL supports multi-layer definition of user interface, and is noted for its independence, scalability, and reusability. With E-UIDL, one can implement pen-based and adaptive user interface as well as interface generation automation [9].

DVDL, an acronym for data visualization description language, combines some of the key features of E-UIDL with characteristics of data visualization to provide a description language for developing visualization systems. DVDL inherits several of main properties from its source. For one, DVDL is modular. With regards to data visualization, it is able to describe each of the sub-systems, such as data source, layout, visualization methods, configuration settings and data association, independently. This modular approach not only improves the readability of DVDL itself, but it also enhances the reusability of each modules. Though, the degree of improvement depends on the granularity of modules. DVDL also supports multi-layer description. This feature allows it to make certain assumptions and basic recommendations in terms of type of visualization based on the description at different abstract layers. Therefore, with DVDL, one can develop data visuals more efficiently. Moreover, DVDL is designed with scalability in mind. Regardless how current visualization and interactive technology evolves or new ones emerge, DVDL is able to continue to provide support given its modular nature.

3.2 Component Modules

Based on the design principles of modularity, hierarchy, and scalability, we are able to offer a graphic interpretation of DVDL (Fig. 1). Figure 1 is a graphic representation of the XML schema that describes the structure of DVDL. In the diagram, each rectangle represents a component. The plus "+" or minus "–" signs following each rectangle indicate whether if the component is expanded. The number values underneath each rectangle represent the number of times the component is permitted to appear. The rectangles marked "S", "C", and "A" signifies "Sequence", "Choice" and "All" models, respectively. DVDL is the root structure of data visualization description language. It includes the basic attributes of a visualization description file, such as visual identifier, name, and version information. As shown in Fig. 1, DVDL consists of five modules: AFUI, CV, ADATAMODEL, CVDATAMODEL and MAPPING. DVDL has a one-to-many mapping with each of its modules. This means that in a DVIZ system, each interface description file may include one or more CV, CVDATAMODEL or MAPPING. Because of the reasonable abstraction of interface description in E-UIDL and similarity between developing visualization and user interface, DVDL inherits the description of AFUI, ADATAMODEL and MAPPING from E-UIDL. For more information regarding E-UIDL description of AFUI, ADATAMODEL and MAPPING, refer to literature [10].

The CV module is defined as the concrete description of the DVDL model, whose XML schema is shown in Fig. 2. From this figure, we see that the CV module stays relatively independent from the individual nodes. Having these modules independent can ensure reusability at an abstract level. Thus, this design gives developers the flexibility to add new visual support, or remove unwanted ones. The nodes currently shown in Fig. 2 include different visualization method such as line chart, histogram, scattered plot, pie chart, radar chart, chord diagram, K-line graph, force graph, point

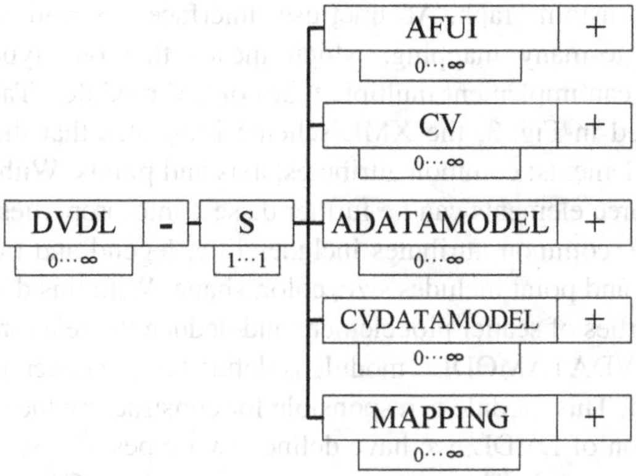

Fig. 1. Graphic representation XML schema of DVDL

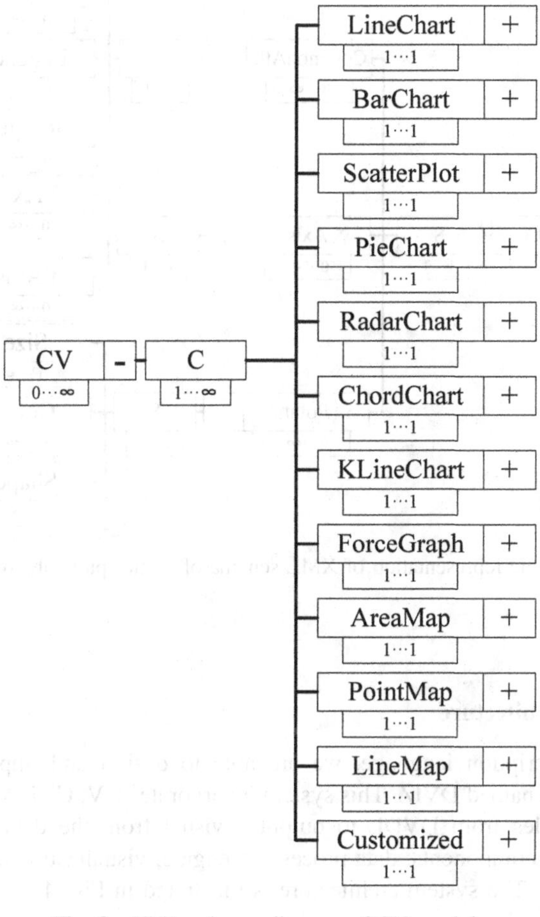

Fig. 2. XML schema diagram of CV module

map, line map and custom graph. Abstract user interface description module and CV module has a one-to-many mapping, which means that one type of abstract UI description module can implement multiple types of CV modules. Take scatter plot for instance, exemplified in Fig. 3, the XML scheme illustrates that the plot consists of three major visual elements: common attributes, axis and points. With certain degree of abstraction, these three elements can be further dissect into properties. For example, as shown in the figure, common attributes includes title, legend and range; axis include both x- and y- axis, and point includes size, color, shape. With this description, one can configure the properties of scatter plot element and deduce the relation between the plot and the data. The CVDATAMODEL module is defined as the concrete data description of the DVDL model. This module is responsible for constructing the visual description. In the current version of DVDL, we have defined two types of visualization structure, namely tabular and network. These two types are denoted as “CTable” and “CGraph”.

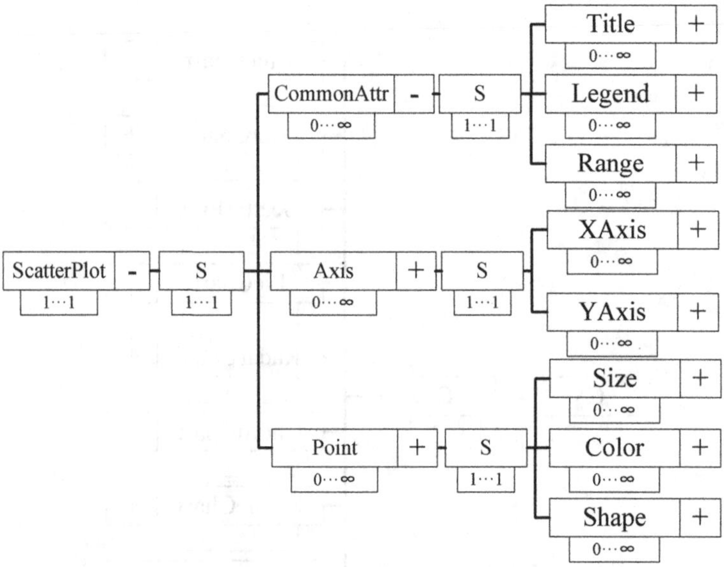

Fig. 3. Graphic representation of XML schema of scatter plot submodule in CV

4 DVIZ

4.1 System Architecture

With DVDL description language, we are able to design and implement a visual generation system named DVIZ. This system incorporates CV, CVDATAMODEL and MAPPING modules from DVDL to output a visual from the data input. DVIZ is divided into three components: data processing engine, visualization engine and result generating engine. The system architecture is illustrated in Fig. 4.

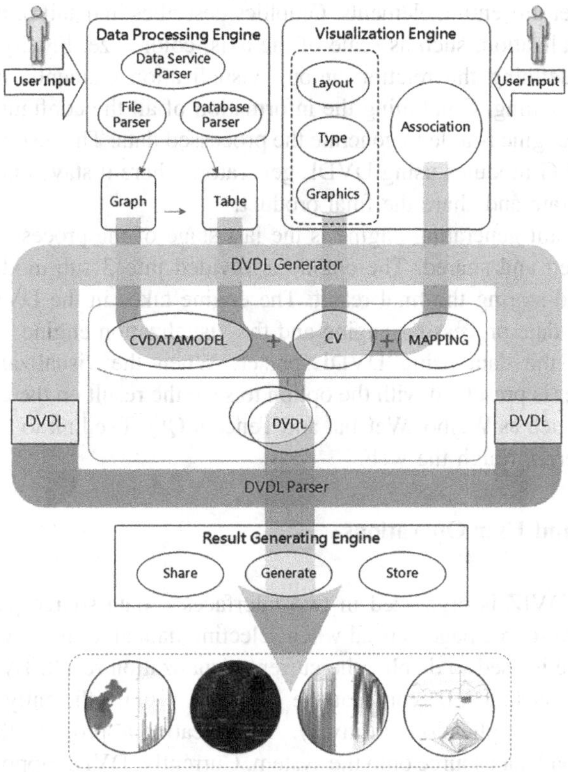

Fig. 4. System architecture

First, the user interacts with the data processing engine. Essentially, the data processing engine takes in the data source and processes it based on a visualization method. While processing, the engine is able to organize the data into tabular structure or network structure, depending on the input data type. The structure of the data can later be altered, thanks to interoperability between the two structure types. The processed data is then stored in the CVDATAMODEL module in DVDL form using DVDL generator, where it will stay until for further operations. The data processing engine is divided into 3 sub-modules, namely file parser, database parser and data service parser. The file parser can read up to four tabular file types (.CSV, .TXT, .XLS, and .XLSX) and two network file types (.GML and .GEXF). The database parser is able to parse relational databases like MySQL, Oracle, SQLServer, as well as NoSQL database types like MongoDB. The data service parser can parse both static and dynamic data service, including those from third-parties.

Second, the user interacts with the visualization engine. The visualization engine is considered to be the core component of DVIZ. It collects the processed data from the data processing engine and generates a series of visualization configurations based on the DVDL description. The engine is comprised of different configuration modules for layout, visual types, graphics, and association. Layout is the overall presentation of the visual result, for instance the visual and controls displayed. Visual type defines the type of visual and other presenting elements. Graphics describes in detail of all the elements required for visualization, such as scale of the axis, color, size. Finally, association is responsible for defining the relation among visualization elements, or between the elements and the setting. Combining the information of all the configuration modules, the visualization engine is able to generate the processed data. The result is stored in the CV and MAPPING modules using DVDL generator, where it stays until the engine is prepared to generate and share the final product.

Lastly, the result generating engine is the last stage of the process where the final visual is generated and shared. The engine is divided into 3 sub-modules for generating, sharing and storing the final result. The engine takes in the DVDL description processed by the data processing engine and the visualization engine, and outputs the visual based on the data using DVDL parser. When the visualization process is complete, the user is presented with the option to save the result on the cloud or share it on social media such as Weibo, WeChat and Tencent QQ. The link to the result can be accessed anywhere through the web.

4.2 Features and User Operations

Loading Data. DVIZ is organized in two interfaces – data source page and visualization page. Data source page is used when selecting data and saving visuals, whereas visualization page is used to display the current visualization result. By organizing the user interface as such, DVIZ can manage data and visual efficiently and users can navigate through the application intuitively. After creating a 'project', the user is given the option to upload data source onto the system. Currently, DVIZ supports up to 5 files, 3 relational databases, 1 non-relational database and 2 data services. Steps to upload data source is illustrated in Fig. 5. First, user selects the data source type (Fig. 5a1). Then the

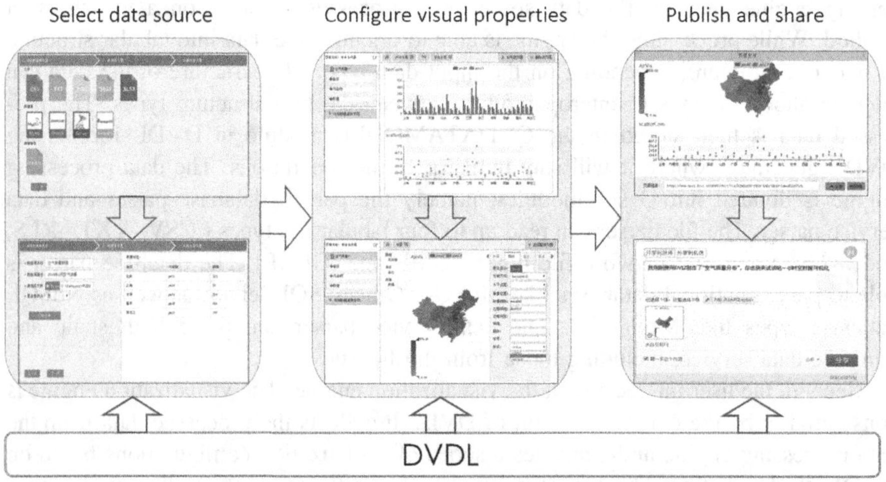

Fig. 5. DVIZ system interface, including options to select (a1), upload and preview (a2) data source, configure layout (b1) and visualization properties (b2), preview (c1) and share (c2) results.

user formulates data details and preview portions of data (Fig. 5a2). Lastly, the user checks for final adjustment. After each step, CVDATAMODEL will automatically update itself and the data is uploaded. Take an arbitrary .CSV file for instance, exemplified in Fig. 5, after step A, CVDATAMODEL would update its unique identifier, column name, column types and other properties (Table 1).

Table 1. CDATAMODEL instance in JSON format


```
{
    id:"cdata1dee4b2c05c5",
    desc:"cdatasample",
    type:"ctable",
    header:["Car", "MPG", "Cylinders", "Displacement", "Horsepower", "Weight", "Accelera-
tion", "Model", "Origin"],
    value:[
        ["Chevrolet Chevelle Malibu", 18, 8, 307, 130, 3504, 12, 70, "US"],
        ["Buick Skylark", 320, 15, 8, 350, 165, 3693, 11.5, 70, "US"],
        ...
        ]
    type:["nominal", "ordinal", "ordinal", "ordinal", "ordinal", "ordinal", "ordinal", "ordinal",
"nominal"]}
}
```


Configuring Visual Settings. After the data is successfully uploaded, the user is able to arrange the presentation of the visualization on the configuration panel. The user has the option to select or reset data source, change layout, adjust data correlation, move visuals, as well as many other features. As demonstrated in Fig. 6, the screen is divided into two sections. On one side, the user is presented with the current visualization, and on the other side, the user is presented with configuration panel that allows the user to "drag and drop" and display changes in real time. The system supports the use of multiple data sources in the same visualization result, and allows user to replace data source if needed. Different diagrams or charts support different configuration items, which also can be accessed via the configuration panel, as shown in Fig. 7. In the figure, the interface is divided in two parts. On the left, the user sees the default scatter plot generated by the application when the dataset is initially uploaded, with elements like x-, y- axis and color pre-defined. On the right, the user is given the option to customize these elements as well as define new ones, such as creating a title, adding grid or highlight data points. If the result contains multiple visuals, then it is necessary to define the relation between them. Association configuration allows multiple graphs to communicate with one another. Thus, when multiple diagrams or charts are associated, any changes or adjustment made on one visual will reflect correspondingly on other one. DVIZ provides four pre-build layout options as well as option to customize layout for users to arrange their data at will. After the layout is finalized, the selected layout is displayed. DVIZ also provides users several theme choices, so that even users with no prior experience in visual design are able to produce an appealing and stylized visual with little effort. The final layout and visual is displayed in the display panel.

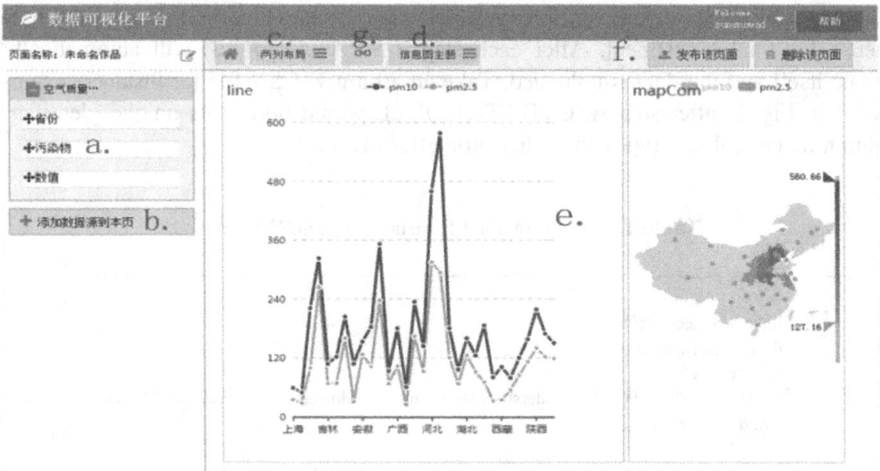

Fig. 6. Visual configuration interface, including options to view data fields (a), change or re-upload data source (b), change layout (c), change theme (d), preview result (e), share or delete page (f) and define data/visual associations (g).

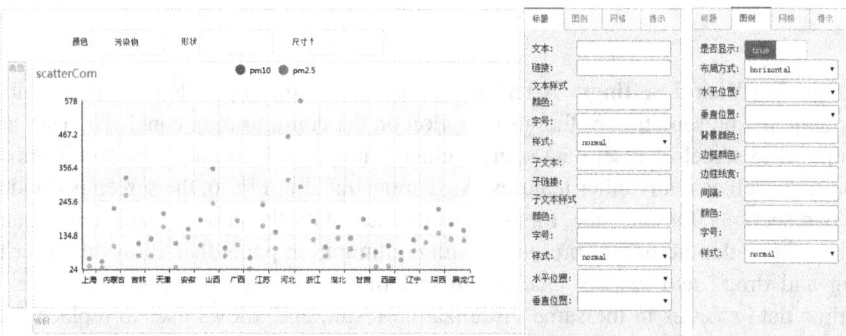

Fig. 7. Configuration interface for a scatter plot, including visual preview (left) and configuration panels (right)

Publishing Result. After the user is satisfied with their visual, the visualization process is complete. DVIZ will then provide the user with an URL link for sharing, as shown in Fig. 6c1. With that URL, the user can import the visual onto their personal web page, presentation or paper, or share link via various social media such as Weibo and WeChat, as shown in Fig. 6c2.

5 Use Cases

DVIZ supports a variety of data types, and both static and dynamic data services. In a static service, the parameter values do not change with respect to time, whereas in a dynamic service, parameter values vary over time. An example of a static service is shown in Fig. 8. Here, we define how DVIZ should treat data service as data source, design and generate visual. In this example, we include two different data services, named service 1 and service 2. Service 1 gives the current nation-wide air quality. It includes a parameter called “type”, which the user can select different air quality index, PM2.5 for example. After connecting to the server, DVIZ will show the generated visual on the display panel, as shown in Fig. 9. After which, user can further design and configure other properties on the visual.

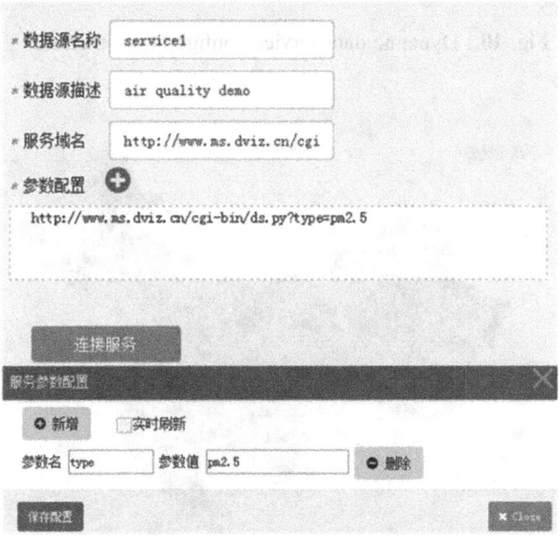

Fig. 8. Static data service configuration interface

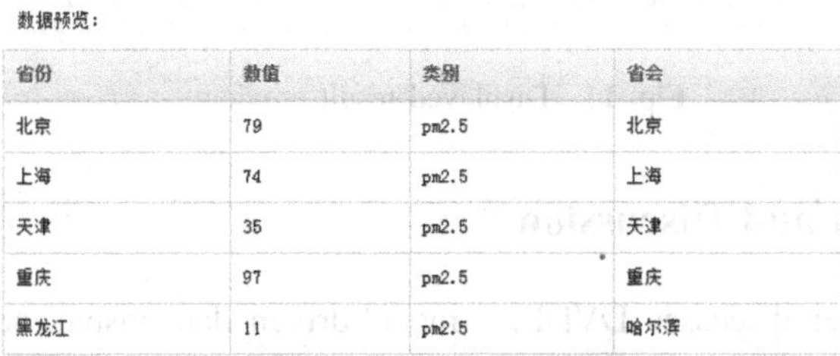
数据预览：

省份	数值	类别	省会
北京	79	pm2.5	北京
上海	74	pm2.5	上海
天津	35	pm2.5	天津
重庆	97	pm2.5	重庆
黑龙江	11	pm2.5	哈尔滨

Fig. 9. Data preview interface

An example of the configuration panel for a dynamic service is displayed in Fig. 10. The data in this Figure shows the nation-wide status of PM2.5 in the period from January 1, 2015 to January 31, 2015. After connecting to the dynamic service, data with corresponding initial parameter is displayed on the preview panel. After further configuring, the visual with dynamic service is shown in the display panel, as shown in Fig. 11. Since this is a dynamic service, the visual will change over time.

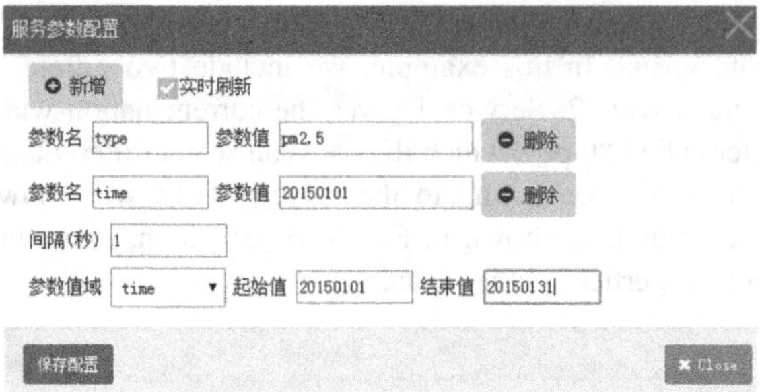

Fig. 10. Dynamic data service configuration interface

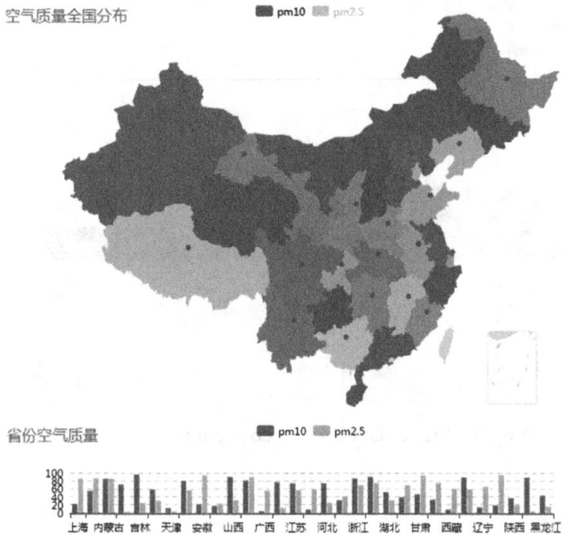

Fig. 11. Displayed result preview

6 Conclusion and Discussion

In brief, this paper discusses DVDL, a model-driven data visualization description language that inherits from E-UIDL. The paper also introduces DVIZ, a visualization system developed with DVDL, and explains its design and implementation. DVIZ uses CV, CVDATAMODEL and MAPPING models from DVDL model, and allows users to generate and configure visuals based on data in real-time. The system supports both static and dynamic data service, creating a visual that varies with time or changes with parameters. The system can also make association between multiple visuals. Finally, since DVIZ is also web-based, it supports sharing and publication of result on social media.

Comparing to other visualization systems currently exist, the most important feature of DVIZ is that the system is based on DVDL, an extensible description language. Because of this flexibility, one can with DVDL to develop other visualization systems, like DVIZ, that are specifically catered to visualization engineers, statisticians or personnel across other professions. For example, if system A and B are both developed with DVDL for statisticians and visualization engineers, respectively, when importing visuals designed by system A to system B, visualization engineers can further investigate the details of a given data along with existing visuals. This way, cost on communication is minimized when a statistician and a visualization engineer collaborate on a visualization task [16]. DVDL's modular and hierarchical design method enables the possibility for conversion and collaboration between multiple systems.

DVIZ also has some shortcomings. For one, DVIZ does not supports operations on the data while in the configuration panel. Also, DVIZ currently only supports 9 visual types. To improve DVIZ for future uses, we can have statistical index of existing data to reflect any changes in configuration in real-time, as well as to add supports for more visual types, such as parallel coordinates.

Although E-UIDL has demonstrated that the modular description language for user interface may expands to new interface elements and interactions, visualization has its own unique characteristics. Based on current investigation and study, the logical next step would be to further explore the applications of all the DVDL modules, and to build on top of the existing functions, for example the option to give recommendations based on data uploaded.

Acknowledgement. This work was supported by the National Key Research Program of China under Grant No. 2016YFB1000600 and No. 2016YFB0501900, Natural Science Foundation of China under Grant No. 61402435 and No. 61572057.

References

1. Shneiderman, B.: The eyes have it: a task by data type taxonomy for information visualizations. In: The Craft of Information Visualization: Readings and Reflections, pp. 364–371 (1996)
2. Heer, J., Card, S.K., Landay, J.A.: Prefuse: a toolkit for interactive information visualization. In: Proceedings of the SIGCHI Conference on Human Factors in Computing Systems, pp. 421–430 (2005)
3. Bostock, M., Ogievetsky, V., Heer, J.: D^3 data-driven documents. IEEE Trans. Vis. Comput. Graph. **17**, 2301–2309 (2011)
4. Stolte, C., Tang, D., Hanrahan, P.: Polaris: a system for query, analysis, and visualization of multidimensional relational databases. IEEE Trans. Vis. Comput. Graph. **8**, 52–65 (2002)
5. Satyanarayan, A., Heer, J.: Lyra: an interactive visualization design environment. Comput. Graph. Forum **33**, 351–360 (2014)
6. Paterno', F., Santoro, C., Spano, L.D.: MARIA: a universal, declarative, multiple abstraction-level language for service-oriented applications in ubiquitous environments. ACM Trans. Comput.-Hum. Interact. **16**, 1–30 (2009)

7. Nichols, J., Myers, B.A.: Creating a lightweight user interface description language: an overview and analysis of the personal universal controller project. ACM Trans. Comput.-Hum. Interact. **16**, 1–37 (2009)
8. Navarre, D., Palanque, P., Ladry, J.-F., Barboni, E.: ICOs: a model-based user interface description technique dedicated to interactive systems addressing usability, reliability and scalability. ACM Trans. Comput.-Hum. Interact. **16**, 1–56 (2009)
9. Yi, D., Tian, F., Ma, C., Dai, G.: A user interface generation framework based on multi-scale description method. Chin. J. Comput. **36**(11), 2179–2190 (2013)
10. Yi, D., Deng, C., Tian, F., Dai, G.: Extensible user interface description language. J. Softw. **24**(5), 1127–1142 (2013)
11. van Wijk, J.J., Nuij, W.A.: A model for smooth viewing and navigation of large 2D information spaces. IEEE Trans. Vis. Comput. Graph. **10**, 447–458 (2004)
12. Satyanarayan, A., Wongsuphasawat, K., Heer, J.: Declarative interaction design for data visualization. Presented at the Proceedings of the 27th Annual ACM Symposium on User Interface Software and Technology, Honolulu, Hawaii, USA (2014)
13. Heer, J., Bostock, M.: Declarative language design for interactive visualization. IEEE Trans. Vis. Comput. Graph. **16**, 1149–1156 (2010)
14. Viegas, F.B., Wattenberg, M., van Ham, F., Kriss, J., McKeon, M.: ManyEyes: a site for visualization at internet scale. IEEE Trans. Vis. Comput. Graph. **13**, 1121–1128 (2007)
15. Zgraggen, E., Zeleznik, R., Drucker, S.M.: PanoramicData: data analysis through pen & touch. IEEE Trans. Vis. Comput. Graph. **20**, 2112–2121 (2014)
16. Yi, D., Tian, F., Dai, G.: A development approach based on extensible user interface description language. J. Softw. **26**(7), 1772–1784 (2015)

A Practical Energy Modeling Method for Industrial Robots in Manufacturing

Wenjun Xu[1,2(✉)], Huan Liu[1,2], Jiayi Liu[1,2], Zude Zhou[1,2], and Duc Truong Pham[3]

[1] School of Information Engineering, Wuhan University of Technology, Wuhan 430070, China
{xuwenjun, jyliu, zudezhou}@whut.edu.cn, huangewanting@foxmail.com

[2] Key Laboratory of Fiber Optic Sensing Technology and Information Processing, Ministry of Education, Wuhan 430070, China

[3] Department of Mechanical Engineering, School of Engineering, University of Birmingham, Birmingham B15 2TT, UK
d.t.pham@bham.ac.uk

Abstract. Industrial robots (IRs) are widely used in modern manufacturing systems, and energy problem of IRs is paid more attention to meet requirements of environment protection. Therefore, it is necessary to investigate the approaches to optimize the energy consumption of IRs, and the energy consumption model is the basis for enabling such approaches. Usually, energy consumption modeling for IRs is based on dynamic parameters identification. Meanwhile, the physical parameters, e.g. angle, velocity, acceleration, torque, etc. are all the necessary data of parameter identification. However, since the parts of IRs are not easy to be disassembled and the sensor modules can not be installed easily inside IRs, it is difficult to obtain all such physical parameters through sensing method, in particular the torque data. In this context, a practical energy modeling method by measuring total power for IRs is proposed. This method avoids the problem of directly measuring relevant parameters inside IRs, and the parameter identification process is gradually carried out by several excitation experiments. The experimental results show that the proposed energy modeling method can be used to predict the energy consumption of the process used in robot movement in manufacturing processes, and it can also efficiently support the analysis of the energy consumption characteristics of IRs.

Keywords: Industrial robots · Energy modeling · Energy consumption · Power measurement

1 Introduction

In recent decades, in the context of the world economic globalization and integration, cloud manufacturing is proposed and developed to transform the way that enterprises do business from traditional production-oriented manufacturing to service-oriented manufacturing [1–3]. Since the industrial robots (IRs) have the advantages of high efficiency, stability, reliability and can work in harsh environment, they have been

L. Zhang et al. (Eds.): Monterey Workshop 2016, LNCS 10228, pp. 25–36, 2017.
DOI: 10.1007/978-3-319-61994-1_3

widely applied in manufacturing systems in order to facilitate the manufacturing intelligence in cloud manufacturing. Meanwhile, the energy consumption optimization of IRs is also becoming an important issue in cloud manufacturing, and it can also be beneficial to the reduction of carbon dioxide emissions. From the viewpoint of economy, energy-efficient operation of IRs is useful to reduce the costs of manufacturing enterprises. The energy consumption modeling of IRs based on mathematical formulas can be more scientific to study the influence of operation states on energy consumption, which provides guides to facilitate the energy-efficient strategies.

Aiming at energy consumption minimization in IRs, many literatures have described effective methods. For instance, in literatures [4, 5], an energy optimization is investigated by hardware replacements. Energy-optimal IRs selection for specific operations is described in [6], and it can be found in literatures [7–10] that many past researches focused on energy-optimal paths and motion profiles, and also considered the system dynamics and control. At last, energy consumption can be regarded as a cost function to be minimized in order to determine optimal design parameters in the field of autonomous IRs for service applications [11, 12], such as gear reduction ratios and/or actuator placements [13, 14].

In most cases, an effective method must synthetically consider the involved cost and the energy consumption reduction results. The hardware modification used in IRs, which always means high cost to the manufacturing enterprises, is not suitable for large-scale practical applications. Hence, the energy consumption analysis of IRs based on no hardware modifications should be paid more attention to. However, energy consumption modeling is a key element to analyze the energy consumption of IRs based on software methods. Energy consumption modeling method of this paper mainly contains joint motor power modeling, the energy consumption of the peripheral equipment, which can be obtained by the methods in [15, 16], is not considered. Because the energy consumption modeling reflects the relationship between the joint motion and power of the IRs, and the joint power can be calculated by joint torque and joint velocity, therefore the main content of this method is joint torque modeling, and the parameter estimation is one of the most important steps in the process of torque modeling.

2 Related Works

As for parameter estimation, it mainly has three kinds of methods, CAD drawings, physical experiments and identifications [17]. For the CAD drawings, an accurate model is needed to obtain the inertial parameters of the IRs in advance from the manufacturer, but most of the time the manufacturer is not willing to provide these parameters, and for the method of physical experiments, the accuracy of its estimation often depends on the accuracy of the measuring devices, plenty physical experiments and priori knowledge of robot mechanical structures are necessary. But the former two cannot consider the actual factors of joints, including the joint friction and elastic, so identification which considered the actual joint characteristics based on dynamic theory and huge amounts of measuring data is discussed in this paper. On the other hand, in terms of torque measurement, literature [18] by measuring current, this method can easily obtain any joint torque value. Literature [19] used the multi-dimension wrist joint torque sensor to measure the torque at the wrist joint, the output only contains information about the terminal mechanical arm's inertial parameters, and base force sensor was used in [20], because the base force sensor installed in the base of IRs, all mechanical arm barycentric parameters will influence the torque output, therefore the usage of the base force sensor can identify all the barycentric parameter values by one-time identification. However, this method suffers from the fact that joint friction parameters cannot be estimated. Literature [21] combines internal current measurement and external base force measurement to improve the accuracy of the parameter identification.

This paper used a ABB industrial robot as the experimental object, which is a commercial product, and it is not easy to install current sensor or torque sensor module inside, thus a practical method by measuring energy consumption from embedded power measurement module is proposed, and this module can monitor the power of IRs in real-time. As only the terminal joint is driven, torque value can be directly calculated by the total power, stationary power and joint velocity, by solving the linear model used the least-square method, identification results are obtained. From the joint which is far away from the base to the joint which is close to the base, the previous identification result should be used to identify the next axis's inertial parameters. Finally, each axis's mathematical model is established. Otherwise, high precision of the model is also necessary for controlling IRs. But in the research of energy consumption of IRs, a high accuracy dynamic model is not needed, more attention should be paid to the general trend of energy consumption. This paper presents this practical method of energy modeling based on power measurement, this method reduces difficulties rather than sensing method and the experimental results show that energy model can be used to calculate energy consumption in the processing of IRs' movement, and it can also efficiently support the analysis the energy consumption characteristics.

The remainder of this paper is listed as follows: Sect. 3 presents the practical energy modeling method. Section 4 describes the experiments and the validation of the results. Finally, conclusions are given in Sect. 5.

3 Practical Energy Modeling Method

The energy consumption modeling of IRs is to establish the mathematical model of the power for the IRs under different operating states as Eq. 1 shows. Where $P_{m,i}$ and τ_i are respectively, the input motor power and actuator torque delivered to the *i*th shaft, whereas $q_i, \dot{q}_i, \ddot{q}_i$ are the *i*th joint angular position, velocity and acceleration, respectively. The input motor power can be calculated by multiplying the actuator torque by joint velocity, and Eq. 2 indicates that actuator torque can be calculated by multiplying coefficient matrix W by unknown dynamic parameters ϕ. It is obvious that the identification of unknown dynamic parameters is one of the most important steps in the processing of power modeling. Energy consumption modeling of IRs based on parameter identification includes linear model of torque, excitation trajectory design, experimental data processing, parameter identification and model validation, the whole process is shown in Fig. 1. In order to establish the linear model of torque,

Denavit-Hartenberg (DH) convention, rigid dynamics, serial robot kinematics and dynamics are needed as priori knowledge, and the coefficient matrix of the linear model can be used to design the objective function of excitation trajectory. The IRs' angle, speed, acceleration limitation are the constraints, so the excitation trajectory can be obtained by solving the optimal problem, by the excitation trajectory, after data processing, the measured power values should be regarded as the input to linear model identification procedure. Finally, it is needed to verify the correctness of the energy consumption model based on the identified parameters, if experimental results are not satisfied, then redesign the excitation trajectory and repeat the experiments.

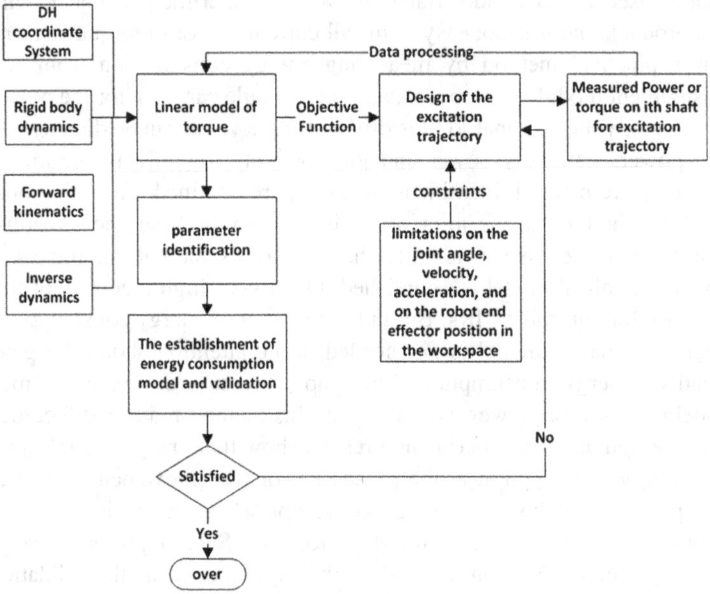

Fig. 1. Structure diagram of modeling

$$P_{m,i} = P_{m,i}(q_i, \dot{q}_i, \ddot{q}_i) = \tau_i(q_i, \dot{q}_i, \ddot{q}_i)\dot{q}_i \tag{1}$$

$$\tau_i(q_i, \dot{q}_i, \ddot{q}_i) = W(q_i, \dot{q}_i, \ddot{q}_i)\phi \tag{2}$$

Based on the *i*th joint motor power or actuator torque, the *i*th joint power model can be established. However, because it is not easy to install current meter or torque sensor modules inside IRs to measure correspondent joint power or actuator torque, thus a practical method by measuring total power from embedded power measurement module is proposed in this paper, Eq. 3 shows the relationship between total power and driving joints actuator torque

$$power_{total} = \sum \tau_i \dot{q}_i + power\_stationary \tag{3}$$

Where $power_{total}$ is the total power of robot, power_stationary is the power when robot is in stationary state. In order to establish each joint power model, as Fig. 2 shows, in this article, only former three joints are considered. When only the terminal joint is driven, torque value can be directly calculated by the total power Power1 minus stationary power and then divide joint velocity, by solving the linear model of torque used the least-square method, identification results are obtained. From the terminal joint to the base, through this direction, the previous identification result should be used to identify the next axis's inertial parameters. Finally, all unknown parameters of former three shafts are identified and the mathematical model of total power is established.

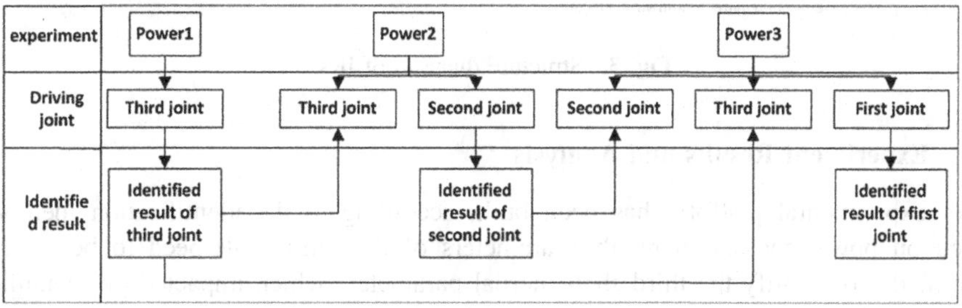

Fig. 2. Power identification process

4 Experiments and Result Analysis

4.1 Experiment Setting

ABB IRB1200 industrial robot is used as experimental object, which has embedded power measurement module and joint encoders by the ABB enterprises. RobotStudio and Matlab are used as simulation tools, the structure diagram of experimental platform is shown as Fig. 3. Since it is unable to set the movement of variable acceleration for ABB robots, excitation trajectory obtained from Matlab can be divided into huge amounts of small linear segments, each segment is set in different velocities, thus excitation trajectory can be fitted in this way, and RobotStudio can observe the motion of the robot in real time. Matlab software can be used for building robot dynamics program and deducing symbolic expression of actuator torque, after building the linear model for dynamic parameter identification based on Matlab, the joint movement parameters monitored from joint encoders and power monitored from embedded power measurement module will be used to calculate corresponding coefficient matrix and torque value, because the sampling data is much, the coefficient matrix is over determined, so then through the least-square method, the value of the inertial parameters can be identified. Refer to the idea of minimum parameter set [22], there are two rules that should be followed: Firstly, an inertial parameter has no effect on the dynamic model if the corresponding coefficient vector is equal to zero, and secondly, an inertial parameter can be regrouped to some other parameters if the corresponding coefficient vector can be linearly dependent on other vectors in coefficient matrix.

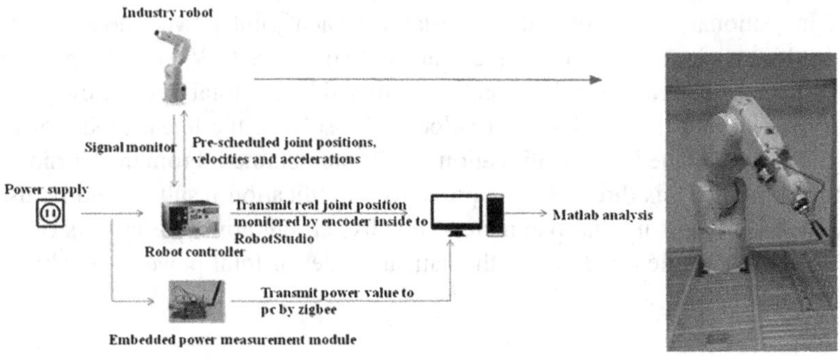

Fig. 3. Structure diagram of IRs

4.2 Experiment Results and Analysis

After experimental platform has been built, according to the identification method based on power measurement, the parameters of the third shaft need to be firstly identified. To identify the third shaft inertial parameters which impacted on dynamic model, the former two joints need to be locked while the third joint should be driven, so $\dot{q}_1 = \dot{q}_2 = 0$, $\ddot{q}_1 = \ddot{q}_2 = 0$. In order to reduce the complexity of the fitting path, the fundamental frequency is set to $f_0 = 0.2\,\text{hz}$, due to the limitations of the robot controller, the measured joint trajectories deviated from the desired trajectories can be shown in Fig. 4(a), and the last three mechanical arms can be regarded as a whole, Fig. 4(b) shows the space trajectory in RobotStudio.

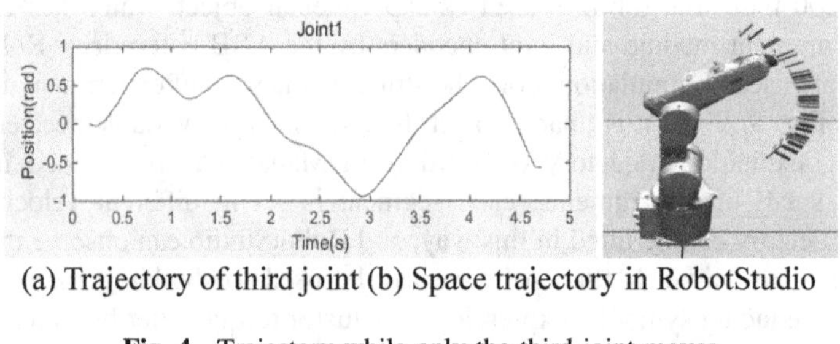

(a) Trajectory of third joint (b) Space trajectory in RobotStudio

Fig. 4. Trajectory while only the third joint moves

Because only the third joint is taken into consideration, torque value can be directly calculated by the total power minus stationary power and then divided by velocity of third joint, by solving the linear model through the least-square method, identification results are obtained as shown in Table 1.

After third shaft' parameters have been identified, the result can be used for second shaft parameters identification. To identify the inertial parameters of second shaft, the

Table 1. The identified inertial parameters while only the third joint moves

Parameter	I_{3zz}	mr_{3x}	mr_{3y}	$k_{c,3}$	$k_{v,3}$
Value	1.6046	−2.1079	−0.9015	34.9987	2.4405

first joint need to be locked while the other two joints should be driven, so $\dot{q}_1 = 0$, $\ddot{q}_1 = 0$ and ensure that the third joint's trajectory is unchanged. Figure 5(a) shows the trajectory of second joint, Fig. 5(b) shows the space trajectory in RobotStudio.

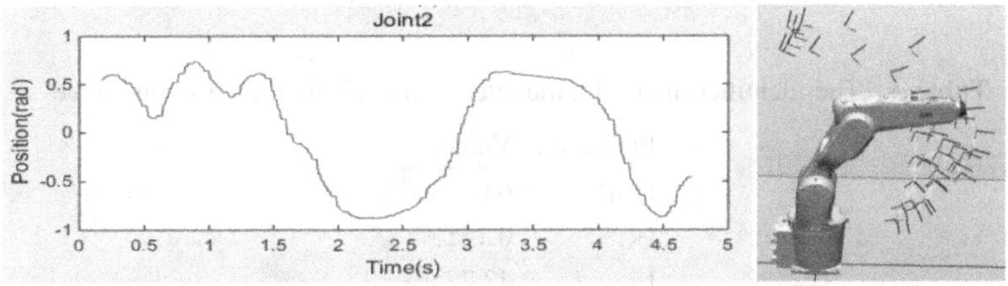

(a) Trajectory of second joint (b) Space trajectory in RobotStudio

Fig. 5. Space trajectory while the second and third joints move

Because the total power obtained from embedded power measurement module contains second and third joints' power, second joint's power can be calculated by total power minus third joint's power which is calculated by identified parameters, then by solving dynamical equation, part of inertial parameters of the second mechanical arms can be calculated, Table 2 shows the identification results, and the parameters with letter R mean the regrouped parameters as follows:

Table 2. The identified inertial parameters while second and third joints move

Parameter	$I_{2zz}R$	$mr_{2x}R$	$k_{c,2}$	$k_{v,2}$
Value	10.8166	0.3806	78.4818	−11.2914

Similarly, based on identification results obtained above, the identification process of the first shaft can be described as follows: All three joints should be driven, ensuring the identification trajectories of second and third joints remain unchanged, Fig. 6 shows the first joint's trajectory and space trajectory in RobotStudio. The identification results are shown in Table 3.

4.3 Validation of Identified Parameters and Power Model

The purpose of dynamic parameter identification is to build energy consumption model used for the prediction in energy consumption of IRs, therefore, it is necessary to verify the energy consumption model established by the identification results.

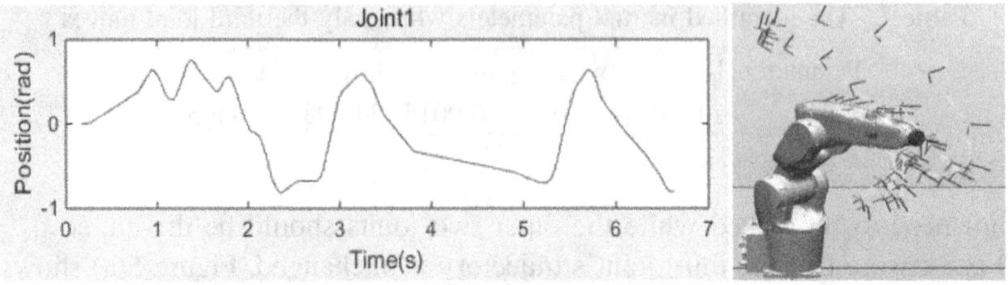

(a) Trajectory of first joint (b) Space trajectory in RobotStudio

Fig. 6. Trajectory while all first three joints move

Table 3. The identified inertial parameters while all first three joints move

Parameter	Value
$I_{1zz}R$	64.8939
I_{2xy}	0.1513
I_{2xz}	42.7756
I_{2yz}	−4.7205
$I_{3yy}R$	−76.7639
$I_{3zz}R$	107.9768
$I_{3xy}R$	−1.0986
I_{3xz}	−12.0371
I_{3yz}	10.4658
mr_{3z}	5.6503
$k_{c,1}$	−61.6334
$k_{v,1}$	65.7696

Firstly, we need to verify the accuracy of the identified parameters obtained in the above mentioned experiments. Due to neither masses, nor moments of inertia or friction losses of IRs are unavailable, it is not easy to compare the error between real parameter values and identified parameter values, so the verify method is to analyze the relative error between the modeling power based on identified parameters and measurement energy consumption for the specified excitation trajectory in each experiment, Fig. 7 shows the compared results.

It is obvious from Fig. 7 that when the third joint moves, the power model based on the identification parameters can predict the trend of the measured power, in the meanwhile, there still exists error in the power model between the other two groups. It is mainly because, when the third joint moves alone, the identification process only includes the inertia parameters of the third joint, there is no coupling effect between the multi-joints. As for the second group of experiments, there is the largest error, in fact, there are some additional parameters which are related to the gravity-compensating factor need to be identified, due to the limitation of torque measurement, these parameters are ignored, but their effects are added to the other parameters. And then, the identification error is accumulated in the third groups of identification experiments, which can also result in the error of the identification results.

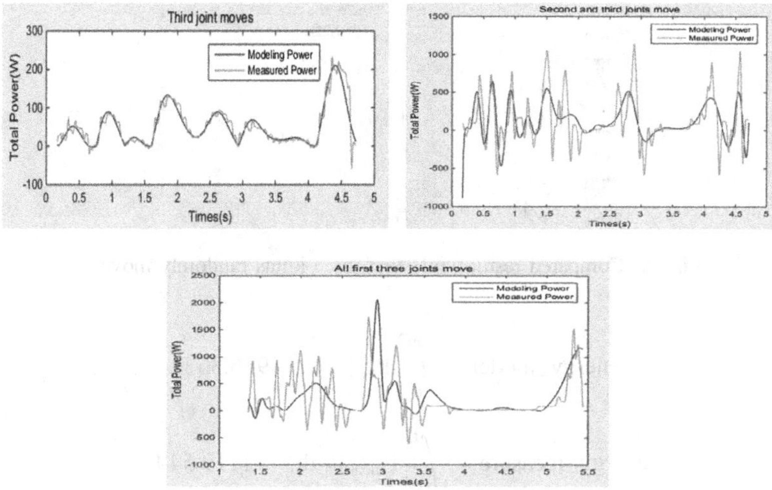

Fig. 7. Model validation for the excitation trajectory

After verifying the accuracy of identified parameters, it is also needed to verify whether the modeling power based on the identified parameters for other trajectory can predict energy consumption of IRs. The following shows the process which compares the modeling power value with the measured power value when the robot arms randomly move. The trajectory of first three joints can be shown in Fig. 8. And Fig. 9 shows the compared results.

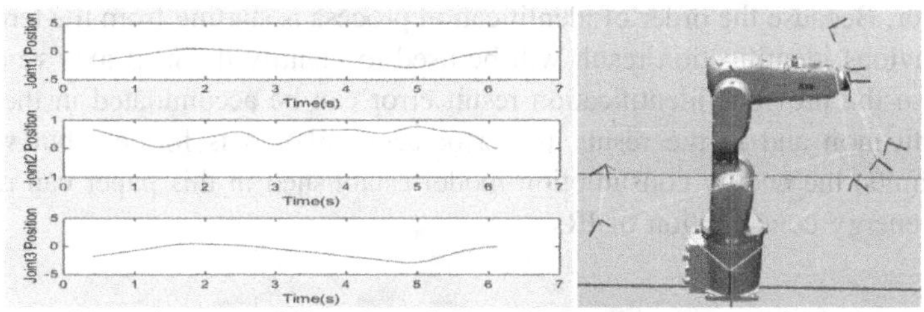

(a) Trajectory of first three joints (b) Space trajectory in RobotStudio

Fig. 8. Random trajectory of first three joints

It can be seen from Fig. 9 that, as the experimental time range is from t1 to t2, in which t1 is equal to 0.40 s and t2 is equal to 6.12 s, the modeling power, P_{model}, can approximately reflect the trend of measured power, $P_{measure}$. Energy consumption is a function of power based on time integral, thus energy_model and energy_measure are the modeling energy consumption and the measuring energy consumption individually, as Eqs. (4) and (5) shown. The Error in Eq. (6) indicates the relative error between those two kinds of energy consumption.

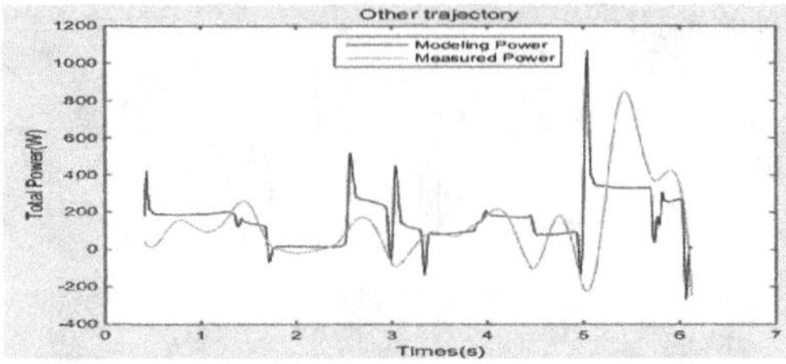

Fig. 9. Compared result while first three joints randomly move

$$\text{energy\_model} = \int_{t1}^{t2} P_{\text{model}}\, dt = 936.36\,\text{J} \tag{4}$$

$$\text{energy\_measure} = \int_{t1}^{t2} P_{\text{measure}}\, dt = 1119.54\,\text{J} \tag{5}$$

$$\text{Error} = \frac{\|\text{energy\_model} - \text{energy\_measure}\|}{\text{energy\_measure}} \times 100\% = 16.36\% \tag{6}$$

Analysis from the entire identification process, the error mainly comes from two aspects. The first aspect is that the power measured includes the power consumption of the motor torque, and the power loss of the motor. In the experiment, we assume that the loss of the motor is constant, which can be regarded as static energy consumption. In fact, the loss of the motor will change with the load, motion parameters, temperature, current changes, *etc.*, but this part of the loss is relatively small compared with the power consumption of torque. Error accumulation, on the other hand, is also a major source of error. Because the order of identification process is starting from the terminal joint, the previous identification result will be used to identify the next axis's inertial parameters, so the previous identification result error can be accumulated in the next axis's identification and in the result, the error accumulation is formed, but within acceptable limits, the energy consumption model established in this paper can reflect the trend of energy consumption of IRs.

5 Conclusion and Future Work

In the conclusion, this paper proposed the identifications method to calculated energy consumption of industrial robots which are highly integrated IRs and whose torques are difficult to be directly measured. Compared to the method of installing sensors to measure torque or current, the experimental cost and the operation difficulty are reduced. Through the results of parameter identification and verified experiment based on ABB IRB1200 robot, because of the change of static power and the error accumulation of the identification process, it causes that the energy consumption model has acceptable error compared with the actual energy consumption, the method can reflect the trend of energy consumption of IRs.

This paper is mainly about the energy consumption modeling based on ABB type IRs, in the future studies, a more accurate energy consumption modeling method, analysis of energy consumption characteristics and energy consumption optimization based on energy consumption model will be the main research direction.

Acknowledgements. This research is supported by National Natural Science Foundation of China (Grant No. 51305319), the International Science & and Technology Cooperation Program of China (Grant No. 2015DFA70340), and Engineering and Physical Sciences Research Council (EPSRC), UK (Grant No. EP/N018524/1).

References

1. Li, B., Zhang, L., Wang, S., Tao, F., Cao, J., Jiang, X., Song, X., Chai, X.: Cloud manufacturing: a new service-oriented networked manufacturing model. Comput. Integr. Manuf. Syst. **16**(1), 1–1343 (2010)
2. Xu, X.: From cloud computing to cloud manufacturing. Rob. Comput.-Integr. Manuf. **28**(1), 75–86 (2012)
3. Ren, L., Zhang, L., Tao, F., Zhao, C., Chai, X., Zhao, X.: Cloud manufacturing: From concept to practice. Enterp. Inf. Syst. **9**(2), 186–209 (2015). Taylor & Francis
4. Saidur, R.: A review on electrical motors energy use and energy savings. Renew. Sustain. Energy Rev. **14**(3), 877–898 (2010)
5. Yang, A., Pu, J., Wong, C., et al.: By-pass valve control to improve energy efficiency of pneumatic drive system. Control Eng. Pract. **17**(6), 623–628 (2009)
6. Maimon, O., Profeta, E., Singer, S.: Energy analysis of robot task motions. J. Intell. Rob. Syst. **4**(2), 175–198 (1991)
7. Diken, H.: Energy efficient sinusoidal path planning of robot manipulators. Mech. Mach. Theory **29**(6), 785–792 (1994)
8. Sergaki, E., Stavrakakis, G., Pouliezos, A.: Optimal robot speed trajectory by minimization of the actuator motor electromechanical losses. J. Intell. Rob. Syst. **33**(2), 187–207 (2002)
9. Huang, M.S., Hsu, Y.L., Fung, R.F.: Minimum-energy point-to-point trajectory planning for a motor-toggle servomechanism. IEEE/ASME Trans. Mechatron. **17**(2), 337–344 (2012)
10. Field, G., Stepanenko, Y.: Iterative dynamic programming: an approach to minimum energy trajectory planning for robotic manipulators. IEEE Int. Conf. Rob. Autom. **3**, 2755–2760 (1996)
11. Kim, C.H., Kim, B.K.: Minimum-energy motion planning for differential-driven wheeled mobile robots. Motion Plan. 192–226 (2008)
12. Yongguo, M., Yung-Hsiang, L., Hu, Y., Lee, C.: Deployment of mobile robots with energy and timing constraints. IEEE Trans. Rob. **22**(3), 507–522 (2006)
13. Roos, F., Johansson, H., Wikander, J.: Optimal selection of motor and gearhead in mechatronic applications. Mechatronics **16**(1), 63–72 (2006)
14. Izumi, T., Zhou, H., Li, Z.: Optimal design of gear ratios and offset for energy conservation of an articulated manipulator. IEEE Trans. Autom. Sci. Eng. **6**(3), 551–557 (2009)
15. Meike, D., Pellicciari, M., Berselli, G.: Energy efficient use of multirobot production lines in the automotive industry: detailed system modeling and optimization. IEEE Trans. Autom. Sci. Eng. **11**(3), 798–809 (2014)

16. Paryanto, Brossog, M., Bornschlegl, M., Franke, J.: Reducing the energy consumption of industrial robots in manufacturing systems. Int. J. Adv. Manuf. Technol. **78**(5–8), 1315–1328 (2015)
17. Wu, J., Wang, J., You, Z.: An overview of dynamic parameter identification of robots. Rob. Comput.-Integr. Manuf. **26**(5), 414–419 (2010)
18. Swevers, J., Verdonck, W., Schutter, J.D.: Dynamic model identification for industrial robots. IEEE Control Syst. Mag. **27**(5), 58–71 (2007)
19. Chen, E.W., Liu, Z.S., Gan, F.J.: Method of identifying inertial parameters of manipulator based on wrist force sensor. Robot **28**(2), 125–129 (2006)
20. Christoforou, E.G.: On-line parameter identification and adaptive control of rigid robots using base reaction forces/torques. In: IEEE International Conference on Robotics & Automation, pp. 4956–4961 (2007)
21. Verdonck, W., Swevers, J., Samin, J.: Experimental dynamic robot identification: advantages of combining internal and external measurements and of using periodic excitation. J. Dyn. Syst. Meas. Control-Trans. ASME **123**(4), 630–636 (2001)
22. Gautier, M., Khalil, W.: Exciting trajectories for the identification of base inertial parameters of robots. Int. J. Robot. Res. **11**(4), 362–375 (1992)

An Optimization Method for User Interface Components Based on Big Data

Fei Lyu[1,2(✉)], Lei Ren[3], and Yi Du[4]

[1] School of Digital Media and Design Arts, Beijing University of Posts and Telecommunications, Beijing, China
FeiLyu@bupt.edu.cn
[2] Beijing Key Laboratory of Network Systems and Network Culture, Beijing University of Posts and Telecommunications, Beijing, China
[3] School of Automation Science and Electrical Engineering, Beihang University, Beijing, China
[4] Department of Big Data Technology and Application Development, Computer Network Information Center, Chinese Academy of Sciences, Beijing, China

Abstract. The efficiency and usability of user interface largely depend on the design and optimization of UI components. This paper proposes an optimization method for UI components based on big data collected from users. First, a user interface components optimization model (UCOM) is proposed which is described from four aspects including user model, task model, interaction model, and component presentation model. Then, based on UCOM, a big data-driven optimization method for user interface component (BOM) is presented. This method defines complete optimizing solution, uses the crowdsourcing to publish solution, gathers and analyzes users' big data, utilizes AHP to develop a weight formula, and finally provides integrated optimization suggestion.

Keywords: Big data · Optimization method · User interface

1 Introduction

The user interface component is one of the most important research topic in human-computer interaction. Researchers construct all sorts of UI components to expand the input channel and raise interaction efficiency. In order to design UI components which match with user's capability, it is necessary to evaluate and optimize components to get the optimal design scheme.

One way to design and optimize components is to use the prediction models. GOMS [1] is one of the most famous models in the era of WIMP, describing user's interaction behavior as a serial sequence of cognitive and motor operations. GOMS can predict the execution time of skilled users' errorless performance, and can be used to evaluate and select UI component design schemes [2]. But since it only focuses on errorless performance of skilled users, it has certain limitations.

Another important way to optimize UI components is the laboratory experiment. The researchers design interface components, recruit users to complete predetermined experimental tasks with the component candidates, and then evaluate and select the optimal

L. Zhang et al. (Eds.): Monterey Workshop 2016, LNCS 10228, pp. 37–42, 2017.
DOI: 10.1007/978-3-319-61994-1_4

design scheme. Tilt Menu [3] is a pen-based component to generate the secondary input channel with a pen tip. Through experiment, researchers explored the usability of orientation and menu size of the Tilt Menu items. HandMark Menu [4], a UI component based on the haptic devices, tested the user's performance on three design schemes. The experiment for Hover Widget compared design schemes of different shapes and directions [5].

Laboratory experiments can evaluate and improve interface components efficiently, but the traditional experiment methods have three issues: 1. the experiments are conducted in laboratory which cannot represent the actual daily workspace of the users; 2. the number of users is limited, so researchers cannot obtain experiment result of large-scale samples; 3. the optimizing solutions have not been modularized, hence it is unable to avoid repeated coding and shortening the cycle.

In order to solve these problems, this paper constructs a User Interface Components Optimization Model (UCOM). Based on this model, we propose a Big Data-Driven Optimization Method for User Interface Components (BOM). This method constructs a complete optimization solution for user interface components, uses crowdsourcing to publish the solution, collects and analyze users' data, and eventually gives the optimal UI component recommendations with AHP integration method. Using this method, researchers and designers can evaluate and optimize the user interface components quickly and efficiently.

2 User Interface Components Optimization Model (UCOM)

According to Puerta' theory, the user interface model need to describe all of the user interface elements in order [6]. Ren et al. proposed a model for cloud-based intelligent user interface [7]. Based on these theories, we build user-big-data orientated interface components optimization model UCOM.

UCOM consists of a series of models, as shown in Fig. 1. It is mainly made up of four sub models, namely User Model (UM), Task Model (TM), Interaction Model (IM), and Component Presentation Model (CM).

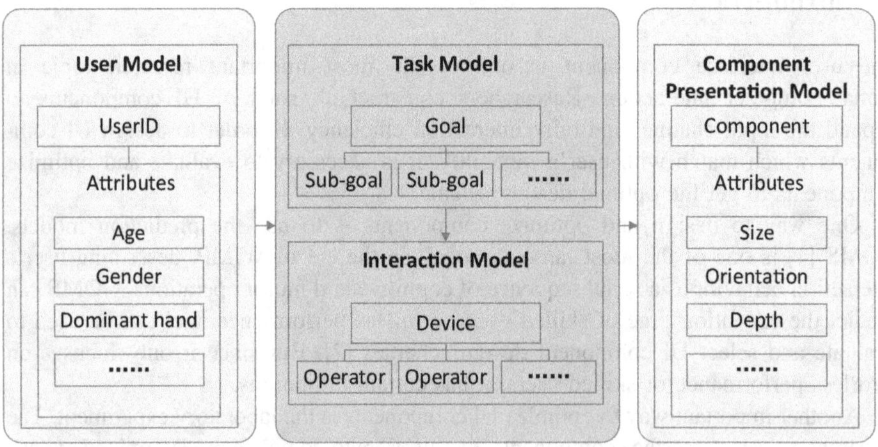

Fig. 1. User interface components optimization model (UCOM)

- User Model
  User Model defines the target user of the interface components, and describes user's characteristics and properties.

  Definition 1: UM= {UserID, UserAttributes}

  Definition 2: UserAttributes = {Gender, Age, DominantHand, …}

- Task Model
  Task Model describes the interactive task sequence with a set of goals and sub-goals based on GOMS. According to GOMS, user starts a task from the goal of highest level which can be decomposed into predefined sub-goals. Sub-goals can be further decomposed until they are indecomposable.

  Definition 3: TM = {Goal, SubGoalSet}

- In the definition, Goal is the highest goal of interaction and SubGoalSet is the set of all sub-goals by time sequence.
- Interaction Model
  Interaction model describes interaction primitives based on physical input devices and is concrete mapping of the task model. According to GOMS, each sub-goal can be accomplished by a serial sequence of operations. Separating them logically facilitates the reuse of code modules.

  Definition 4: IM = {DeviceSet, OperatorSet}

- In the definition, DeviceSet represents the set of physical input devices and OperatorSet is the set of operators based on the sub-goals, namely the interaction primitives.

  Definition 5: DeviceSet = {Mouse, Keyboard, Haptic Devices, Somatosensory Devices, Pen Interaction Devices, …}

- Users can use certain interaction device to complete tasks, including the keyboard, touch device, gestures device, and so on.

  Definition 6: OperatorSet = {Single Click, Double Click, Tilt, Long Press, Drag, Rotate, Single Finger Rotate, Double Finger Rotate, …}

- Component Presentation Model
  Component Presentation Model describes Components' visual presentation. It shows the characterization of the structure and properties of the interface components, and gives specific interface component parameters as well.

  Definition 7: CM = {ComponentID, ComponentAttributes}

- In the definition, ComponentID is the Components identification set and Component ID number identifies user individuals.

  Definition 8: ComponentAttributes = {Size, Orientation, Depth, …}

- Component's presentation includes multiple attributes and the designer can set those attributes into multiple representation forms.

3 Big Data-Driven Optimization Method for User Interface Components (BOM)

Big Data-Driven Optimization Method for User Interface Components (BOM) mainly includes four key steps, namely model-based solution design, release user experiment by crowdsourcing and acquire multiple types of data, process and analysis data, and finally give integrated optimization suggestions by AHP method, as shown in Fig. 2.

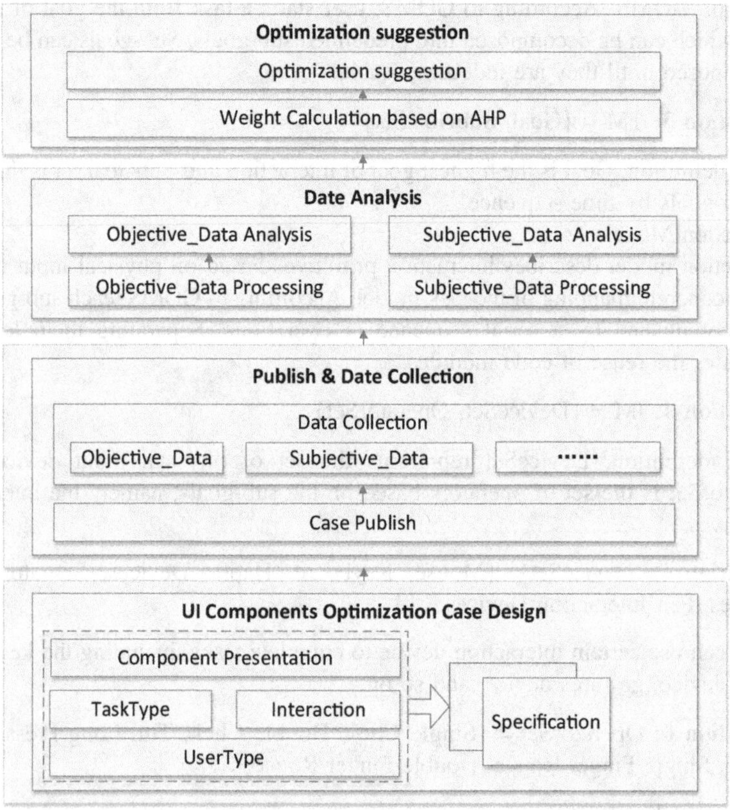

Fig. 2. Big data-driven optimization method for user interface components (BOM)

Step 1. Optimization Solution Design based on UCOM

Based on UCOM model, we construct the optimization solution for user interface component, According to four sub-models in the UCOM model, we give definition as following:

Definition 9: C = {U, T, I, P}

C represents the user interface Components optimization solution which includes not only the visual design to be optimized, but also an integrated solution design.

A complete user interface Components optimization solution includes user type, task types, interactions, Component characterization and data types.

U represents the type of user. Before the experiment task began, we screened the target user and recorded the characteristics of the user attributes, such as gender, age, occupation, technical background and handedness preferences. These properties will be used in subsequent optimization analysis.

T stands for the task flow, corresponding with the task sub-model. Task flow is user's interactive task sequence. We set specific beginning and ending tips of the task in the solution and require the user to follow the prompts to complete the scheduled tasks.

I represents the interaction primitive, corresponds with the interaction sub-model, and defines interactive primitives depending on the different types of interaction and interactive devices.

P describes the visual presentation design to be optimized and corresponds with the component presentation sub-model. Users will be provided with several visual solutions.

Step 2. Solution Release and Data Collection

Release optimization solution by crowdsourcing. Users test each visual design solution included in the interface components utilization solution, and complete pre-designed task flow by interaction operation on their own terminal devices which can represent real work environment. During the task, the system automatically collects data on the user's performance. After the task is completed, the user fills in a subjective questionnaire and the system records the subjective data.

Definition 10: Objective_Data = {Time, X_coordinate, Y_coordinate, …}.

Step 3. Data Process and Analysis

The collected objective data and subjective data are processed separately. Objective data is generally used for performance metrics to evaluate the effectiveness and efficiency of the interface components, while Subjective data is typically used to evaluate the user perception of products which leave them impression.

Definition 11: Performance_Index = {Task time, Error rate, Accuracy, Learnability, …}

Definition 12: Perception_Index = {Usefulness, Comfortableness, Enjoyment, …}
For continuous data, feature extraction is needed; and for discrete data, the feature extraction can be done directly by the normalization. Statistical methods may be used to further analyze the relationship between the data.

Step 4. Give Integrated Optimization Recommendations

With AHP method [8], we construct the weight of all kinds of data types and propose the weight formula

$$\mathrm{W} = (w_1, w_2, \ldots w_{\mathrm{n}})^T \tag{1}$$

After normalizing the data, we substitute them into the formula and give the specific suggestions on optimization solution of interface components design.

4 Conclusions and Future Work

In this paper, we first introduce User Interface Components Optimization Model (UCOM), and on this basis we present a Big Data-Driven Optimization Method for User Interface Components (BOM). This method designs optimization solution based on UCOM, gathers data by crowdsourcing, and gives final interface optimization solution by AHP method. Overall, this method can effectively overcome the disadvantage of traditional user interface optimization method: lacking sufficient experimental data and having duplication in experimental program development.

In the next step, we will further study and evaluate this method by examining its performance on different user interfaces, for instance, pen-style user interface or reality-based user interface.

Acknowledgement. This work is supported by National Natural Science Foundation of China (Grant No. 61303162, No. 61402435), the Fundamental Research Funds for the Central Universities, and Beijing Municipal Social Science Foundation (Grant No. 16YTC033).

References

1. Card, S.K., Newell, A., Moran, T.P.: The Psychology of Human-Computer Interaction. Lawrence Erlbaum Associates Inc., Mahwah (1983)
2. Olson, J.R., Olson, G.M.: The growth of cognitive modeling in human-computer interaction since GOMS. Hum.-Comput. Interact. **5**, 221–265 (1990)
3. Tian, F., Xu, L., Wang, H., Zhang, X., Liu, Y., Setlur, V., Dai, G.: Tilt menu: using the 3D orientation information of pen devices to extend the selection capability of pen-based user interfaces. In: Proceeding of the Twenty-Sixth Annual SIGCHI Conference on Human Factors in Computing Systems, pp. 1371–1380 (2008)
4. Uddin, M.S., Gutwin, C., Lafreniere, B.: HandMark Menus: rapid command selection and large command sets on multi-touch displays. In: Proceedings of the 2016 CHI Conference on Human Factors in Computing Systems, pp. 5836–5848 (2016)
5. Grossman, T., Hinckley, K., Baudisch, P., Agrawala, M., Balakrishnan, R.: Hover components: using the tracking state to extend the capabilities of pen-operated devices. In: Proceedings of the SIGCHI Conference on Human Factors in Computing Systems, pp. 861–870 (2006)
6. Puerta, A., Eisenstein, J.: Towards a general computational framework for model-based interface development systems. In: Proceedings of the 4th International Conference on Intelligent User Interfaces, pp. 171–178 (1999)
7. Ren, L., Cui, J., Li, N., Wu, Q., et al.: Cloud-based intelligent user interface for cloud manufacturing: model, technology and application. Trans. ASME J. Manuf. Sci. Eng. (2015). ISSN:1087-1357. doi:10.1115/1.4030332
8. Salmeron, J.L., Herrero, I.: An AHP-based methodology to rank critical success factors of executive information systems. Comput. Stand. Interfaces **28**(1), 1–12 (2005)

Clustering-Based Data Aggregation and Routing for Real-Time WirelessHART Communication

Feng Li, Chunhui Wang, Lei Ju(✉), and Zhiping Jia

School of Computer Science and Technology,
Shandong University, Jinan, China
lifeng0799@126.com, julei@sdu.edu.cn

Abstract. Clustering-based routing strategies have been widely studied in the context of wireless sensor network for energy-efficient data communication. However, application of clustering-based routing to hard real-time wireless network is still an open challenge. In this work, we study the integration of clustering-based routing with WirelessHART for energy-efficient real-time wireless data communication. We re-design the clustering strategy to incorporate node transmission frequency so that the end-to-end delay of each data delivery is captured early in the clustering phase. Moreover, the data aggregation within a cluster is taken care of in the superframe design phase to ensure the stringent timing requirements are met. Experimental results show that the proposed data communication framework prolongs the WirelessHART network by effectively reducing the number of data packages transmitted. Meanwhile, the end-to-end delay of each data delivery can be always guaranteed.

Keywords: WirelessHART · Clustering · Data aggregation · Routing

1 Introduction

WirelessHART communication specification has been adopted by the International Electrotechnical Commission (IEC) as the first open-ended real-time wireless Mesh network communication protocol for industrial automation and control system. WirelessHART is capable of meeting the essential requirements of reliability, stability and safety on wireless communication of real-time factory application of process industry. With the centralized control system, WirelessHART, compared with the immobilized link of tree-shape network or star-shape network, can transmit or retransmit data through different paths and redundant path to ensure the high robustness and fault-tolerant ability of the WirelessHART network. The network manager controls the entire network information and dispatches the communication resources in a centralized way, thus optimizing the network and meeting the hard real-time requirement. In particular, WirelessHART precisely dispatches communication of the network by the method of time division multiple access (TDMA) and enables network communication with no conflict.

With the large number of field devices in today's process automation control network, energy-efficiency becomes an increasing challenge for reliable WielessHART

L. Zhang et al. (Eds.): Monterey Workshop 2016, LNCS 10228, pp. 43–51, 2017.
DOI: 10.1007/978-3-319-61994-1_5

communication. Many techniques have been proposed in the literature for energy-efficient wireless communication, including energy-efficient routing path selection, data aggregation/fusion techniques, as well as clustering-based routing [1, 2]. In particular, data aggregation is a process of fusing data collected by several sensors into one network package in order to decrease data transmissions in the network. By using data fusion techniques, the data package transmitted in the network can be effectively decreased and the lifetime of the entire network can be increased. The idea of clustering in wireless sensor has been well-studied for wireless sensor networks (WSNs). A cluster is a collection of nodes with some relationships in the network. Each cluster has one cluster head and several cluster members; the cluster members send the collected data to cluster head and the cluster head will fuse these data and transmit them to network manager. This algorithm divides the entire network into conjoint sections. Many clustering routing algorithms have been proposed for WSNs, including LEACH [3], LEACH-C [4], UCS [5], HEED [6]. However, the requirement is quite strict on timeliness and reliability in industrial production, but these traditional clustering algorithms didn't take timeliness and reliability into account, so they cannot be used directly in the WirelessHART communication.

In this paper, we integrate clustering based routing algorithm into the WirelessHART for real-time and energy-efficient data communication. Our technical contributions are as follows.

- We combine the cluster head election process into the up-link path selection phase of WirelessHART protocol. In particular, the node transmission frequency is used as an extra criterion in the cluster head election in order to facilitate the superframe scheduling phase in meeting the real-time constraints.
- We redesign the superframe scheduling phase of the WirelessHART communication protocol to incorporate clustering-based data aggregation. The package size and node frequency are both considered to ensure the end-to-end package delay while minimizing the package transmissions in the network.
- Experimental evaluation shows that the proposed clustering-based routing algorithm improves the network lifetime by 40% compared with the state-of-the-art WirelessHART communication protocol, and the imposed end-to-end delay constraints are always met.

2 Related Work

The research on routing strategy of wireless sensor network can be classified into two categorizations: single path routing and multipath routing algorithm. Single path routing algorithms include AODV [7], ABR [8], SSR [9], DSR [10], DSDV [11], etc. But low reliability and low adaptability to topological changes make it difficult to adapt to constantly changing industrial environment. Compared with single path routing selection algorithm, multipath routing selection algorithm has more obvious advantage in network robustness and adaptability to topological changes. In multipath routing selection algorithm, if the transmission of the data is failed, the data can be transmitted through another redundant path in the network. At present, the most widely used multipath routing selection algorithms are the extension of some single path routing selection algorithms, such as M-DSDV [12], AOMDV [13], AMOR [14] and so on.

[15] puts forward a superframe schedule algorithm based on routing map to improve the robustness of WirelessHART, which can avoid time slot conflict and channel disturbance existing in the network. It improves robustness and decreases network communication delay to a large extent. But this algorithm doesn't optimize routing selection. [16] proposes an algorithm by adding node's surplus energy in routing selection to improve Guaranteed Bit Rate (GBR). Under the same circumstances, the node with higher surplus energy is more likely to become the choice of next hop, which balances the load of the entire network node and relieves the pressure of bottleneck nodes in the network to some extent. [17] presents a multi-hop routing algorithm called HBRRP, which can improve the robustness of the entire network. This algorithm regards the shortest path as the primary element of the data transmission, and comprehensively takes link quality, surplus energy and load balancing into account, but its drawback is that it can't evaluate the impact of various elements on the network. [18] puts forward a reliable and low-energy-consumption routing algorithm, considering the routing algorithm and the superframe design phase.

Earlier clustering algorithms mainly adapt uniform distribution clustering algorithm and divide the entire network into clusters of the same size. The numbers of nodes in these clusters are almost the same and the radiuses of these clusters are also the same. LEACH algorithm [3] is the typical even-distributed clustering algorithm which adopts random clustering strategy and periodicity cluster head rotating method. UCS [5] proposes non-even clustering idea to balance node energy consumption of cluster head which use multi-hopping method. The consumption of the cluster head includes intra-cluster communication and inter-cluster communication consumption. HEED clustering algorithm [6] divides the entire network into uneven cluster heads through completely distributed cluster generation method.

3 System Model

In this Section, we first introduce the proposed clustering-based link selection algorithm, followed by the redesigned superframe scheduling algorithm.

3.1 Link Selection

When there are several routing candidates for a node to upload its data, we should take each node into account and ensure that each transmission has at least two uploading paths. In terms of path selection, three essential elements should be taken into consideration: communication cost, node's residual energy, and clusters selection.

Communication Cost

In one time slot, the sender and the acceptor should finish the transmission of data and affirmation frame. Energy consumption in finishing one communication is directly related to distance among the two sides and the size of the data that need to be transmitted; the farther the distance among the two sides is, the more energy it will consume; the more data is transmitted, the more energy will be consumed. However, WirelessHART has requirement on transmission rate, and the data package transmitted in one time slot should not be bigger than 127 B, thus limiting the number of data in one data package.

$$E = 1 - \frac{E_j}{\sum_{k=1}^{n} E_k} \tag{1}$$

In Eq. 1, E_j is energy consumed when joining node j; $\sum_{k=1}^{n} E_k$ is the total energy consumption that can be joined into cluster.

Node's Residual Energy

In the process of WirelessHART network data transmission, residual energy is an important consideration. When selecting node for data transmission, we will select those with high residual energy to avoid the early death of some nodes and prolong the lifetime of the entire network.

$$R = \frac{enery_{cur}}{enery_{init}} \tag{2}$$

In Eq. 2, $enery_{cur}$ is the current surplus energy of the node; $enery_{init}$ is the initial energy of the node.

Clusters Selection

In the process of clustering, we first take frequency into consideration. We can know it from Data Aggregation Framework for Energy-efficient WirelessHART Networks. We select father node as the sink node, as the data transmission frequency of the node is comparatively high and the father node may fuse the data of child node instead of solely transmitting the data uploaded by the child node. In this way, the transmission times will be decreased, and the consumption of the node will be lowered.

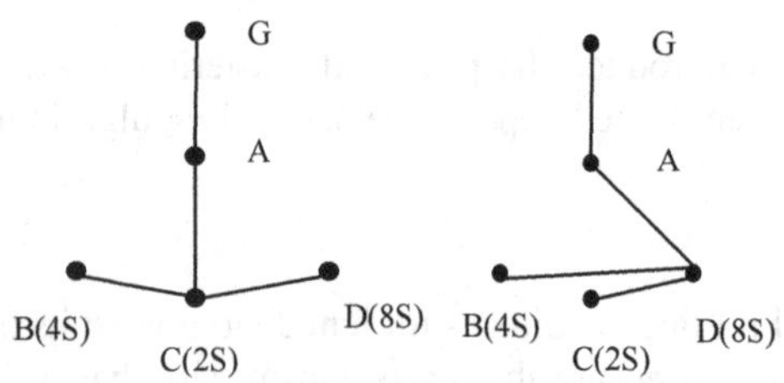

Fig. 1. Select cluster node by frequency

As shown in Fig. 1, we will present the differences of network transmission times when selecting nodes of different frequency as cluster head.

Table 1 shows that when selecting nodes with high transmission frequency as cluster head, the network can transmit 11 times in 8 s. However, as shown in Table 2, when selecting nodes of low transmission frequency as cluster head, the network transmits 14 times in 8 s. When the number of network nodes increases, the difference

Table 1. Select high frequency node as cluster head

Time slot	Transmission in the WirelessHART Network	Times
2 s	C→A, A→G	2
4 s	B→C, C→A, A→G	3
6 s	C→A, A→G	2
8 s	B→C, D→C, C→A, A→G	4

Table 2. Select low frequency node as cluster head

Time slot	Transmission in the WirelessHART Network	Times
2 s	C→D, D→A, A→G	3
4 s	C→D, B→D, D→A, A→G	4
6 s	C→D, D→A, A→G	3
8 s	B→D, C→D, D→A, A→G	4

of the transmission times will be more obvious. Then we can know that selecting nodes of high transmission frequency may decrease the data transmission times, thus decrease energy consumption and prolong the lifetime of the entire network.

$$F = \begin{cases} 1 & f_c \leq f_{ic} \\ \frac{f_{ic}}{f_c} & f_c > f_{ic} \end{cases} \quad (3)$$

In Eq. 3, f_c is the frequency of cluster head; f_{ic} is the frequency of the nodes in clusters. When the node selects cluster head, if its transmission frequency is lower or equal to transmission frequency of the cluster head, then set F as 1; if its transmission frequency is higher than that of the cluster head, then set F as $\frac{f_{ic}}{f_c}$.

3.2 Superframe Design

Superframe routing is a special form of routing. It is a reliable path for data generated by a field device to be sent to the gateway. It is created by the network manager. Each data transmission is scheduled by a superframe. In this paper, data transmission is divided into two types: inner cluster data transmission and inter-cluster data transmission. Inner cluster data transmission uses single-hop transmission mode, and inter cluster data transmission uses multi-hop transmission. In order to avoid conflict, this paper arranges superframe for the inner cluster and inter cluster data transmission simultaneously. The superframe is mainly divided into two parts. One is the super-frame of the inner cluster, and the other is the superframe between the cluster heads.

Within the cluster, each node in the cluster transmits the data directly to the cluster head, so the route is relatively simple. When the data is transmitted between the cluster heads, each cluster head selects two nodes with the best link quality upload, and ensures that the data can be uploaded to the gateway node via a redundant path.

As shown in Algorithm 1, we propose superframe algorithm which can arrange superframe for inner nodes and cluster heads uniformly. In the initial stage, the whole superframe *SF* is null (line 1), then we traversal all cluster heads from highest to lowest according to frequency (line 2), then we traversal all inner cluster nodes of n_i from highest to lowest according to frequency, and create superframe for node n (lines 3–4). If the data of cluster head n_i can be uploaded to the AP point timely, we combine the superframe of node n to the superframe of cluster head n_i (lines 5–6); if can't, we combine the superframe of node n to the whole superframe *SF* (lines 7–8). Finally, we combine the superframe of n_i to the whole superframe *SF* (lines 11–13).

```
Algorithm 1: Superframe Arrangement
Notations:
  N is the set of cluster heads
  E_i is the upload links from node n_i∈N to an access point
  SF_i is the superframe of n_i
  SF is the total superframe of the WirelessHART network
Begin:
1:  SF = Ø
2:  for each node n_i∈N from highest to lowest do
3:    for each inner cluster node n of n_i from highest to
      lowest do
4:      create SF_n for n
5:      if E_i is schedulable then
6:        E_i = combine (E_i, n);
7:      else
8:        SF = combine (SF, n);
9:      end if
10:   end for
11:   if SF_i is schedulable then
12:     SF = combine (SF, n_i)
13:   end if
14: end for
End
```

4 Experimental Evaluation

In the simulation-based experiment, we assume that all the nodes are randomly distributed in the 400 × 400 areas; the communication radius of the device is 80 m; the number of nodes in the network changes among 100–200. Other parameters are as follows (Table 3):

In this section we evaluate our proposed clustering-based WirelessHART algorithm compared with the algorithms presented in [18] (referred as the Re-add algorithm) and [6] (referred as the Heed algorithm). In Fig. 2, we show the lifetime of the network

Table 3. Network and parameters

Parameters	Value
Simulation area	400 m × 400 m
communication radius	100 m
The number of node	100, 125, 150, 175, 200
Initial power E_0	1
E_{elec}	50
ε_{fs}	10
ε_{amp}	0.0013

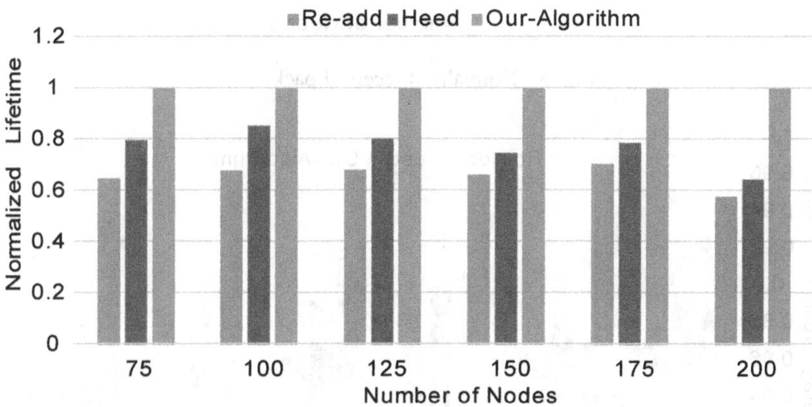

Fig. 2. Normalized lifetime of the network (when the first dead node appears)

(till the first node dies) with different network sizes for various routing algorithms. Since the network workload will also increase with the size of the network increases, the lifetime of network is not proportional to the increase of the network size. The lifetime of our algorithm is improved by 40% compared with the Re-add algorithm, and is about 20% higher than the Heed algorithm.

As shown in the Fig. 3, we count the number of packets received by the gateway within the lifetime of the network. Compared with Re-add, our algorithm leads to 1.19X more packets received, due to the prolonged network lifetime. Furthermore, compared with Heed, we are able to receive 1.09X more packages received, due to the increased network lifetime as well as high transmission reliability.

Finally, we compare the average residual energy. As shown in Fig. 4, we know that by using our algorithm the average residual energy is obviously less than Re-add and Heed, this is why our algorithm's lifetime is longer than them.

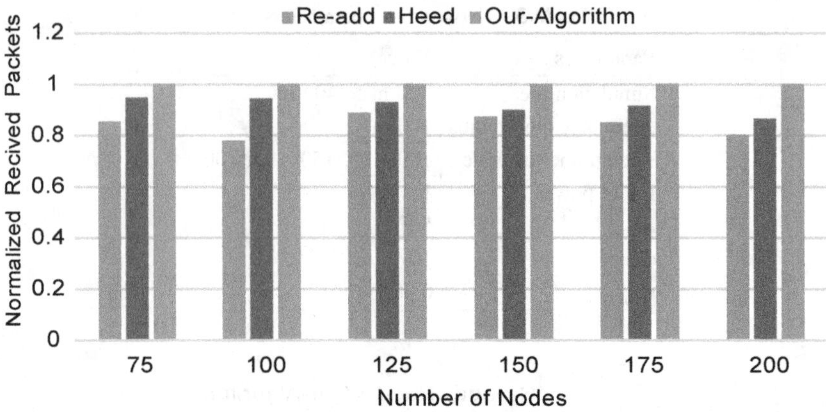

Fig. 3. Normalized received packets

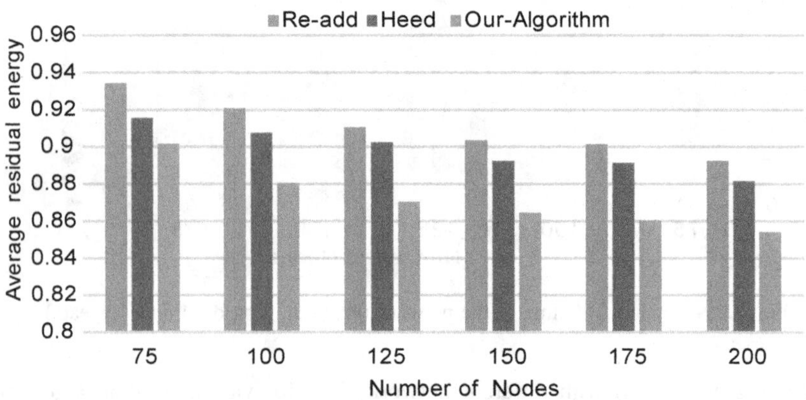

Fig. 4. Average residual energy

5 Conclusion

Clustering algorithm can significantly improve the lifetime of WSNs. Considering the frequency of sensors, we create a new clustering algorithm of real-time WirelessHART communication in this paper. Through our algorithm, we reduce the number of data package transmissions and improve energy efficiency of WirelessHART network, while ensuring the hard real-time constraints are met.

References

1. Patil, M., Biradar, R.C.: A survey on routing protocols in wireless sensor networks. In: 18th IEEE International Conference on Networks (ICON), pp. 86–91. IEEE Press (2012). doi:10.1109/ICON.2012.6506539

2. Al-Karaki, J.N., Kamal, A.E.: Routing techniques in wireless sensor networks: a survey. IEEE Wirel. Commun. **11**(6), 6–28 (2004)
3. Heinzelman, W.R., Chandrakasan, A., Balakrishnan, H.: Energy-efficient communication protocol for wireless microsensor networks. In: 33rd Annual Hawaii International Conference on System Sciences, pp. 10–20 (2000). doi:10.1109/HICSS.2000.926982
4. Singh, S.K., Singh, M.P., Singh, D.K.: A survey of energy-efficient hierarchical cluster-based routing in wireless sensor networks. Int. J. Adv. Netw. Appl. **2**(02), 570–580 (2010)
5. Zang, Z., Qi, J.D., Cao, Y.J.: A robust routing protocol in wireless sensor network. In: IET International Conference on Wireless Sensor Network, pp. 276–279. (2010). doi:10.1049/cp.2010.1066
6. Younis, O., Fahmy, S.: HEED: a hybrid, energy-efficient, distributed clustering approach for ad hoc sensor networks. IEEE Trans. Mobile Comput. **3**(4), 366–379 (2004). doi:10.1109/TMC.2004.41
7. Perkins, C., Belding-Royer, E., Das, S.: Ad hoc on-demand distance vector (AODV) routing (2003). doi:10.17487/RFC3561
8. Toh, C.K.: Associativity-based routing for ad hoc mobile networks. Wirel. Pers. Commun. **4**(2), 103–139 (1997). doi:10.1023/A:1008812928561
9. Chen, G.G., Branch, J.W., Szymanski, B.K.: A self-selection technique for flooding and routing in wireless ad-hoc networks. J. Netw. Syst. Manag. **14**(3), 359–380 (2006). doi:10.1007/s10922-006-9036-7
10. Johnson, D.B., Maltz, D.A.: Dynamic source routing in ad hoc wireless networks. In: Imielinski, T., Korth, H.F. (eds.) Mobile Computing, pp. 153–181. Springer, New York (1996). doi:10.1007/978-0-585-29603-6_5
11. Perkins, C.E., Bhagwat, P.: Highly dynamic destination-sequenced distance-vector routing (DSDV) for mobile computers. ACM SIGCOMM Comput. Commun. Rev. **24**(4), 234–244 (1994). doi:10.1145/190809.190336. ACM
12. King, P.J.B, Etorban, A., Ibrahim, I.S.: A DSDV-based multipath routing protocol for mobile ad-hoc networks. In: Proceedings of the 8th Annual Post Graduate Symposium on the Convergence of Telecommunications, Networking and Broadcasting, pp. 93–98 (2007)
13. Marina, M.K, Das, S.R.: On-demand multipath distance vector routing in ad hoc networks. In: Ninth International Conference on Network Protocols, pp. 14–23. IEEE (2001). doi:10.1109/ICNP.2001.992756
14. Mateen, W., Raza, S., Uzmi, Z.A.: Adaptive multi-path on-demand routing in mobile ad hoc networks. In: Eighth IEEE International Symposium on Object-Oriented Real-Time Distributed Computing, pp. 237–244 (2005). doi:10.1109/ISORC.2005.8
15. Dang, K., Shen, J.Z., Dong, L.D.: A graph route-based superframe scheduling scheme in WirelessHART mesh networks for high robustness. Wirel. Pers. Commun. **71**(4), 2431–2444 (2013). doi:10.1007/s11277-012-0946-2
16. Shao-Shan, J., Huang, C.H., Guangqiong, Z.: A minimum hop routing protocol for wireless sensor networks. Hua Univ. **24**(2007.12), 45–57 (2007)
17. Soro, S., Heinzelman, W.B.: Prolonging the lifetime of wireless sensor networks via unequal clustering. In: 19th IEEE International on Parallel and Distributed Processing Symposium, pp, 8–16 (2005). doi:10.1109/IPDPS.2005.365
18. Zhang, Q., Li, F., Ju, L., Jia, Z., Zhang, Z.: Reliable and energy efficient routing algorithm for WirelessHART. In: Sun, X.-h., et al. (eds.) ICA3PP 2014. LNCS, vol. 8630, pp. 192–203. Springer, Cham (2014). doi:10.1007/978-3-319-11197-1_15

Big Data Management

Constrained Semantic Grammar Enabled Question Answering System

Dongsheng Wang[1,2(✉)], Shi Wang[3], Weiming Wang[1], Jianhui Fu[3], and Yun Dai[4]

[1] Department of Computer Science and Engineering, Jiangsu University of Science and Technology, Zhenjiang 212003, China
wds_ict@163.com, wangweimin@gmail.com

[2] International WIC Institute, Beijing University of Technology, Beijing 100022, China

[3] Institute of Computing Technology, Chinese Academy of Sciences, Beijing 100190, China
{wangshi, fujianhui}@ict.ac.cn

[4] Jiangsu Justice Police Advanced Vocational School, Zhenjiang 212003, China
21325005@qq.com

Abstract. Restricted domain question answering (QA) system is a hotspot in the natural language processing area. Correct understanding of the users' intentions is the key to such QA systems while open domain QA can always make use of data redundancy. In this paper, a robust but highly constrained semantic grammar and corresponding matching algorithm are proposed. On the basis of the domain ontology constructed by domain experts, the grammar experts creat the core semantic grammar, which describes patterns of expression about properties of concepts or relationships between concepts in the interested domain. In order to verify the validity of the proposed method, the method is applied to mobile service consulting area, experimental results show that the proposed method has strong practicability as well as maintainability.

Keywords: Ontology · Semantic grammar · Question answering · Restricted domain

1 Introduction

With the rapid development of internet-based information systems, information query technology based on natural language interface has been put forward more and more requirements, while currently general natural language understanding technology can not fully meet actual demands, especially domain-related applications [1].

Domain-specific applications can take many different forms, and if they are developed as case-by-case, it will be a time-consuming and labor-intensive task which can always be done only by experts. We hope to focus on a class of systems that are common but also widely used, namely information query system based on natural language interface, which can be used for intelligent customer service, flight information query service, tourist attractions information query service. Such systems have the following

L. Zhang et al. (Eds.): Monterey Workshop 2016, LNCS 10228, pp. 55–65, 2017.
DOI: 10.1007/978-3-319-61994-1_6

characteristics: (1) They are oriented to a specific task or a particular area; (2) Spoken natural language are used for human-computer interaction. Choosing such systems as study object has the following reasons: firstly, from a practical point of view, such systems used in practice can save a lot of resources for the community and improve the quality of information services. Secondly, from a research strategy point of view, such systems have a certain degree of representation, which is the basis for further research on open domain QA system. Thirdly, from the perspective of application, natural language is the most convenient and most used way of communication [3].

Based on the above points of view, this paper presents a domain-restricted natural language understanding technology including constrained semantic grammar and the corresponding semantic grammar matching algorithm. In order to verify the effectiveness of the method, it is applied to mobile service consulting area, results show that the method presented in this paper is effective.

2 Related Work

According to the application field of QA system, QA systems can be divided into two categories: restricted domain QA system and open domain QA system. Frequently Asked Question (FAQ) is the most commonly used techniques for restricted domains, and it can be used as an effective complement to the open domain question answering system. If similar questions are asked more frequently, the question-answer pairs can be stored as FAQs. When newly sumbitted questions match some FAQs, answers can be directly fed back to users, no need to re-organize the answer which can improve the efficiency of the system [8]. At present, most of FAQ systems only provide keyword search, which is difficult to accurately capture the true intentions of users. In addition, such methods usually can not provide a variety of operators, such as ‘AND’, ‘OR’, ‘NOT’, etc., to construct complex queries. An effective solution is to provide a natural language query interface for the system, and users are usually able to express their intentions in a natural and concise manner without the need for special training.

The techniques used for question answering system can be mainly divided into three types: traditonal natural language understanding (NLU) technology, information retrieval and template matching. At the present stage, the technology of natural language understanding is not yet mature, deep semantic analysis of sentences has not yet reached the practical requirements [4]. Meanwhile, information retrieval based question answering system can not effectively process some types of questions, Such as HOW-TO, WHY questions, the accuracy of such systems is far from being able to meet the actual needs, especially for domain specific applications.

Jimmy [5] pointed out the reason for the effectiveness of template-based QA system is that distribution of user questions is likely to obey zipf law, i.e., most questions only correspond to a small part of the question type set, the statistics of TREC-2001 question set showed that 50 question types cover more than 45% of whole question set, and they propose a centralized and distributed QA system, in which the centralized method uses a small number of question templates to cover a lot of online databases, while information retrieval is technique used as distributed method. Winiwarter [6] made syntax, semantic and pragmatic analysis to history user queries so as to establish a FAQ XSE (eXtended Semantic Enumeration) tree, then the same analysises are made for the newly summited questions to match to FAQs. Sneiders [1] proposed an approach by using question template with entity slots to match user questions, in which slots are matched with entities in the question so as to match the database model, templates are considered as assertions (predicates) with fixed parameters and variables, so the process of matching templates with user questions is to make the assertions to be true. Yu [7] proposed a restricted domain FAQ model, ontology was used to organise FAQs so as to build a domain knowledge base, domain characteristics of questions, lexical relationships, syntax dependencies and relationships between concepts in the domain are considered into question simmilarity model. HowNet was used as a semantic knowledge resource to calculate the semantic similarity between users' questions and FAQs in Chinese [8]. Yang [9] proposed a ontology-based query templates and interface modeling techniques, in which interface agents act as adjuncts to the FAQ system to obtain streaming FAQs from personal computer domain.

3 Proposed Method

3.1 Domain Modeling

In the field of artificial intelligence, ontology is closely related with knowledge representation, which is defined as 'formal, conceptual system for sharing a clear and detailed explanation'. It is seen as an important tool to support knowledge sharing and reuse. Domain ontology is modeled for an interested domain or a part of the real world, which expresses the special meaning of those terms that are appropriate to the domain. In this paper, we apply the proposed method to Mobile Service Consulting (MSC) domain while considering the general principles of ontology modeling [2] and the characteristics of the interested domain. Figure 1 is a part of the MSC ontology hierarchy.

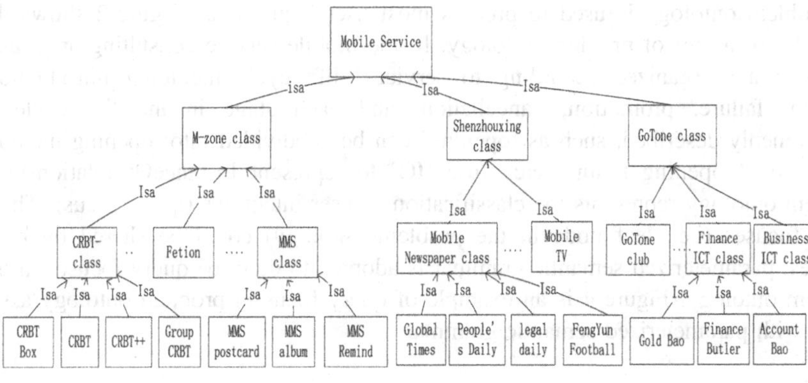

Fig. 1. MSC domain ontology

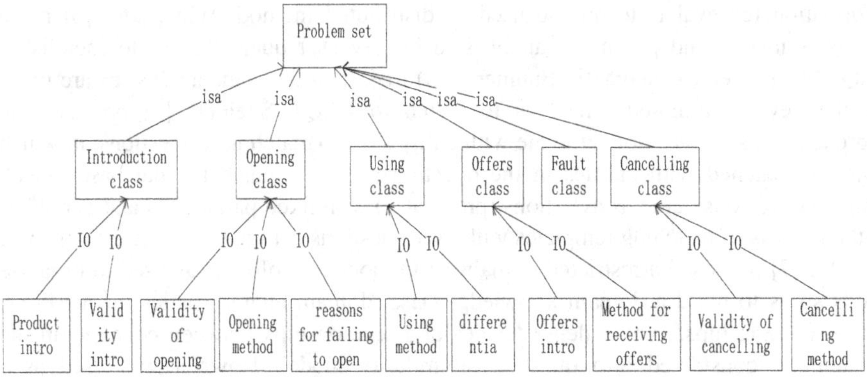

Fig. 2. MSC problem ontology

As can be seen from the ontology hierarchy, mobile service related concepts are modeled as ontology classes, and relationships between child services and parent services are modeled as 'isa' relation, so properties of parent services can be inherited to their children. For each class, user interested and application related aspects are selected as class attributes. Different with traditional modeling methods, only some typical and special attributes or relationships are selected to describe classes in domain ontology while other general ones (i.e., shared by many classes) are maintained in the problem ontology.

When users consult about these special and personalized aspects of mobile services, terminologies and expression patterns in user questions are usually very different with others. For example, CRBT service has a special property 'CRBT song audition method', which is not shared with other services. In this paper, non-parameterized semantic grammar is used to describe class attributes in domain ontology. Since these class attributes are always user concerned aspects, also be called 'query focus'. Detailed definition of semantic grammar will be given in next section. Figure 3 is an example of CRBT service and its attribute associated with non-paramiterized semantic grammar.

Problem ontology is used to process most users' questions. Figure 2 shows the hierarchy of a part of problem ontology. In the mobile service consulting area, user questions are organized according to services' life cycle including introduction, opening, failure, promotion, cancellation. and each stage in the life cycle is fine-grainedly described, such as 'opening' can be subdivided into: opening method, the cause of opening failure, etc., (use 'IO' to represent InstanceOf relationship). Problem ontology represents the classification of user intentions (query focus). These query focuses (i.e., leaf node in the problem ontology) could be shared by most services, parameterized semantic grammar is adopted to describe query focuses in the problem ontology. Figure 4 is an example of query focus in problem ontology associated with parameterized semantic grammar.

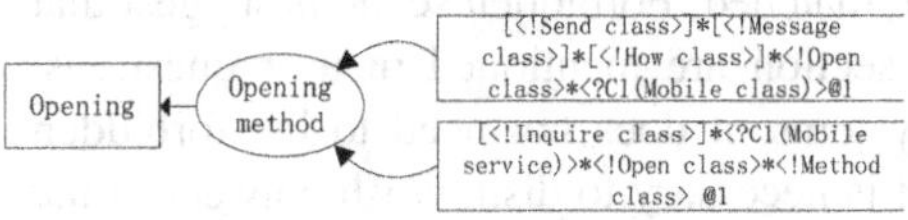

Fig. 3. Example of non-parameterized semantic grammar

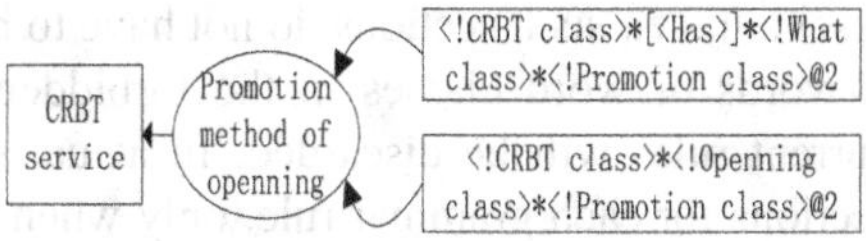

Fig. 4. Example of parameterized semantic grammar

Users always refered the same concept with different expressions, for example, when users describe 'opening' of services, words with same or similar meanings would be used, such as handling, openning, turn on, etc. In this paper, a thesaurus is created to link words with semantic similarity, which is also known as shallow lexical semantics, because these links are established directly between words. Semantic classes are created to represent a cluster of synonymous words, which would be cited in semantic grammar.

3.2 Definition of Semantic Grammar

Semantic grammar represents static relationships between non-static entity slots or non-static entity slots and attributes, in which the entity slots can be filled with various instances that is consistent with slot type constraints. Semantic grammar consists of parameterized and non-parameterized rules, parameterized rules are mainly used to describe query focuses in the problem ontology while non-parameterized rules are adopted to describe properties in the domain ontology. Semantic grammar is usually associated with the leaf node (i.e., query focuses in the problem ontology). Its BNF definition is as Fig. 5.

<SG>::=<SGBody>"@"<SGControl>"#"<SGAction>
<SGBody>::=<Required section>"*"<Slot>|
<Required section>"*"{<Optional section>} "*"
<Slot>"*"{<Optional section>"*"
{<Forbidden section>}
<Slot>::=?C"("<Entity class>")"
<Entity class>::= "Mobile service"|...
<SGAction>::=<Action>"("<Parameter list>")"
<Action>::= "GenAnswer"|...
<Parameter list>::= "?C",<GFocus>,...
<GFocus>::="Opening"|"Closing"|...

Fig. 5. Definition of semantic grammar

Set of required sections in semantic grammar rules expresses the core meaning of grammar, which should be matched to one word in questions; Optional sections refer to components that may assist in expressing the meaning of user intentions, but not essential, i.e., such sections do not have to be matched; Forbidden sections suggest that if words or word classes in the forbidden section are mentioned in user questions, current rules will be discarded. In actual systems, it does not need to list forbidden sections for each grammar rule, only when it is necessary to distinguish between some similar rules associated with different query focuses. Each semantic grammar rule contains one or more entity slots with constraints, and semantic actions would be executed on the matched entities if the entire rule is matched.

Design of semantic grammar is closely related with domain modeling. Domain modeling (conceptual model) consists of extracting concepts (C), properties (A), relationships (R) and restrictions (axioms) from interested domains, and users' questions about a certain domain are always related with the elements in the conceptual model. The function of semantic grammar is to map concepts, attributes, relations mentioned in users' questions to corresponding elements in the domain model. One complete semantic grammar should be one-to-one correspondence with the conceptual model of the domain. In this way, semantic grammar can be associated with structured data, such as relational database, grammar rules can be used to describe relationships between many concept instances or concept instances and attributes. Figure 6 is an example of mapping between conceptual model and grammar fragment.

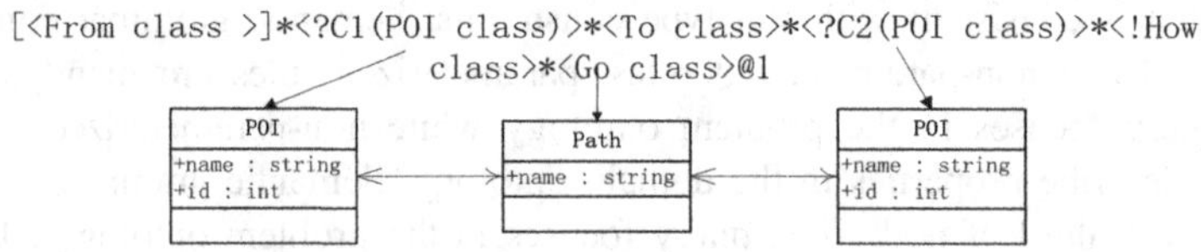

Fig. 6. Example of mapping between conceptual model and grammar fragment

3.3 Semantic Grammar Matching

Considering the matching efficiency, inverted indexes are created for the semantic grammar rules, that is, rules are indexed by words or word classes which constitute them. only words or word classes appeared in required sections are used for indexing. The slots are also deemed as required sections, so slot types are used for indexing. The benefit is that the number of candidate rules is greatly reduced in the matching process while not reducing the matching accuracy. Questions are segmented and labeled with semantic classes based on knowledge base, all candidate semantic grammar rules are selected according to QTM algorithm [10], a core sub proces *SGM-Filtering (CQWs, WP)* should be called, in which rules are filtered according to several principles, such as rule control, semantic constraints etc. *SGM-Filtering (CQWs, WP)* is shown in Algorithm 1.

Algorithm 1 Outline of the SGM-Filtering algorithm

```
Input: Orderly word sequence labeled with semantic classes:CQWs;
Grammar rule:R;
Output: TRUE(Pass) or FALSE(Filtered);
Begin
For i=1 to length(forbiddenR)
  For j=1 to length(CQWs)
    if (forbiddenR[i]= CQWs[j].Word OR contains(forbiddenR [i] ,
        CQWs[j].WordClass) Return False;
  end
end
For i=1 to length(requiredR)
  For j=1 to length(CQWs)
    If requiredR[i]= CQWs[j].Word OR contains(requiredR [i] ,
       CQWs[j].WordClass) then
        Remove CQWs[j] from CQWs;
        Set pose[i]= j ;
        M++;
     end
  end
end
If M<length(requiredR) then Return False;
If (M<length(requiredR) Return False;
If (R.SGControl==1)
  If (numbers in pose is increasing) Return False;
  else Return True;
else Return False;
End.
```

After rule filtering, there may still be serveral rules meeting the matching requirements, Matching score for the matching between questions and grammar rules is calculated, and top ranked rules will be returned, detailed description of matching score model can be found in [10]. Entities Satisfied constraints of slots will be extracted and are assigned to parameters in SGAction. SGAction can be interpreted according to specific demands and requirements, for example, computing sub/super classes, part-of relations with other entities.

3.4 Semantic Grammar Enabled QA System Building Process

Figure 7 is an overview of the process of building a constrained semantic grammar enabled QA system (CSG-QA).

Specifically, The first step is to analyze interested domain and creat domain model (such as domain ontology), then design DB schema according to domain model and create semantic grammar based on FAQs. Entities or relations mentioned in user

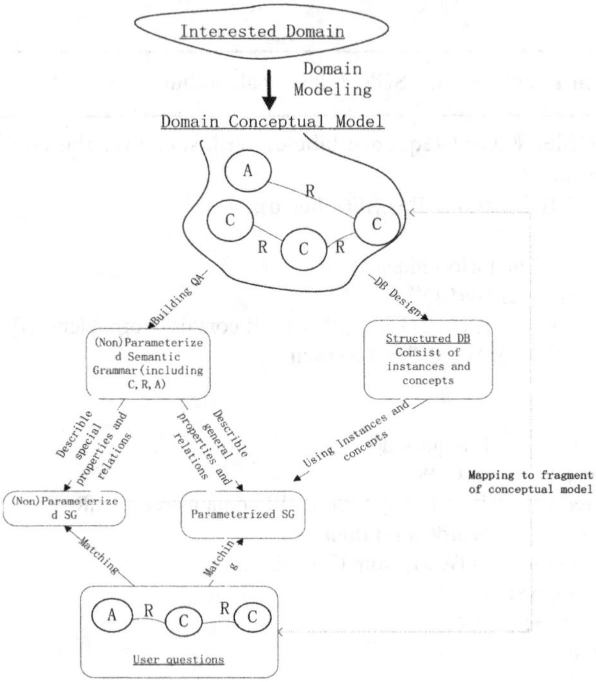

Fig. 7. System building process

questions are mapped to fragment of domain conceptual model through matching questions to semantic grammar. And ultimately pre-organized answers in DBs are returned to users. Layered matching strategy was adopted to process user questions, i.e., general and parameterized semantic grammar which can cover most questions are firstly matched, if has successful matching, answers will be returned to users directly, otherwise, special and non-parameterized semantic grammar will be matched, if the match is successful, answers will be returned. Figure 8 shows the overall work flow of CSG-QA system.

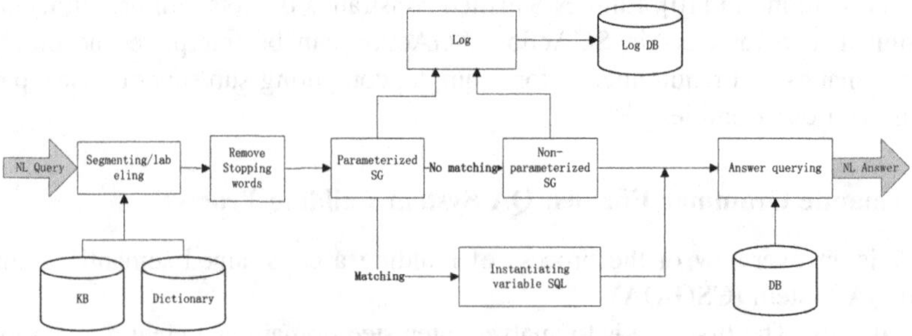

Fig. 8. Workflow of CSG-QA

4 Experiment

4.1 Data Set

In order to verify the effectiveness of the proposed method, the system was applied to the mobile services consulting area. In this application, accuracy of answers to users' request should be 100%, So answers generated by CSG-QA system will be confirmed by CSRs first, if answers generated by the system is correct, it will be directly sent to users, otherwise, CSRs will do some modifications to the auo-generated answers. In this process, the system automatically generates realtime accuracy report of CSG-QA system according to operations done by CSRs, and the higher the recognition rate and accuracy of CSQ-QA, the higher efficiency of CSRs'. Meanwhile, CSRs feedback accurately about the auto-generated answers, so the system can extract unmatched or wrongly matched questions along with corresponding grammar rules, which is helpful for purposefully optimizing the knowledge base, by manually modifying semantic grammars or automatic learning semantic grammars.

Currently the total number of services maintained in the system is 1296, the average number of query focus is about 8.7 (including properties in the domain ontology and query focus in the problem ontology), total daily consultation is about 130,000. Hardware configuration of the system is: HP DL580 servers, 4*Way Intel Xeon CPU 2.70 GHz processor, 73G*4 hard disks, 4G memory, efficiency of CSG-QA is about 20 questions/s.

4.2 Results

Accuracy and recognition rate are used to measure the performance of the proposed algorithm. Definitions are as follows:

$$Accuracy = \frac{\#\text{Questions matched correctly}}{\#\text{Identified questions}} \tag{1}$$

$$Recognition\ rate = \frac{\#\#\text{Identified questions}}{\#\text{Total test questions}} \tag{2}$$

Two experiments are carried out to evaluate the algorithm. The first experiment is to test the impact of average number of grammar rules associated with each query focus on the accuracy and recognition rate of CSG-QA.

Figures 9 and 10 respectively show the relations between number of grammar rules and accuracy/recognition rate. Experimental results show that when the average number of grammar rules for each query focus are increased, accuracy and recognition rate are greatly improved.

The second experiment is to evaluate the stability of the system according to time period, Fig. 11 shows the accuracy and recognition rate corresponding to different time point in one month. From the figure we can see that the system maintained a relatively stable accuracy and recognition rate, indicating that the overall performance of the

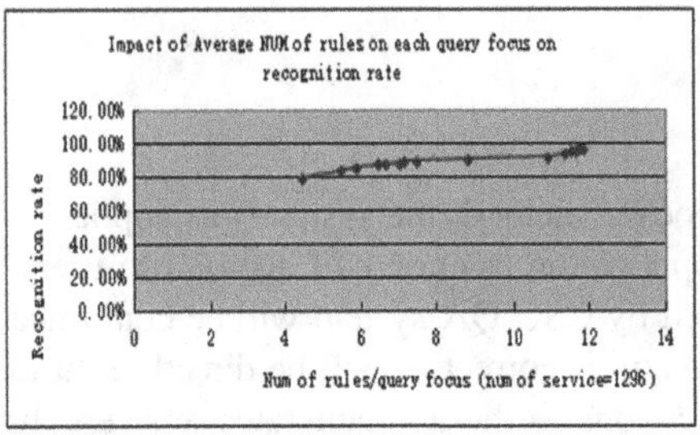

Fig. 9. Relations between number of rules and accuracy

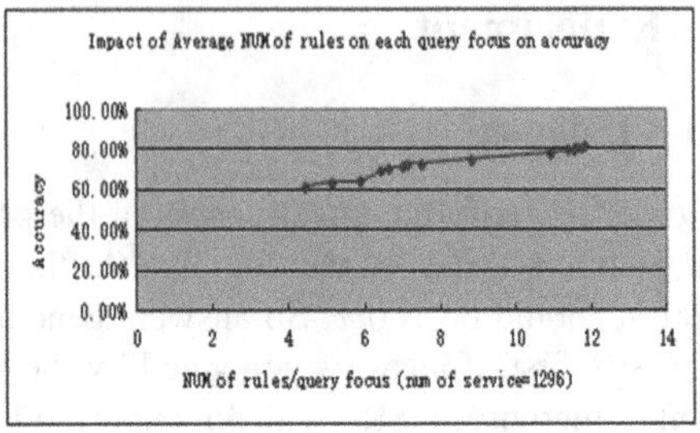

Fig. 10. Relations between number of rules and recognition rate

system is much stable. During this experiment, the average number of services is about 1296, average num of query focus for each business is about 8.7 and average num of grammar rules per query focus is about 10.1.

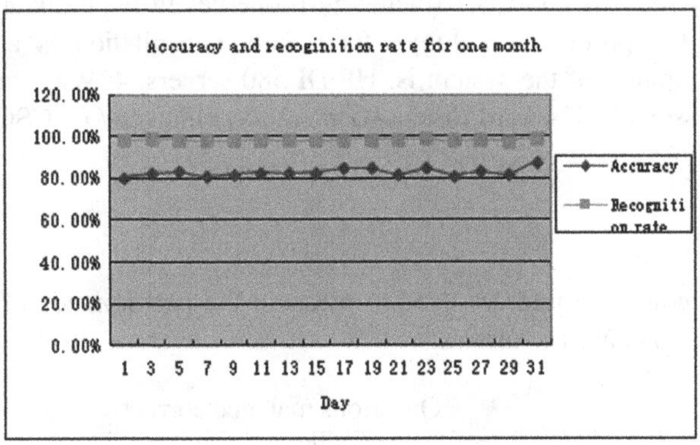

Fig. 11. Performances over one month

5 Conclusion

Compared with other languages, expressions in Chinese are more diverse. The same meaning can be conveyed using same words but with totally different orders, indicating that the syntax for Chinese are more flexible. In this paper, an ontology and semantic grammar enabled QA method is presented, experimental results show that this method has higher accuracy and recognition rate as well as stability. Meanwhile, the system has high maintainability, which does not require special skills for maintainers, they just need to adjust some ambiguous rules according to feedbacks from CSRs. Future work will be focused on automatic or semi-automatic learning semantic grammar from histroy user queries and CSRs' feedbacks.

References

1. Sneiders, E.: Automated FAQ Answering: Continued Experience with Shallow Language Understanding. Technical report FS-99-02. AAAI Press, North Falmouth, Massachusetts, USA, pp. 97–107 (1999)
2. Noy, N.F., McGuinnes, D.L.: Ontology Development 101: A Guide to Creating Your First Ontology. Stanford Knowledge Systems Laboratory Technical report KSL-01 -05 and Stanford Medical Informatics Technical report (2001)
3. Wu, X., Xu, M., Wu, A.W.: Preparing for evaluation of a flight spoken dialogue system. In: International Symposium on Chinese Spoken Language Processing (2002)
4. Wu, Y., Zhao, J., et al.: Research on question answering & evaluation: a survey. J. Chin. Inf. Process. **19**(3), 2–14 (2005)
5. Lin, J.: The Web as a resource for question answering: perspectives and challenges. In: Proceedings of the Third International Conference on Language Resources and Evaluation (2002)
6. Winiwarter, W.: Adaptive natural language interface to FAQ knowledge bases. Int. J. Data Knowl. Eng. **35**(2), 181–199 (2000)
7. Yu, Z., Deng, J., et al.: A FAQ question answering system based on restricted domain. J. Comput. Res. Dev. **2**, 388–393 (2007)
8. Qin, B., Liu, T., et al.: Research of question answering system based on frequently asked questions. J. Harbin Inst. Technol. **35**(10), 1179–1182 (2003)
9. Yang, S.Y., Chiu, Y.H., Ho, C.S.: Ontology-supported and query template-based user modeling techniques for interface agents. In: The 12th National Conference on Fuzzy Theory and Its Applications, pp. 181–186 (2004)
10. Wang, D.S.: A domain-specific question answering system based on ontology and question templates. In: 2010 11th ACIS International Conference on Software Engineering Artificial Intelligence Networking and Parallel/Distributed Computing (SNPD), pp. 151–156. IEEE (2010)

Information Composition Analysis and Adaptation Access of CNC Lathes in Cloud Manufacturing Environment

Lei Qiu[1], Chao Yin[1], and Xiao-bin Li[2(✉)]

[1] State Key Laboratory of Mechanical Transmission, Chongqing University, Chongqing, China
[2] School of Economics and Business Administration, Chongqing University, Chongqing, China
xiaobin_lee@cqu.edu.cn

Abstract. Aiming at the complicated information composition and the features such as high-degree autonomous, disperse, dynamic and changeable, and adaptive function of CNC lathes in cloud manufacturing environment, a framework for Adaptation Access of CNC lathes is proposed, which could support various types of information modular, dynamic virtual access. The key technologies such as service modeling approach of CNC lathes based on Web Service Modeling Ontology (WSMO) and Adaptation Access of CNC lathes based on Open Service Gateway Initiative (OSGI) are researched. Finally, an experimental case is used to verify the above research results.

Keywords: Cloud manufacturing · CNC lathes · Information composition · Adaptation Access

1 Introduction

Small and Medium-sized Enterprises (SME) as the main components of China's manufacturing industry, the situation such as lack of innovative capacity, poor product quality and reliability, and low resource utilization are ubiquitous [1]. For this reason, cloud manufacturing as a new internet-based and service-oriented manufacturing mode has been proposed, which could organize and optimize manufacturing resource in wide range by cloud manufacturing platform, and provide various types of manufacturing service for users [2–5]. In cloud manufacturing environment, there are lots of advanced manufacturing resources under inactivity, which can be founded, selected and used by SME by registration in the cloud manufacturing platform [6–8].

In recent years, experts and scholars have done lots of research on manufacturing resource modeling and Adaptation Access, and obtained the relevant research results. In order to solve the manufacturing resource integration problems of multi-application system, the author proposed a service-oriented manufacturing resource based on meta-model, and built meta-model of manufacturing which was abstracted from basic data, business process and application extension [9]. [10] proposed a description framework of machine tools resource based on WSMO, and studied the key technologies such as meta-data ontology representation approach and service-oriented

L. Zhang et al. (Eds.): Monterey Workshop 2016, LNCS 10228, pp. 66–76, 2017.
DOI: 10.1007/978-3-319-61994-1_7

packaging of machine tool resource. [11] put forward adaptation approach of analysis-specification-design-realization in cloud manufacturing environment for realizing scalable and virtual manufacturing resources sharing, and built cloud manufacturing resource model based on ontology. Aiming at all kinds of existing problems during heterogeneous sensor data access procedure, the author designed information model of heterogeneous sensor, and proposed a dynamic Adaptation Access method for heterogeneous sensing data [12].

In summary, the main researches are focus on semantic framework building, semantic description and Adaptation Access system developing and applying. In cloud manufacturing environment, the manufacturing resources have complicated information composition and feature, such as high-degree autonomous, disperse, etc. So it is important research significance on studying all kinds of manufacturing resources information modular, dynamic virtual access based on cloud services instance of manufacturing resource. Therefore, focus on the CNC lathes, the paper proposes a framework for Adaptation Access of CNC lathes, and study some key technologies, which could support various types of information achieve virtual access.

2 Information Composition of CNC Lathes in Cloud Manufacturing Environment

In traditional manufacturing environment, there always need to analyze the information composition of single CNC lathe in a limited area, which leads the information composition is simple. In addition, the data of CNC lathes is mainly handled by the manual method, and the dynamic information such as status, ability, alarm and load

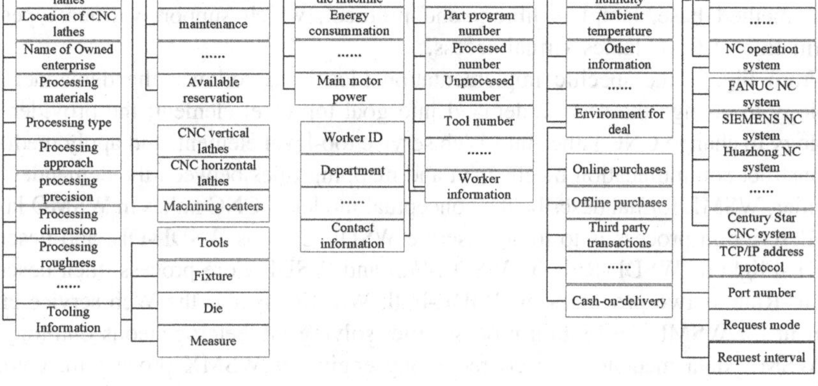

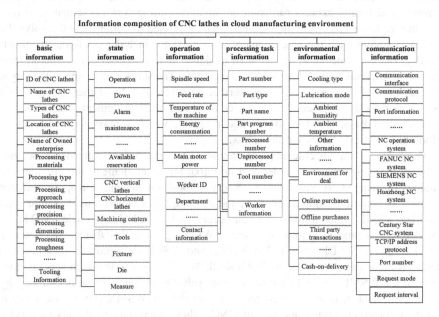

Fig. 1. Information composition of CNC lathes in cloud manufacturing environment

information couldn't be uploaded timely, which bring management barriers for enterprises and customers. In cloud manufacturing environment, there have lots of different types of CNC lathes, which make the information data is rich and huge. But the enterprises and customers can real-time control the CNC lathes information by Internet. So the paper analyzes the information composition of CNC lathes, which include basic information, state information, operation information, processing task information, environmental information and communication information. As shown in Fig. 1.

According to the analysis of complicated information composition of CNC lathes in cloud manufacturing environment, it is concluded that the rich feature of CNC lathes, such as high-degree autonomous, heterogeneous, disperse, service diversity, dynamic and changeable, adaptive function, etc.

3 Adaptation Access of CNC Lathes in Cloud Manufacturing Environment

3.1 Adaptation Access Framework of CNC Lathes in Cloud Manufacturing Environment

A framework for Adaptation Access of CNC lathes in cloud manufacturing environment is proposed, as shown in Fig. 2. The service modeling at the bottom of the framework is realized by applying Web Service Modeling Ontology (WSMO). The conceptual model of WSMO is used to define the four top-level elements, they are goal, mediator, ontology and web service [13, 14], among which ontology is the basic element. The function of ontology is to define semantic term for other three top-level elements and formal express exchange information during web implementation process; the mediator is a connection element, which is used to eliminate and resolve the mismatch among each top-level element. The mediator includes goal-goal mediator, ontology-ontology mediator, service-goal mediator and service-service mediator, their function is to contact other three top-level elements. The service modeling at the top of the framework is on basis of cloud service instance of CNC lathes, using OSGI specification to dynamic configure and combine connection element, analytical element, method base, template library and protocol, which support various types of information of CNC lathes virtual access.

From Fig. 2, the specific implementation idea is as follows: the demander use ontology to change the service demand into goal top-level element; the provider use ontology to change CNC lathes into Web service top-level element, and apply mediator to construct communication mechanism and mapping rules between the demander and provider; WSML formal describe the conceptual model of CNC lathes in WSMO layer. The description process is to logic describe WSDL-Core as WSDL-DL, and describe WSDL-Flight as WSDL-Rule by WSDL-Full and WSDL-Core process, then describe WSDL-Rule as two processes of WSDL-Full; WSMX layer is the Web service environment for WSML description process, after solving the heterogeneous ontology by the WSMX data mediator, the choreography engine of WSMX process mediator is called to construct service instance of CNC lathes. According to the above service

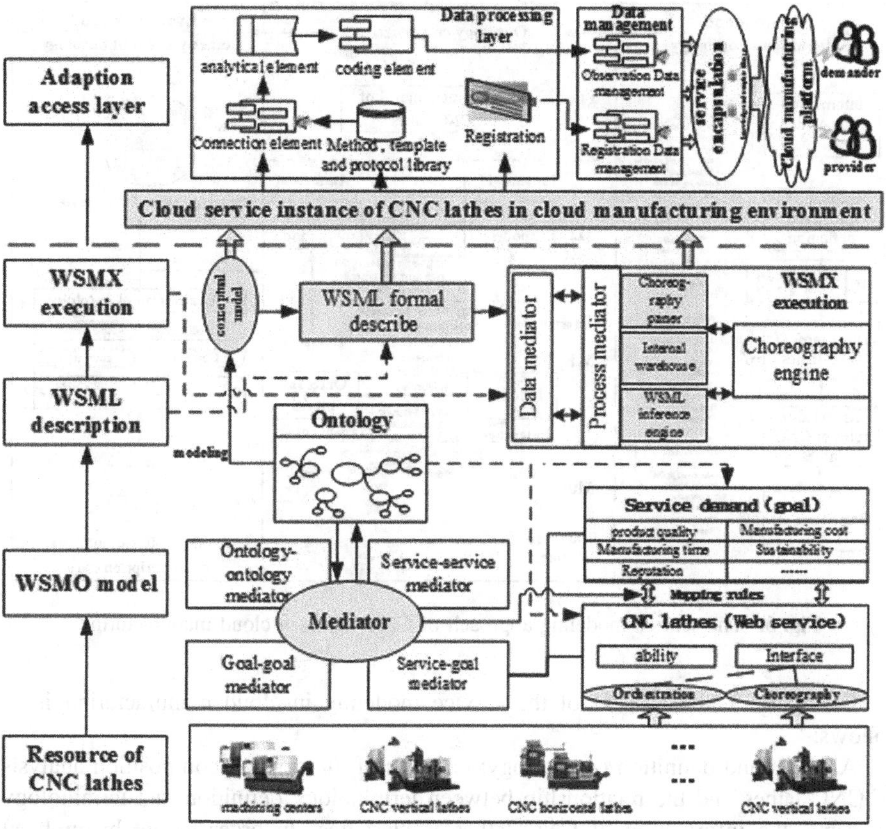

Fig. 2. A framework for access adaptation of CNC lathes in cloud manufacturing environment

instance of CNC lathes, the service instance is registered and the method base, template library and protocol are queried by using OSGI specification; communication protocol of CNC lathes with required plug-in formats is encapsulated and stored in the protocol library. Then, according to the XML documents of the above instance, from connection element, analytical element, coding element to Registration Information management module and Observation Data management module, the available virtual knowledge base and template library for cloud manufacturing platform are formed.

3.2 WSMO-Based Service Modeling Approach of CNC Lathes

The service modeling approach of CNC lathes is realized by a four meta-modeling architecture. Mainly include analysis and definition of ontology, ontology construction and evaluation and improvement of ontology. The process of the service modeling is shown in Fig. 3.

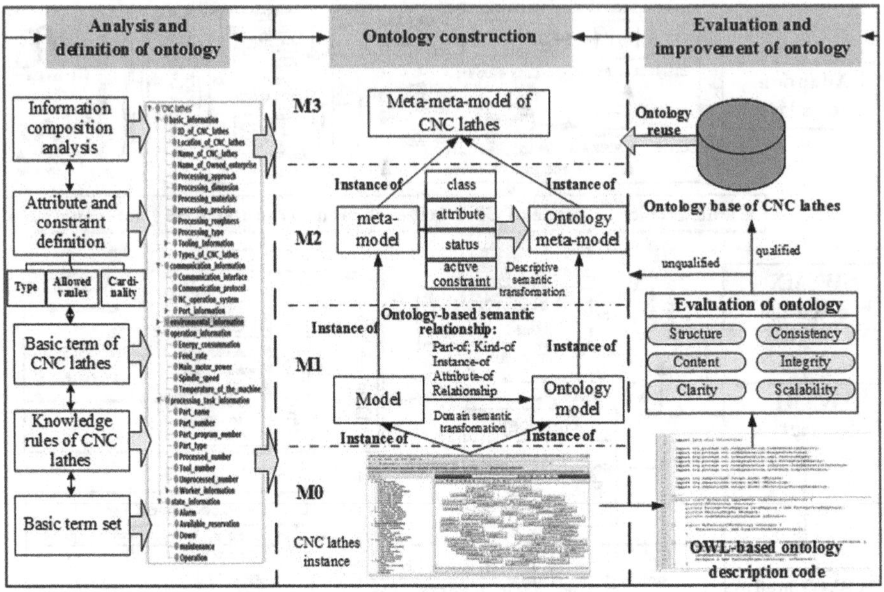

Fig. 3. The service modeling approach of CNC lathes in cloud manufacturing

From Fig. 3, the process of the service modeling in cloud manufacturing is as follows:

Analysis and definition of ontology: on basis of information composition analysis of CNC lathes and the relationship between terminology definition and terminology concepts, the information of CNC lathes is classified. In order to get hierarchical structure, the information of CNC lathes is divided from abstract to the concrete; after that, the attribute classification of CNC lathes is valuated based on constraint and attributes, and the attributes is divided into type, allowed value and cardinality.

Ontology construction: on basis of analysis and definition of ontology of CNC lathes, the paper constructs the ontology of CNC lathes, mainly including instance layer (M0), model layer (M1), meta-model layer (M2) and meta-meta-model layer (M3), among which the meta-meta-model layer is the basis of the whole ontology construction, and the elements of the meta-meta-model layer contains class, attribute and association; the meta-model layer is instance of every element in meta-meta-model layer, the main elements have class, attribute, status and active constraint. In the layer, ontology meta-model is described; the model layer is further instance of ontology meta-model, and the ontology model is built by ontology semantic conversion, such as part-of, kind-of, instance-of, attribute-of and relationship. Finally, ontology instance of CNC lathes is obtained by using protégé software.

Evaluation and improvement of ontology: after getting ontology instance of CNC lathes, the OWL ontology description code will be obtained by protégé directly. In order to get ontology set of CNC lathes, OWL ontology description code will be imported into WSMO model tool, and realize formal description of WSML semantics and syntax. Then does evaluation and improvement of ontology in structure and content, the knowledge base of CNC lathes is formed for the qualified ontology, the unqualified ontology will be rebuilt until there is available ontology instance.

On the basis of the above approach, ontology meta-model example of CNC lathes and corresponding parts of OWL-based ontology description code are obtained, as shown in Fig. 4.

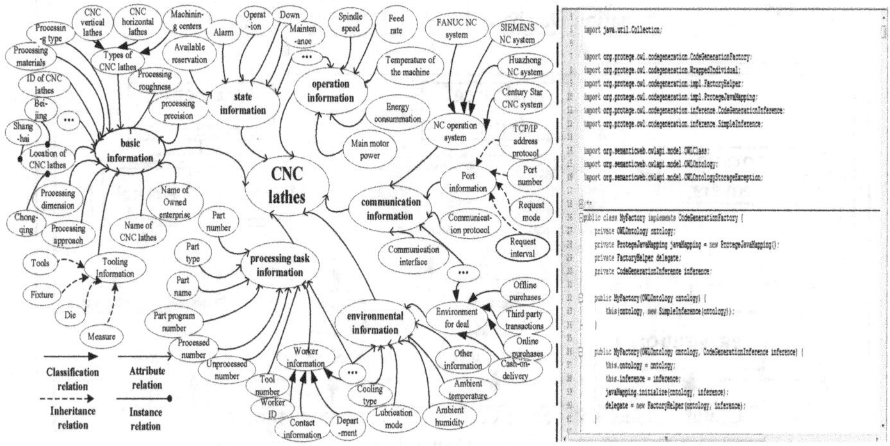

Fig. 4. Ontology meta-model example of CNC lathes and corresponding parts of OWL-based ontology description code

3.3 OSGI-Based Adaptation Access of CNC Lathes

Due to the difference of the operator interface, serial ports, protocol and the complex information composition of CNC lathes, the ontology instance of CNC lathes is different. Therefore, the paper proposes an OSGI-based Adaptation Access framework of CNC lathes [15], as shown in Fig. 5.

From Fig. 5, according to the cloud service instance in cloud manufacturing, CNC lathes is registered, and the registration information is managed by registration information management module. Based on the dynamic characteristic and module development of OSGI, the communication mechanism between the connection element of adaption process and communication of data port is built.

After connecting CNC lathes, the information analytic template is called by inquiring the information template. During the analytical procedure, the instantiated data of CNC lathes is parsed and changed to unified structure. Then, the converted data is coded and delivered to Observation Data management module, and in the procedure, there is no interference among the basic information, state information and communication information, furthermore, this information could be plugged dynamically. In the end, the data in Registration Information management module and Observation Data management module is encapsulated as virtual access knowledge base and template library, and it will be uploaded to cloud manufacturing platform.

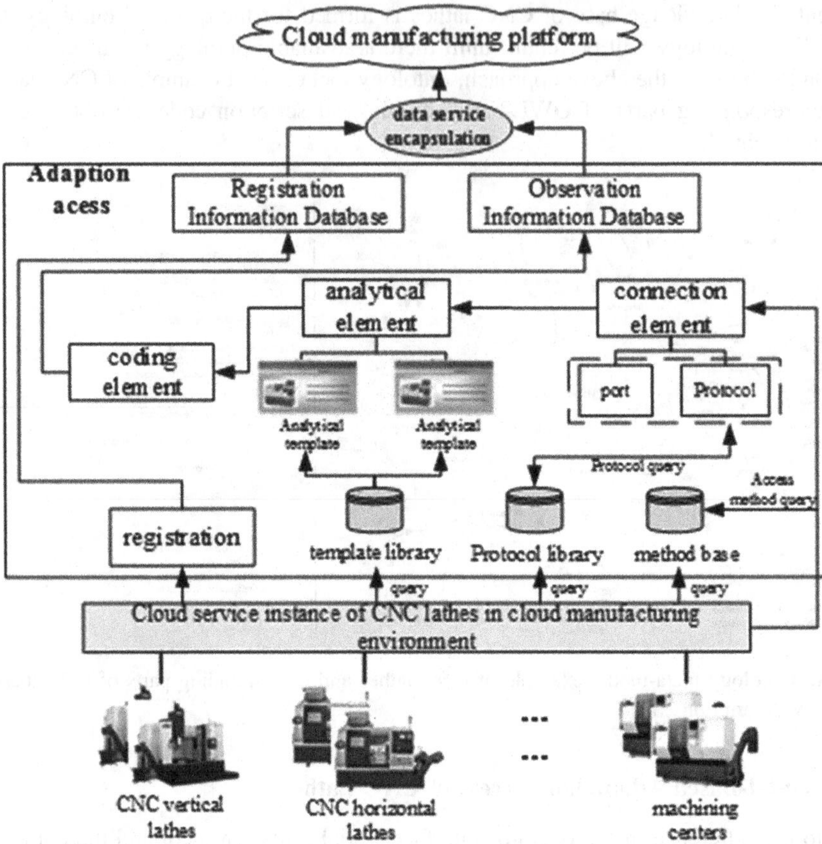

Fig. 5. An OSGI-based Adaptation Access framework of CNC lathes

During the Adaption Access process, the ontology instance data of various complex CNC lathes are connected and parsed by connection element, connection queue and analytical element, furthermore, the protocol of each CNC lathes is encapsulated in accordance with the provisions of OSGI plugins requirements and stored in Protocol Library. In general, because of the difference of the data communication protocol and port of CNC lathes, the Adaption Access and analytical procedure are realized by independent connection and parsing component. For example, there's a CNC lathes with TCP, HTTP and UDP, the connection, parsing and adaption access procedure are handled by TCP, HTTP and UDP monitor. Combine the above idea, take a 4-axis NC Machine Tool (TV5) as research objects, and the IP is 172.20.68.1, the port is 102. The XML program of adaption access and parsing are given, as shown in Fig. 6.

In order to accomplish the information of CNC lathes of connecting with the cloud manufacturing platform seamlessly and exchanging information with the cloud manufacturing platform easily, the data in Registration Information Database and Observation Information Database should be encapsulated. So the paper proposes a data service encapsulation framework based on Mobile Agent, as shown in Fig. 7.

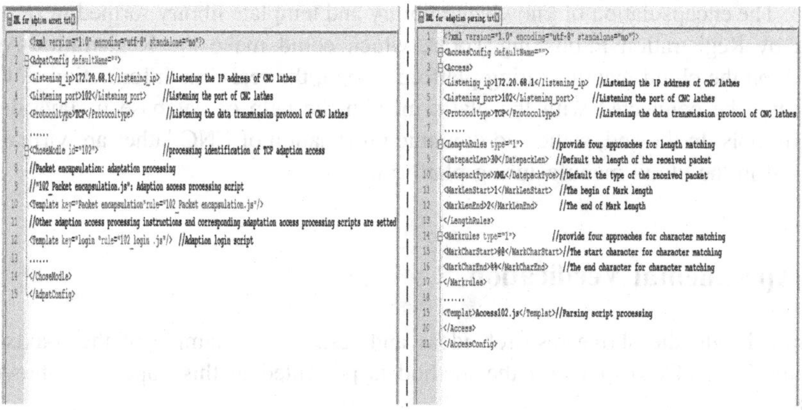

Fig. 6. The XML program of adaption access and parsing

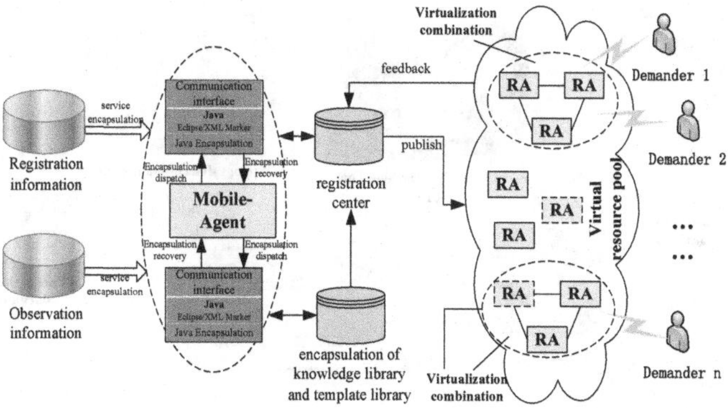

Fig. 7. A data service encapsulation framework based on Mobile Agent

The procedure of data service encapsulation can be divided into three steps:

Step 1: For realizing the service encapsulation, the Mobile Agent should be connected with the XML formed in the Adaption Access process by communication data interface.

Step 2: According to the XML attribute document of CNC lathes information, taking the communication information encapsulation as an example, the main process is as follows: First, semantic XML data document of communication information is encapsulated by using Java development tools, and Java implementation class is compiled; Second, using Aglets parse the formed Java implementation class, and the response Encapsulated Dispatch, Recovery and Communication Mechanism are defined; Third, the encapsulated Agent of communication information is obtained, which is stored at the encapsulation of knowledge library and template library, and it is used at the next encapsulation process. The other information of CNC lathes' encapsulation process is the same as above.

Step 3: The encapsulation of knowledge library and template library formed in step 2 is called by Registration Publishing Tools, which could make the Registration-Agent publish on the cloud manufacturing platform. Then, the real-time information of CNC lathes will be connected with the platform with the help of database in Java development tools. In the end, static and dynamic information of CNC lathes are virtualized accessed in the cloud manufacturing platform.

4 Experimental Verification

Combined with the above research ideas and results, an example of the 4-axis NC Machine Tool (TV5) to verify the method is presented in this paper. As shown in Fig. 8.

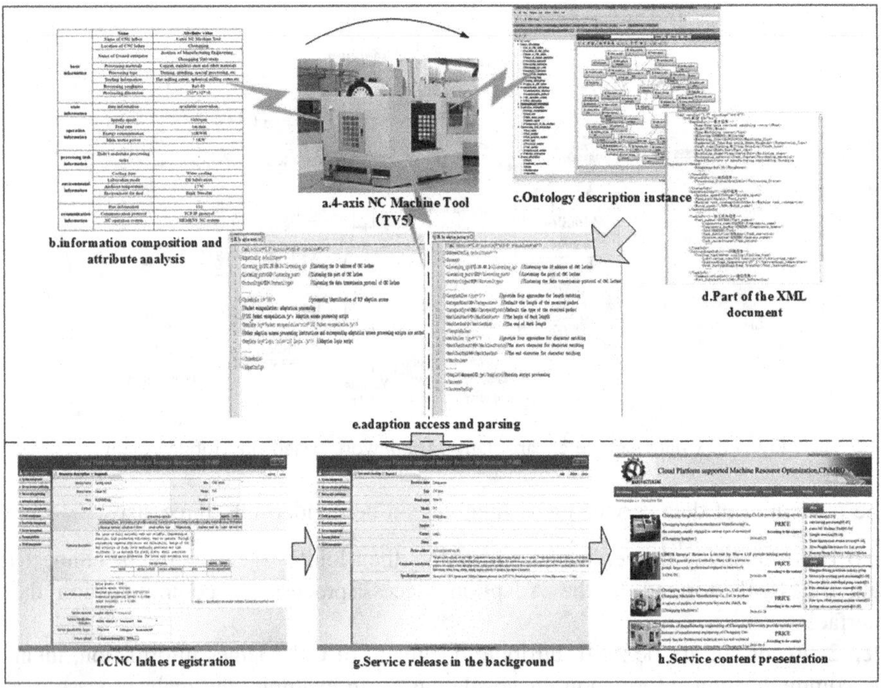

Fig. 8. The adaption access of 4-axis NC Machine Tool (TV5)

The specific process is as follows:

(1) Analysis of information composition and feature. According to the specification parameter, technical parameter, processing method of the TV5, the information composition and feature are analyzed, and the related concepts and concepts of attribute values of the TV5 are developed and complemented, as shown in Fig. 8b.

(2) Service modeling. Based on the information composition and feature analysis document of the TV5, the ontology of CNC lathes is described and built by WSMO Studio and protégé. In the end, the XML description documents of the TV5 are formed combined with XML mapping rules. As shown in Fig. 8c–d.
(3) Adaption access and service encapsulation. In order to realize the connection, parsing and coding of the data, based on the dynamic characteristic and module development of OSGI, the communication information of the TV5 is extracted by querying method base, template library and protocol, as shown in Fig. 8e. Then, the data in Registration Information Database and Observation Information Database are encapsulated to Java Implementation Class, and these encapsulate data will be stored at the encapsulation of knowledge library and template library.
(4) Service registration and publication. The information of TV5 such as registration information is published to the cloud platform to support the manufacturing resource optimization, as shown in Fig. 8f–h.

The experimental verification shows the Adaption Access of TV5 has been initially realized, so the method proposed in this paper is correct and feasible, which will offer the theory and technical guidance in Adaption Access of manufacturing resources in the future.

5 Conclusions and Future Work

In this paper, the information composition of CNC lathes in cloud manufacturing environment is analyzed, which includes the basic information, operation information, etc. Based on the above results, the paper puts forward a framework for Adaptation Access of CNC lathes, and the key technologies such as WSMO-based service modeling approach of CNC lathes and OSGI-based Adaptation Access of CNC lathes are studied. Finally the paper verifies the correctness and feasibility of the proposed method by experiments. The results of the above research can support all kinds of CNC lathes information modular, dynamic virtual access. The future work of the project will mainly explore and research the matching, optimization and service composition and other aspects of CNC lathes in cloud manufacturing environment.

Acknowledgment. This work was supported by the National High-Tech. R&D Program, China (No. 2015AA042102), and the Science and Technology Program of Guangdong Province (No. 2015A010103022).

References

1. Yin, C., Huang, B.-Q., et al.: Common key technology system of cloud manufacturing service platform for small and medium enterprises. Comput. Integr. Manufact. Syst. **17**(3), 495–503 (2011)
2. Li, B.-H., Zhang, L., Wang, S.-L., et al.: Cloud manufacturing: a new service-oriented networked manufacturing model. Comput. Integr. Manufact. Syst. **16**(1), 1–7 (2010)

3. Ren, L., Zhang, L., Tao, F., Zhao, C., Chai, X., Zhao, X.: Cloud manufacturing: from concept to practice. Enterprise Information Systems. **9**(2), 186–209 (2015). Taylor & Francis
4. Ren, L., Zhang, L., Wang, L., Tao, F., Chai, X.: Cloud manufacturing: key characteristics and applications. Int. J. Comput. Integr. Manufact. (2014). doi:10.1080/0951192X.2014.902105
5. Xun, X.U.: From cloud computing to cloud manufacturing. Robot. Comput.-Integr. Manufact. **28**(1), 75–86 (2012)
6. Ren, L., Cui, J., Wei, Y., LaiLi, Y., Zhang, L.: Research on the impact of service provider cooperative relationship on cloud manufacturing platform. Int. J. Adv. Manufact. Technol. (2016). doi:10.1007/s00170-016-8345-6
7. Li, X.-B., Yin, C., Gong, X.-R., et al.: Cloud manufacturing service platform for machine tool and processing operation. Comput. Integr. Manufact. Syst. **18**(7), 1604–1612 (2012)
8. Yin, S., Yin, C., et al.: Outsourcing resources integration service mode and semantic description in cloud manufacturing environment. Comput. Integr. Manufact. Syst. **17**(3), 525–532 (2011)
9. Wei, W., Li, D.-B., Tong, Y.-F.: Service-oriented unified manufacturing resource modeling based on meta-model. China Mech. Eng. **15**, 1818–1824 (2012)
10. Li, X.-B., Yin, C., Yin, S.: Semantic description and characteristics of machine tool resources in cloud manufacturing environment. Comput. Integr. Manufact. Syst. **20**(9), 2164–2171 (2014)
11. Talhi, A., Huet, J.C., Fortineau, V., Lamouri, S.: Towards a cloud manufacturing systems modeling methodology. Orig. Res. Art. IFAC-PapersOnLine **48**(3), 288–293 (2015)
12. Wang, Z.-L., Pu, F.-L.: Dynamic adaptation accessing method for heterogeneous sensing data. Transducer Microsyst. Technol. **36**(6), 13–16 (2015)
13. Wei, L., Wang, X.-L.: The theoretic framework and application of WSMO. J. Mod. Inf. **30**(8), 19–24 (2010)
14. Roman, D., Keller, U., Lausen, H., et al.: Web service modeling ontology. Appl. Ontol. **1**(1), 77–106 (2005)
15. Wu, J., Wang, D., Sheng, H.-Y., Siror, J.: Toward an SCA-OSGi based middleware for radio frequency identification applications. J. Shanghai Jiaotong Univ. (Sci.) **15**(2), 199–206 (2010)

Interactive Animation Editing Based on Sketch Interaction

Yan Huang[1,2](✉), Ti Zhou[2], Yanfeng Li[1], Yan Zhang[1], and Cuixia Ma[2,3]

[1] Nanjing Software Research Institute, Nanjing, China
huangyanl14@mails.ucas.ac.cn
[2] University of Chinese Academy of Sciences, Beijing, China
cuixia@iscas.ac.cn
[3] Institute of Software, Chinese Academy of Sciences, Beijing, China

Abstract. User-centric interactive system shows potential in allowing users facilely access to the experience of natural interaction appropriate to user's intention with a low cognitive load. A novel approach, central to the user's experience, is presented based on knowledge reuse, user interaction model and sketch-based interaction. A proposed sketch platform for animation editing provide the key to instantiating typical application within the reuse methods. The sketch-based interface explores a point in the tradeoff between expressiveness and naturalness to provide users a natural interactive environment. It helps to fill in the gaps of traditional WIMP (Window Icon Menu Pointing Device) pattern in the process animation drawings by sketching, exploring and modifying their ideas interactively with immediate and continuous visual feedback, and validate existing efforts and provide impetus for future work in the area of natural interaction research.

Keywords: Knowledge reuse · User-centric · Sketch · Natural user interface

1 Introduction

The booming of portable devices and networks helps to the development of innovative interaction pattern and operation behavior in the area of human-computer interaction. The design thinking of man-machine interface is being migrated from the pattern research of graphical interface to user-centric interactive design [1]. For improving the efficiency of knowledge utilization on a user-centric interface, a lack of an available method for knowledge induction, sorting, archiving may make a contribution to the poor reuse of existing data in the process of user interactive design. Since knowledge reuse, with its guidance, foreseeability and reappearance, is instructive for the interface design and interaction theory. In this paper, taking animation cases as application background, we make the most of knowledge reuse to present a sketch animation editing method that supports user with simple, natural sketch drawing on operating and organizing animation appropriate to user's intention with a low cognitive load. As animations are ubiquitous in modern visual media, the animation editing is an interactive, visual prototype with an interface resembling a sketch editor or drawing

L. Zhang et al. (Eds.): Monterey Workshop 2016, LNCS 10228, pp. 77–86, 2017.
DOI: 10.1007/978-3-319-61994-1_8

application, which provides an open work surface similar to the user's sketching lines. The user can sketch static illustrations or outline annotations directly on the objective animation using a simple sketch operation. The editing metaphor is extended with tools for sketching, interactive visual elements on the animation surface. Considering that user's editing stroke represents the timeline of an animation that can be used to achieve any operation like cutting, splicing, selecting or modification, We take advantage of the ability of sketching to provide efficient interaction directly to perform knowledge reuse for user design with the animation elements in order to make it easier and faster to work with animation editing.

The main contributions of this paper include: (1) Analysis the interactive behavior of user-computer to provide a sketch-based user model, which provides available theoretical guidance and assessment principles for the natural sketch editing method. (2) Demonstrate a sketch modeling of the multi-layered solution mechanism to achieve sketch structural recognition and understanding. (3) Provide a sketch-based animation editing platform that supports knowledge reuse for user facilely access to animation design in a natural environment. The work we conducted shows that it enhances the accessibility and individualization during the process of user drawing design and helps to enhance user experience in human computer interaction.

2 Related Work

Animation design is one of the most challenging problem-solving activities that the modern system faces. The cognitive complexity of design problems and the respond-time pressure due to improved interactive efficiency force designers to pursue efficient processes and strategies [2]. Natural editing method have become the central feature of user intention expression and are becoming the more fundamental and critical part in human interaction [3]. The traditional freehand writing on a paper is that simple and provides good user experience during the knowledge understanding. Most current animation designs for interactive interface are intuitive and multi-style which present different, rich menu items for users accessing operations. But they cannot support the interactively creative ideas description and achieve natural interaction well, which is important for user experience in the process of communicating with system. With the popularity of computers and pen interaction technologies, ideas of new methods and interactive technologies are incited to aid the sketch design and application. We prefer combining technologies of sketch-based recognition and understanding to explore an effective knowledge reuse in natural animation editing system. Some related techniques are involved, such as cognitive model, knowledge reuse and sketching technology.

Cognitive Model. Since the user tasks in the systems are becoming more complex, the benefit of systematic interface design receives more emphasis [4]. A good interface design procedure should elicit the user's task needs and task knowledge, which to some extent, leads to the demand of user cognitive factor on the special interactive interface [2]. To establish effective design strategies, the practical cognition of different users' needs to be considered [5]. Exploring cognition mechanism of user behavior helps to illustrate the user cognition model in the calculation process of user analysis, modeling and decision-making [6] when they interact with the interface. To realize natural and efficient interaction, we need to build the mapping mechanism to make computer understand the human cognitive process and shorten the cognitive distance between themselves thus reducing the burden of users' cognition. In this paper, we explore the user behavior and characteristics in the cognitive process to provide a sketch user model.

Knowledge Reuse. Natural interface design is becoming a more complex task due to the increasing needs of functionality and convenience of animation editing systems. Since User's constrained cognitive capability has made natural interface challenge further, we should optimize the interaction between the user and interface considering user goals, cognitive capabilities and available interface intention in the process of animation editing. Thus the concept of knowledge reuse has been proposed to minimize many redundant works and save the time cost for user editing and drawing [7, 8]. Among the existing approaches to achieve systematic knowledge reuse, some may appropriately focus on the preservation of design rationale for the issue-based information systems [9–11], some may consider the component-based software development with reusable modularized components practiced to depict object-oriented modelling techniques [12, 13], and others may prefer case-based reasoning techniques to find a prior problem similar to the current problem and provide a modified solution [14, 15]. This techniques have been applied to various design domains such as architecture, mechanical or physical devices and software [16–18]. In this paper, we probe the opportunity to achieve better user design by presenting relevant design cases based on sketch-related method. The sketch knowledge representation is therefore taken as the most important success factor, for which we propose organization of cases for users efficiently access to the animation design.

Sketching Interface. Sketch-based interaction presents a new generation natural user experience that breaks the bottleneck of current WIMP pattern and adopt the nature and efficiency of pencil and paper based interaction. Freehand sketching is a natural and crucial part of everyday human interaction, especially in early design processing [5]. Sketching technique mimics the tradition pen and paper that represents a natural way of thinking about ideas, its interface satisfies users in a freeform and flexible manner, allowing them to use their pen to draw sketches actively when interacting with computer systems [19]. With sketch interaction and recognition method, we provide user feedbacks to improve and enhance the learning process. By creating sketch-based interface, users can editing data more easily while keeping a natural style of interaction [20, 21]. Sketching technology has become popular for interactively design in different domains, like animation [22, 23], garment design, mathematics sketching, botanical modeling [24], floral modeling [25], hair style modeling [26, 27] and so on. In these systems, sketching can be used to create the prototype of design quickly. However, in our work, recognizing and understanding of sketches user depicting and designing can be performed based on the animation design.

3 Knowledge Reuse for Adaptive Sketching User Interface

3.1 Sketch-Based User Interaction Model

User model aims to explore the user characteristics in the process of the interaction by grasping user's cognitive habits, predicting their behaviors, thus to provide theoretical guidance for reuse design of user interface. User plays a central role in generating knowledge information from the snippets of data emerging from visual interaction, which enables users to analyze huge information spaces in order to support complex decision making and data exploration. Exploring the process of knowledge generation based on user's cognition helps to effective modeling of user visual analysis and interaction. In this paper, we adhere to the principle of user-centered interactive characteristics and rule of sketch-based editing method, referenced to the knowledge generation process [28] to provide a sketch-oriented user interaction model (see Fig. 1), which illustrates the usual interactive process that enables users to interact with the system using sketch interaction. The model demonstrates the cyclical process of user-computer interaction, the user part illustrates the knowledge generation process of the human, which depicts a reasoning process composed of exploration, verification, and knowledge generation loops. The interaction part presents the interactive information on the sketch interface with its different context provided so that a sketch-oriented object can be developed to support various operations and applications. The contexts contained in the system includes, **User context:** experienced designers or novice. **Environment context:** devices, pen locations, pen-styles, colors, symbol, diagram etc. **Sensed context:** time, sequence, color and positioning information etc. **Interpreted context:** first level derived context from sense context: classification of texts, symbols, drawings, gestures, etc. Second level derived from first level: geometry, topological relations, and sketch constraints.

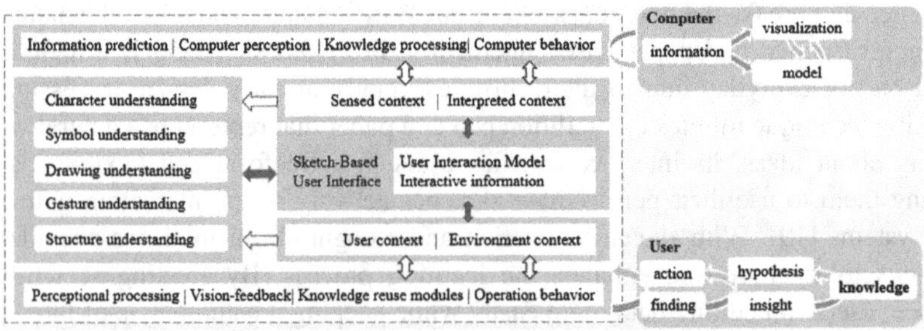

Fig. 1. Sketch-based user interaction model

3.2 Adaptive Sketch Recognition and Understanding

Due to the various ways user depicting sketches and its intentions, uncertainties over the process of interaction make it appropriate to consider the dissimilarity among users to develop knowledge reuse sketch context and constraint [29]. Thus to achieve an adaptive sketch-based interface for facilitating the design reuse process, modeling the sketching process is of great significance to improve the sketch recognition and understanding in the process of animation editing and interaction. We define the sketch including strokes that involves different constraints, strokes should be operated in the vector format, since a stroke is a set of sequent points captured from an input device during a time period between a pair of pen-down and pen-up events. Each point has a time stamp, with which we can recognize and compute the stroke to understanding the whole sketch structure. Admitting that different users may draw several strokes continuously or overlapping when they are required to finish a straight line, we need to group some strokes into different edges, which is a high level geometrical concept. Any modifications in either sketch strokes may contribute to the corresponding changes in another, which demonstrates the necessity of sketch modeling (Fig. 2 shows the corresponding sketch modeling).

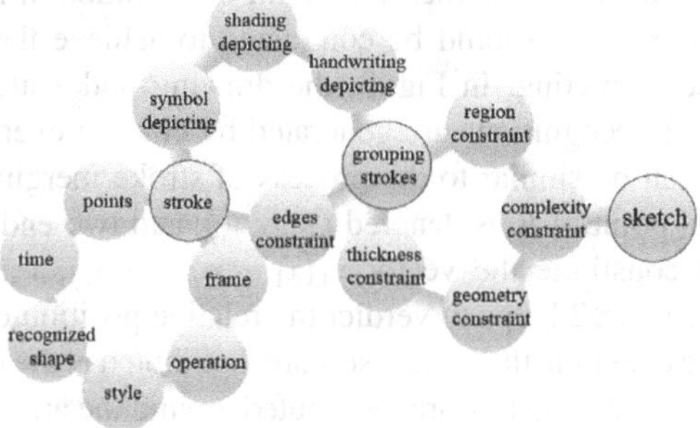

Fig. 2. The sketch modeling for recognition and understanding

To reuse the knowledge in interface design that users input the sketch data, system adaptively responds the retrieval and recognition for providing the existing similar recommendations. Adaptive recognition and understanding here means it can spontaneously adjust to variations of any sketches the user editing and provide optimal result realignment. Since the sketches users depicting presents the integrated concepts of their intents, we need to split them into every single meaningful pieces and then support a partial matching for sketch recognition [30, 31]. Figure 3 gives examples of a sketch drawings, structural recognition and understanding. For a set of sketches, detection and segmentation of pieces (nodes) should be first conducted. Considering that close distance between strokes among every piece may lead to inefficiency of recognition by simply computing the distance of strokes, we propose a new method to confirm the relative position of sketch nodes and use RNN classifier to train and recognize the feature vector of that obtained position. On the basic of recognition for connecting lines, we aim to merge the strokes according to the distance of strokes and the density of a stroke set. Denote that $dist(S_i, S_j)$ as the distance between stroke set S_i and S_j, *stroke_thres* as the merging threshold, while $dist(S_i, S_j) < stroke\_thres$, taking the merging operation since $stroke\_thres = \frac{3}{2n}\sum_{i=1}^{n} d_i$, where n represents the total number of strokes in a sketch, d_i represents the diagonal length of the select box that can contain

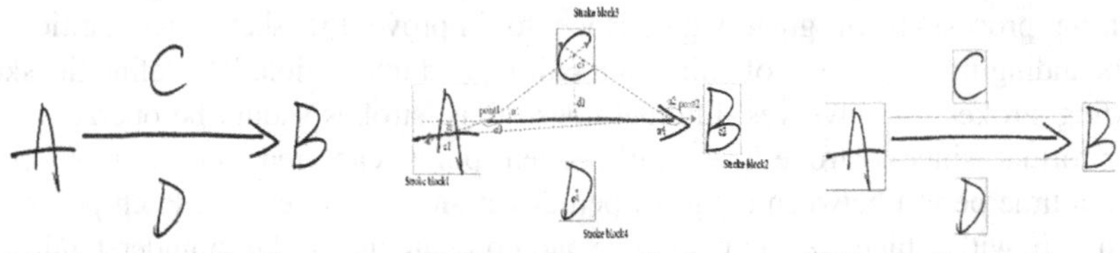

(a) Original input sketches (b) Recognition method (c) Result of recognition

Fig. 3. An example of sketch drawings, recognition and understanding

stroke i. Meanwhile, computing the stroke density $den(B_i)$ that has been merged and its density threshold $block\_thres$ using $den(B_i) = \frac{\sum_{j=1}^{k} len_j}{dia_i}$, in which len_j is the length of stroke j, $j \in B_i$, dia_i *is* the diagonal length of the bounding box of stroke set B_i. If $den(B_i) < block\_thres$, abandon the merging. With the iteration of recognition for each piece of strokes, further work should be conducted to achieve the recognition of the whole sketches a user depicting. In Fig. 3, the drawing nodes are shown on the left side, the corresponding recognitions are generated by circling every piece on the right side. Its recognition can be similar to the process of stroke merging to obtain a set of stroke B_i. The central point of B_i is denoted $C_i(x_i, y_i)$, and two endpoints of the arrow, $p_1(x_1, y_1)$, $p_2(x_2, y_2)$ constitute the vector $v_1(x_1 - x_i, y_1 - y_i)$, $v_2(x_2 - x_i, y_2 - y_i)$, in which their angles $\alpha 1$ and $\alpha 2$ helps to verdict the relative position of each stroke set. If $cos\alpha 1 * cos\alpha 2 < 0$, we conclude that stroke sets are distributed at the top or bottom side of the arrow. If $cos\alpha 1 * cos\alpha 2 \geq 0$, they are distributed around the arrow. Among of which,

$$cos\alpha 1 = \frac{(x_1 - x_i) \times (x_2 - x_1) + (y_1 - y_i) \times (y_2 - y_1)}{\sqrt{(x_1 - x_i)^2 + (y_1 - y_i)^2} \times \sqrt{(x_2 - x_1)^2 + (y_2 - y_1)^2}}$$

$$cos\alpha 2 = \frac{(x_2 - x_i) \times (x_2 - x_1) + (y_2 - y_i) \times (y_2 - y_1)}{\sqrt{(x_2 - x_i)^2 + (y_2 - y_i)^2} \times \sqrt{(x_2 - x_1)^2 + (y_2 - y_1)^2}}$$

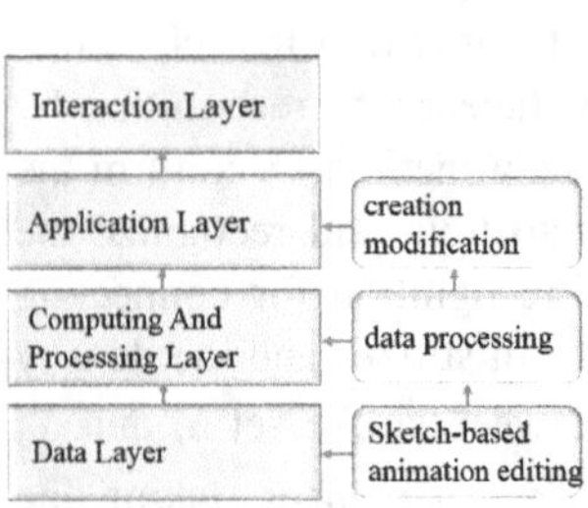

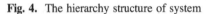

Fig. 4. The hierarchy structure of system

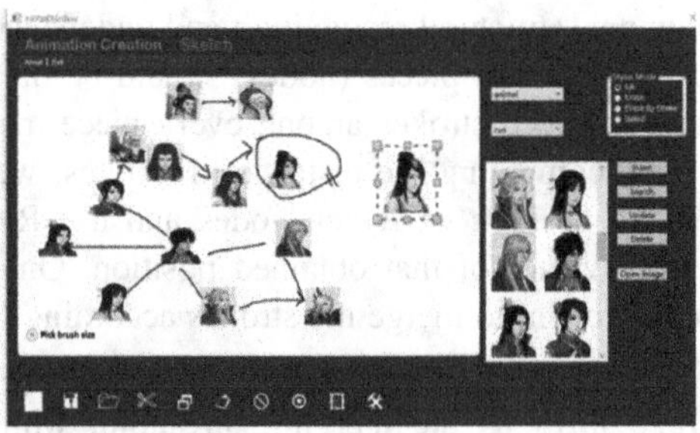

Fig. 5. Example of sketch editing and processing

After obtaining the relative position of the stroke sets, we can confirm whether they belong to the arrow by judging that distance $d \leq$ *threshold* or $d >$ *threshold* thus to achieve the recognition of each piece of strokes.

3.3 Knowledge Reuse for User Interface Design

The objective of the sketch-based animation editing system is to provide users with benefits of a traditional pen-pencil tool that has taken the effective design knowledge reuse into a consideration. The design of history backtracking develops effective means of adapting to the history information reuse for it helps to amend the sketch editing at any time in history in the process of interactive design. An orderly history backtracking means that stretching the design process back to previous drawing result in the form of backtracking command. For achieving the history knowledge reuse in the sketch interface, we provide a backtracking algorithm of random concept based on user's design intent as follow.

Denote the current collection of selected objects as $P = \{\psi_1, \psi_2, \ldots, \psi_m\}$, $j, k \in (1, n)$, FirstPrev = null, SecondPrev = null, the design node of conceptual object ψ_i :<eleId, attributes, head>. ψ_i.head shows the head pointer of the constraint chain, the constraint node is defined as Cons: *<Type, ElefirstID, ElesecondID, Attributes, ConsNextforfirst, ConsNextforsecond>*, in which ConsNextforfirst points to the next constraint node of object ElefirstID, and ConsNextforsecond points to the next constraint node of ElesecondID,

- For step 1, *j = k, if j > n*, it goes to step 4, *i = j + 1*, the current design object is ψ_j, with the index value, the current object and its mapping constraint chain can be available.
- For step 2, searching for the constrain chain of current object, if *i > n, k = k + 1*, then it goes back to step 1, and taking search matching of the two design objects that the constrain nodes had recorded as <ψ_j, ψ_i> (<ψ_i, ψ_j>). If it succeed, goes to step 3, or *i = i + 1,* then goes to step 2.
- For Step 3, the current constrain node is Con, FirstPrev records the previous constrain pointer or the mapping head pointer of ψ_j, SecondPrev records the previous constrain pointer or the mapping head pointer of ψ_i, FirstPrev = Con.ConsNextforfirst, SecondPrev = Con.ConsNextforsecond, then delete Con, goes to step 2.
- Step 4, end of the program.

The sketch-based backtracking in the process of drawing design helps to enhance the users' thinking process, with which users can take advantage of the ability of the reuse of history information to achieve an effective design on sketch editing. The system we provide allows users to input their own sketch knowledge to design and editing the animation, which includes animation importing and modification on the input knowledge by only using sketch interaction. The input knowledge they produce can in turn be added to the knowledge base for further reuse and reedit. If a regular user leaves, the loss will be prevented because his/her entering knowledge and experience will have already been saved for reuse. Figure 4 demonstrates the hierarchy structure of the editing system for knowledge design process, which includes four layers: data layer, computing and processing layer, application layer and interaction layer, in which, data layer depicts the animation knowledge and experience during the inputting process, as well as the original (reuse) input animation the system had provided before. It provides general data access for the external application. Computing and processing layer provides functions to recognize and process the inputting data collected by sketching from the users. As leading to the personalities of the systemic achievement. Application layer provides functions of creation, modification, save of the animation input drawings. And interaction layer provides the flexible sketch-based interaction to improve the natural human interaction with the purpose of reducing the cognitive load of different users. Figure 5 illustrates an example of the sketching editing of the animation and their structural recognition. When designing and editing any animation using sketches, users can save the depicting into the sketchborad for their reusing and editing with the functions toolbar for modification.

4 Conclusion and Future Work

A user-centric natural interaction, has the potential to alter the way that user's usual access to the knowledge creation process with distinct advantages. In this paper we present a natural sketch-based animation editing and design based on knowledge reuse, aiming to improve the design efficiency and user experience since sketch-based interaction helps to achieve the fact that reducing the user's cognitive load. The research involved detailing and demonstrating a sketch-based user interaction model, a method of sketch modeling and a supporting knowledge reuse user interface. It is capable and applicable for modeling various sketching interfaces and knowledge modeling applications. Of course, various input constraints for sketch structure recognition and understanding can be considered as one kind of improvement for our future work. A long term goal is to explore the algorithms of extending the abilities of adaptation and recognition of complex sketches, enriching them with further user interaction model. These characters would be beneficial to improvements of more natural interactive applications, capable of addressing the limits due to different users' cognitive ability, capturing users' intentions and then performing available presentations.

Acknowledgments. This work was supported by Jiangsu Province Colleges Natural Science Major Project under Grant No. 16KJA520003.

References

1. Ghasemifard, N., Shamsi, M., Kenari, A.R.R., et al.: A new view at usability test methods of interfaces for human computer interaction. Glob. J. Comput. Sci. Technol. **15**(1) (2015)
2. Kim, H., Wan, C.Y.: Supporting the cognitive process of user interface design with reusable design cases. Int. J. Hum.-Comput. Stud. **62**(4), 457–486 (2005)
3. Feng, S., Wan, J.: User interface knowledge reuse and multi-device user interface development. In: IEEE International Conference on Automation and Logistics, pp. 1203–1208. IEEE (2007)

4. Kalawa, A., Occello, Derypinna, A.M., et al.: Reusing user interface across devices with different design guidelines. In: Fourth International Conference on Knowledge and Systems Engineering, pp. 211–216 (2012)
5. Ma, C., Wang, H., Teng, D., Dai, G.: Design and analysis of conceptual sketches based on context awareness. In: Lee, S., Choo, H., Ha, S., Shin, I.C. (eds.) APCHI 2008. LNCS, vol. 5068, pp. 328–335. Springer, Heidelberg (2008). doi:10.1007/978-3-540-70585-7_37
6. Fu, X.L., Cai, L.H., Liu, Y., Jia, J., Chen, W.F., Yi, Z., Zhao, G.Z., Liu, Y.J., Wu, C.X.: A computational cognition model of perception, memory, and judgment. Sci. China Inf. Sci. **57**(3), 1–15 (2014)
7. Ockerman, J.J., Mitchell, C.M.: Case-based design browser to support software reuse: theoretical structure and empirical evaluation. Int. J. Hum.-Comput. Stud. **51**, 865–893 (1999)
8. Sutcliffe, A.G., Carroll, J.M.: Designing claims for reuse in interactive systems design. Int. J. Hum.-Comput. Stud. **50**, 213–241 (1999)
9. Lee, J., Lai, K.Y.: What's in design rationale? In: Moran, T.P., Carroll, J.M. (eds.) Design Rationale: Concepts, Techniques, and Use, pp. 271–289. Lawrence Erlbaum Associates, Mahwah (1996)
10. Chen, G., Lu, R., Jin, Z.: Constructing virtual domain ontologies based on domain knowledge reuse. J. Softw. **3**, 007 (2003)
11. Pathak, A., Patra, B.K.: A knowledge reuse framework for improving novelty and diversity in recommendations. In: Proceedings of the Second ACM IKDD Conference on Data Sciences, pp. 11–19. ACM (2015)
12. Lubars, M.D., Harandi, M.T.: Knowledge-based software design using design schemas. In: Proceedings of the Ninth International Conference on Software Engineering, California, USA, pp. 253–262 (1987)
13. Sutcliffe, A.: On the effective use and reuse of HCI knowledge. ACM Trans. Comput.-Hum. Interact. (TOCHI) **7**(2), 197–221 (2000)
14. Domeshek, E.A., Kolodner, K.L.: The designers' MUSE: experience to aid conceptual design of complex artifacts. In: Maher, M.L., Pu, P. (eds.) Issues and Applications of Case-Based Reasoning in Design, pp. 11–38. Lawrence Erlbaum Associates, New York (1997)
15. Wahid, S.: Investigating design knowledge reuse for interface development. In: Conference on Designing Interactive Systems, pp. 354–356. ACM (2006)
16. Mou, Y., Cao, J., Zhang, S.: A process component model for enterprise business knowledge reuse. In: Proceedings of the 2004 IEEE International Conference on Services Computing, pp. 409–412. IEEE Computer Society (2004)
17. Cheung, P.K, Chau, P.Y.K., Au, A.K.K.: Does knowledge reuse make a creative person more creative? In: Pacific Asia Conference on Information Systems, PACIS 2005, Bangkok, Thailand, 7–10 July 2005, pp. 219–227 (2005)
18. Zelewski, S., Kowalski, M., Bergenrodt, D.: "Intelligent" knowledge reuse for complex logistics projects: an application of ontology-driven and case-based reasoning. J. Control Sci. Eng. **1**, 23–37 (2013)
19. Ma, C., Du, Y., Teng, D., et al.: An adaptive sketching user interface for education system in virtual reality. In: IEEE International Symposium on IT in Medicine & Education, ITIME, vol. 1, pp. 796–802 (2009)
20. Shesh, A., Chen, B.: Smartpaper: an interactive and user friendly sketching system. Comput. Graph. Forum **23**(3), 301 (2004)
21. Ma, C., Dai, G., Teng, D.: Gesture-based interaction computing in conceptual design. J. Softw. **16**(2), 303–308 (2005)

22. Thorne, M., Burke, D., van de Panne, M.: Motion doodles: an interface for sketching character motion. ACM Trans. Graph. **23**(3), 424–431 (2004)
23. Igarashi, T., Moscovich, T., Hughes, J.F.: Spatial keyframing for performance-driven animation. In: Proceedings of the 2005 ACM SIGGRAPH/Eurographics Symposium on Computer Animation, SCA 2005, pp. 107–115. ACM Press, New York (2005)
24. Okabe, M., Owada, S., Igarashi, T.: Interactive design of botanical trees using freehand sketches and example-based editing. In: Eurographics 2005 (2005)
25. Ijiri, T., Owada, S., Okabe, M., Igarashi, T.: Floral diagrams and inflorescences: interactive flower modeling using botanical structural constraints. ACM Trans. Graph. **24**(3), 720–726 (2005)
26. Mao, X., Kato, H., Imamiya, A., Anjyo, K.: Sketch interface based expressive hairstyle modeling and rendering. In: Proceedings of IEEE Computer Graphics International (CGI), pp. 608–611 (2004)
27. Malik, S.: A sketching interface for modeling and editing hairstyles. In: Eurographics Workshop on Sketch-Based Interfaces and Modeling (2005)
28. Sacha, D., Stoffel, A., Stoffel, F., et al.: Knowledge generation model for visual analytics. IEEE Trans. Vis. Comput. Graph. **20**(12), 1604–1613 (2014)
29. Davis, R.: Magic paper: sketch-understanding research. Computer **40**(9), 34–41 (2007)
30. Ma, C.-X., Liu, Y.-J., Yang, H.-Y., Teng, D.-X., Wang, H.-A., Dai, G.-Z.: KnitSketch: a sketch pad for conceptual design of 2D garment patterns. IEEE Trans. Autom. Sci. Eng. **8**(2), 431–437 (2011)
31. Bresler, M., Průša, D., Hlaváč, V.: Online recognition of sketched arrow-connected diagrams. Int. J. Doc. Anal. Recogn. (IJDAR) **19**(3), 253–267 (2016)

Manufacturing Service Reconfiguration Optimization Using Hybrid Bees Algorithm in Cloud Manufacturing

Wenjun Xu[1,2(✉)], Xin Zhong[1,2], Yuanyuan Zhao[1,2], Zude Zhou[1,2], Lin Zhang[3], and Duc Truong Pham[4]

[1] School of Information Engineering, Wuhan University of Technology, Wuhan 430070, China
{xuwenjun, yuanzhao, zudezhou}@whut.edu.cn, phoebezx@foxmail.com
[2] Key Laboratory of Fiber Optic Sensing Technology and Information Processing, Ministry of Education, Wuhan 430070, China
[3] School of Automation Science and Electrical Engineering, Beihang University, Beijing 100191, China
johnlin9999@163.com
[4] Department of Mechanical Engineering, School of Engineering, University of Birmingham, Birmingham B15 2TT, UK
d.t.pham@bham.ac.uk

Abstract. During the execution process of a cloud manufacturing (CMfg) system, manufacturing service may become faulty to cause the violation of whole production processes against the predefined constraints. It is necessary to timely adjust service aggregation process to the runtime failure during manufacturing process. Therefore it is significant to do service reconfiguration to enhance the reliability of service-oriented manufacturing applications. The issues of the runtime service process reconfiguration based on QoS and energy consumption have been studied. In this paper, by contrast, an effective reconfiguration strategy is proposed to identify reconfiguration regions rather than the whole service process. Moreover, a hybrid bees algorithm (HBA) combining discrete bees algorithm (DBA) with discrete particle swarm optimization (DPSO) is developed to explore the replaceable services during service reconfiguration process. The experiment results show that most of manufacturing service aggregation processes can be repaired by replacing only a small number of services, and HBA is more efficient when finding the replaceable manufacturing services set compared with the existing algorithms.

Keywords: Cloud manufacturing · Manufacturing service reconfiguration · Reconfiguration optimization · Hybrid bees algorithm

1 Introduction

Cloud manufacturing (CMfg) aims to realize the full sharing and seamless collaboration, high utilization, and on-demand use of various manufacturing resources and capabilities in the form of manufacturing service to users [1, 2]. During the practical

L. Zhang et al. (Eds.): Monterey Workshop 2016, LNCS 10228, pp. 87–98, 2017.
DOI: 10.1007/978-3-319-61994-1_9

industry activities, there is a large amount of industrial data arising from the course of manufacturing process, which can be used to support service management and implementation [3]. In the CMfg environment, service aggregation optimization technology is the enabling technology to realize optimal allocation of resource. However, during the process of service aggregation execution, the service failure may occur due to the uncertain factors of the manufacturing resource service or the operating environment. Therefore, in order to ensure the liability of manufacturing service aggregation process, it is significant to adjust the process to uncertain and changeful environment.

Service reconfiguration has been proved to be feasible to solve this issue under the support of manufacturing resource aware technology and industrial big data technology. With aware technology, the service aggregation process and service operation status can be monitored. During the management and execution of manufacturing resource service, a large amount of industrial data would be perceived, which can be handled by related technologies of big data to analyze the status of manufacturing service. When the failing service is detected, service reconfiguration mechanism would be triggered in the process of service aggregation optimization to repair the failure service. However, service aggregation is regarded to be time-consuming because the optimal service aggregation problem is NP-hard [4]. A minimum system reconfiguration is always expected to keep most existing manufacturing service unchanged. Hence, it is not desirable to stop and recompose the entire process all the time when errors happen for the sake of efficiency and productivity. For this consideration, in this paper, an effective reconfiguration strategy is proposed to identify reconfiguration regions rather than the whole service process.

In addition, during the process of manufacturing service aggregation, a lot of works have been done mostly based on the quality of service (QoS), ignoring the importance of energy consumption. In order to reduce energy consumption cost to promote the sustainable and green manufacturing, energy consumption is required to be considered during reconfiguration process. In this case, a multi-objective service optimization algorithm based on a hybrid bees algorithm is developed to improve the quality of manufacturing service provided and reduce energy consumption cost.

The paper is organized as the following structure. The related works of service reconfiguration optimization are introduced in Sect. 2. In Sect. 3, a system framework of manufacturing service reconfiguration is illustrated. And in Sect. 4, the aggregation model and reconfiguration strategy are presented. The reconfiguration optimization algorithm is described in Sect. 5. Then, case study and experimental result is shown in Sect. 6. Finally, conclusion and future work are discussed and introduced in Sect. 7.

2 Related Works

A general monitoring model for the failure monitoring of web service is presented in [5]. When dealing with the faulty service, different from the previous method based on re-compositing the web process, an approach to discovering the "same skill" web services for the replacement of the failed and unavailable components is presented in [6]. In [7], Ramacher and Monch proposed a time-sensitive reconfiguration, which takes into account the uncertainty of response times and the temporal conditions found at execution time of a time-critical service composition. In addition to an execution time restriction, the reconfiguration of a service aggregation is also driven by the cost that results from the process of reconfiguration and other QoS attributes that are also subject to global constraints. Taking into account these aspects, the reconfiguration has to decide which services have to be reconfigured and which services are subject of an re-execution in [8, 9].

An issue of service reconfiguration optimization, which is also the challenge in this paper, is to reconfigure service in the conditions of multiple objectives and with multiple indexes constraints. Due to the complexity of service reconfiguration optimization problem, it is difficult to solve it by linear method. Hence, many intelligent optimization algorithms, such as bees algorithm (BA) [10], particle swarm optimization (PSO) algorithm [11], ant colony algorithm (ACA) [12], genetic algorithm (GA) [13], etc., have been applied to solve the multi-objective optimization problem. Bees algorithm (BA) is an optimization algorithm with the combination of neighborhood searching and random global searching by mimicking the food foraging behavior of swarms of honey bees. Castellani et al. use an improved bee algorithm to solve the dynamic optimization problems in [14]. The results show that the performance of the improved algorithm is superior to the standard bees algorithm, GA and PSO. Tian et al. used an improved discrete bees algorithm to solve multi-objective manufacturing service aggregation problem in [15]. Inspired by these previous works, in this paper, a hybrid bees algorithm which combines the advantage of discrete bee algorithm and discrete particle swarm optimization is proposed in this paper, in order to solve the multi-objective manufacturing service reconfiguration optimization problem.

3 System Framework

In engineering applications, service-oriented manufacturing processes need to adapt to the dynamic changes of the manufacturing environment so as to ensure successful execution. Figure 1 presents an overview of manufacturing service reconfiguration system Framework.

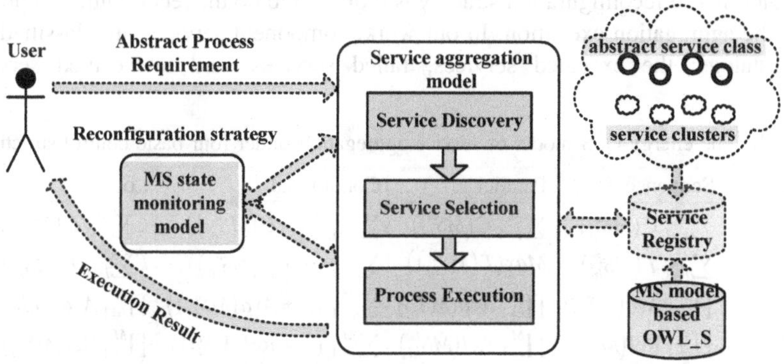

Fig. 1. Manufacturing service reconfiguration system framework

In the framework, the manufacturing services (MS) are described by the multi-dimension model based OWL-S [16]. Manufacturing resources and abilities are encapsulated into manufacturing services that are registered to the service register. In CMfg service resource pool, there are many kinds of abstract service classes that describe the common functions of the certain service cluster. Service cluster is the set of services that have the same or similar functionalities grouped together. Manufacturing tasks can be applied to a small number of abstract services and then mapped to the actual manufacturing services.

The manufacturing service aggregation execution process is monitored and managed based on the perception of the running state of manufacturing services until the manufacturing task is successfully executed. As a faulty manufacturing service of a component node is monitored, the service reconfiguration process is performed to rebind a new manufacturing service selected from the candidate services set to replace the faulty service. The corresponding reconfiguration strategy and optimization algorithm are used in the service reconfiguration process to ensure the normal implementation of the service aggregation process and reduce the reconfiguration cost. Finally, the execution result is returned to the user.

4 Aggregation Model and Manufacturing Service Reconfiguration Strategy

Given that a CMfg Task is decomposed into M sub-tasks. For each sub-tasks, there are a set of candidate services with similar function. After choosing M services from each corresponding candidate service set, a manufacturing service aggregation execution path (MSAP) is generated. In theory, there will be. $\Pi_{j=1}^{M} h_j$ possible MSAP. A MSAP is: $\{MS_{h_1}^{1}, \ldots, MS_{h_i}^{i}, \ldots, MS_{h_M}^{M}\}$. For QoS evaluation, four quality indexes are considered: execution cost (C), response time (T), availability (Ava) and reliability (Rel). Energy consumption (En) of CMfg lifecycle was studied by Xiang et al. in [17]. The energy-QoS model of service aggregation under four basic control structures is shown in Table 1. γ_i means the corresponding probability that $MS_{h_i}^{i}$ been selected and $\Sigma_{i=1}^{M} \gamma_i = 1$, where k is the cycle times.

Region-based reconfiguration strategy is proposed to do the reconfiguration process during the aggregation execution. In our work, component services are classified into three catalogs: the executed services, failed services, and unexecuted services.

Table 1. The energy-QoS model of service aggregation under four basic control structures

Attribute	Sequence	Parallel	Conditional	Loop
C	$\sum_{i=1}^{M} C(MS_{hi}^{i})$	$\sum_{i=1}^{M} C(MS_{hi}^{i})$	$\sum_{i=1}^{M} (\gamma_i * C(MS_{hi}^{i}))$	$k\sum_{i=1}^{M} C(MS_{hi}^{i})$
T	$\sum_{i=1}^{M} T(MS_{hi}^{i})$	$Max(T(MS_{hi}^{i}))$	$\sum_{i=1}^{M} (\gamma_i * T(MS_{hi}^{i}))$	$k\sum_{i=1}^{M} T(MS_{hi}^{i})$
Ava	$\prod_{i=1}^{M} Ava(MS_{hi}^{i})$	$\prod_{i=1}^{M} Ava(MS_{hi}^{i})$	$\sum_{i=1}^{M} (\gamma_i * Ava(MS_{hi}^{i}))$	$\prod_{i=1}^{M} Ava(MS_{hi}^{i})$
Rel	$\prod_{i=1}^{M} Rel(MS_{hi}^{i})$	$\prod_{i=1}^{M} Rel(MS_{hi}^{i})$	$\sum_{i=1}^{M} (\gamma_i * Rel(MS_{hi}^{i}))$	$\prod_{i=1}^{M} Rel(MS_{hi}^{i})$
En	$\sum_{i=1}^{M} En(MS_{hi}^{i})$	$\sum_{i=1}^{M} En(MS_{hi}^{i})$	$\sum_{i=1}^{M} (\gamma_i * En(MS_{hi}^{i}))$	$k\sum_{i=1}^{M} En(MS_{hi}^{i})$

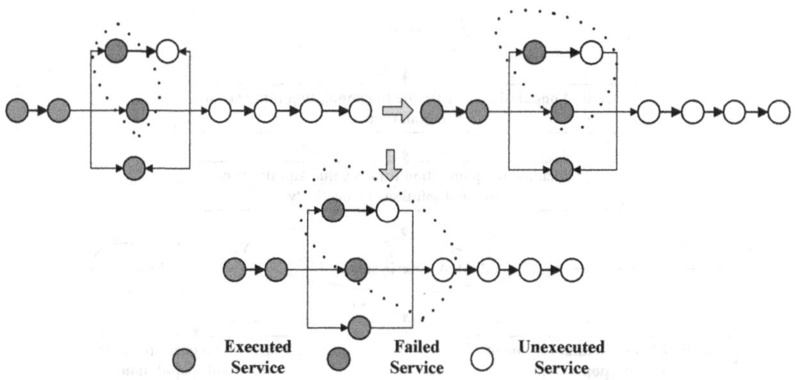

Fig. 2. Diagram of the region based reconfiguration process

The reconfiguration region is expanded continuously to cover more services, including unexecuted services and the executed services. The diagram of the region based reconfiguration process is shown in Fig. 2.

5 Reconfiguration Optimization Algorithm

In order to quickly and effectively find the replaceable services set for enriching reconfiguration region, a hybrid bees algorithm (HBA) is proposed. During the process of identifying the reconfiguration region, HBA is continued to be called to find optimal replaceable services to repair faulty services. The main steps of HBA are shown in Fig. 3.

In step 1, population is initialized and divided into two sub-populations. In step 2, calculate the fitness of the sub-populations is calculated to obtain the non-dominated solutions respectively based on Pareto dominance relationship among individuals. In step 4 and step 5, DBA and DPSO execute parallel search together. In step 4, the whole structure of DBA algorithm is re-adjusted while VNS (Variable Neighborhood Search) [18] search and crossover mechanism [15] is used in the neighborhood searching. VNS can enhance the local searching ability of bee algorithm through changing neighborhood structure. In the early iterations, the number of Pareto set of population may be relatively small. The part of remaining individual is selected to perform crossover operation which can increase the search scope of such algorithm. The detailed flowchart for DBA used in HBA is shown in Fig. 4.

In step 5, improved inertia weight ω, learning factor c_1, c_2 are used in the DPSO algorithm [19]. For step 6 and step 7, as the information exchange iterations N_{cmu} is satisfied, the sub-populations would go to step 8 to update the non-dominated solutions and population of the sub-populations. Through such information exchange mechanism to exchange the search results, it can overcome the shortcomings of falling into local extreme value of respective populations.

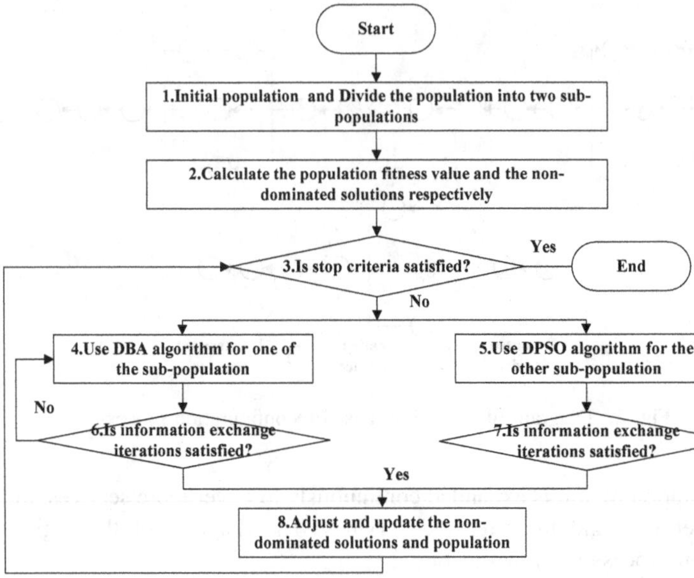

Fig. 3. HBA flowchart

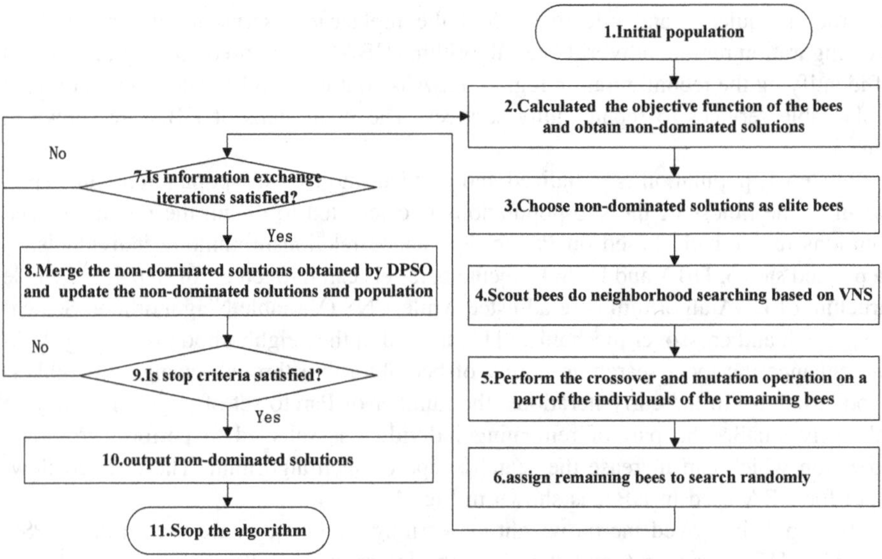

Fig. 4. Flowchart of DBA used in HBA

6 Case Study and Performance Evaluation

6.1 Case Study

The structure assembly of magnetic bearing is used as study case. In order to verify the proposed multi-objective service reconfiguration model and optimization algorithm, the representative 10 assembly activities are selected to build the manufacturing equipment service aggregation process, as shown in the following Fig. 5. MSS^1 is the assembly process design and simulation resource service set. MSS^2–MSS^8 represent different parts assembly services sets respectively. MSS^9 is the final assembly task resource service set. MSS^{10} is the assembly testing and evaluation service set.

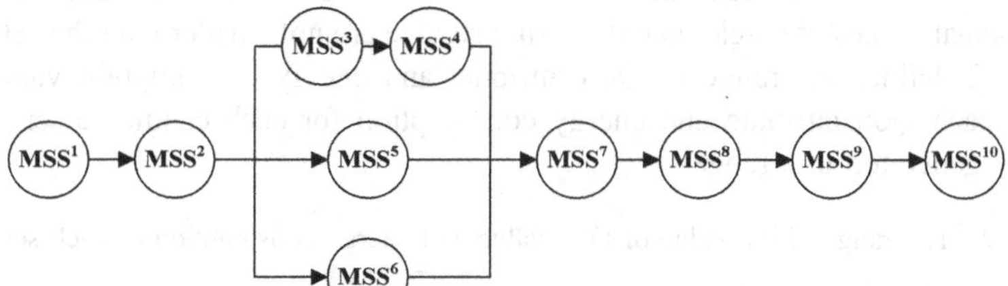

Fig. 5. Service aggregation process of magnetic bearing assembly

The fitness function for the service aggregation is as follows:

$$\begin{cases} f_{QoS}(MSAP) = \alpha C'(MSAP) + \beta T'(MSAP) + \eta Ava'(MSAP) + \theta \mathrm{Rel}'(MSAP) \\ f_{En}(MSAP) = \sum_{i=1}^{10} En(MS^i) \end{cases} \quad (1)$$

Specific formula corresponding to the above-described fitness function is as follows:

$$\begin{cases} T'(MSAP) = \sum_{i=1}^{2} T'(MS^i) + Max(\sum_{i=3}^{4} T'(MS^i), T'(MS^5), T'(MS^6)) + \sum_{i=7}^{10} T'(MS^i) \\ C'(MSAP) = \sum_{i=1}^{10} C'(MS^i) \\ Ava'(MSAP) = \sum_{i=1}^{10} Ava'(MS^i) \\ \mathrm{Rel}'(MSAP) = \sum_{i=1}^{10} \mathrm{Rel}'(MS^i) \end{cases} \quad (2)$$

$T'(MSAP), C'(MSAP), Ava'(MASP), \mathrm{Rel}'(MSAP)$ represent the normalized time, cost, availability and reliability of MSAP respectively. The related constraints for service aggregation process are as follows:

$$\begin{cases} T(MSAP) \le T_{\max}(MSAP) \\ C(MSAP) \le C_{\max}(MSAP) \\ Ava\left(MS_j^i\right) \ge Ava_{\min}\left(MS_j^i\right) \\ \mathrm{Re}l\left(MS_j^i\right) \ge \mathrm{Re}l_{\min}\left(MS_j^i\right) \end{cases} \tag{3}$$

T(MSAP), C(MSAP) represent the actual aggregation execution time and cost involved before normalized. T_{max}(MSAP), C_{max}(MSAP) are the maximum value of constraints set by user. The above two functions mean the actual execution time and cost are not bigger than the set value. $Ava_{\min}(MS_j^i)$ and $\mathrm{Re}l_{\min}(MS_j^i)$ mean the pre-supposed minimum value of availability and reliability. The lower two functions mean that the actual values of single manufacturing service are not smaller than the set value.

Table 2 defines the range of QoS attribute and energy consumption value; The value of each QoS attribute and energy consumption for each candidate service are randomly generated in a range.

Table 2. The range of the value of QoS value and energy consumption of each service

Candidates	*QoS of MS*				*En(MS)*
	T(MS)	*C(MS)*	*Ava(MS)*	Re*l(MS)*	
$MS \in MSS^1$	[20 33]	[50 70]	[0.5 1]	[0.5 1]	[50 80]
$MS \in MSS^2$	[8 14]	[90 120]	[0.5 1]	[0.5 1]	[20 35]
$MS \in MSS^3$	[10 13]	[70 90]	[0.5 1]	[0.5 1]	[70 90]
$MS \in MSS^4$	[15 30]	[100 125]	[0.5 1]	[0.5 1]	[30 50]
$MS \in MSS^5$	[25 40]	[70 110]	[0.5 1]	[0.5 1]	[80 120]
$MS \in MSS^6$	[16 25]	[120 140]	[0.5 1]	[0.5 1]	[30 45]
$MS \in MSS^7$	[30 40]	[70 120]	[0.5 1]	[0.5 1]	[40 60]
$MS \in MSS^8$	[16 25]	[50 60]	[0.5 1]	[0.5 1]	[20 30]
$MS \in MSS^9$	[30 35]	[180 200]	[0.5 1]	[0.5 1]	[80 130]
$MS \in MSS^{10}$	[10 15]	[40 80]	[0.5 1]	[0.5 1]	[10 20]

The value of the parameters used in the HBA algorithm are as follows: $\alpha = 0.5$, $\beta = 0.3$, $\eta = 0.1$, $\theta = 0.1$, $T_{max}(MSAP) = 170$, $C_{max}(MSAP) = 920$, $Ava_{\min}(MS_j^i) = 0.6$, $\mathrm{Re}l_{\min}(MS_j^i) = 0.6$, $N_{cmu} = 20$.

6.2 Experimental Results and Analysis

- Verifying the effectiveness of HBA algorithm in finding non-dominated solutions for multi-objective Service Aggregation Problem

For multi-objective optimization problem, Set Coverage (CS) [20] is used to compare the quality of solutions of different algorithms. The formula is as follows:

$$C(S_1, S_2) = |\{x_2 \in S_2 | \exists : x_1 \in S_1, x_2 \preceq x_1\}| / |S_2| \quad (4)$$

Where the value $C(S_1, S_2) = 1$ means that all solutions in S_2 are dominated by or equal to solutions in S_1. The opposite, $C(S_1, S_2) = 0$, represents the situation when none of the solutions in S_2 are covered by the set S_1.

Since the number of the candidate service for corresponding component node is 5 accurate non-dominated solutions can be obtained by using Enumeration method (Enu) which will take $1 * 5^{10}$ times to search. When population size is 120, the number of iterations is 200. The non-dominated solutions can be obtained by HBA in average 2.278 s. However, the solution is approximate optimal solution. Obviously the value of C(HBA, Enu) which represents the set coverage of non-dominated solutions for HBA and Enu is higher, the quality of the HBA obtained non-dominated solutions is better.

When the iterations is 200, population size is 80, 120, 160, 200, 240, 280 respectively, the result of C(HBA, Enu) is shown in Fig. 6. The results show that with the increasing in population size, the value of C(HBA, Enu) is increasing, finally is close to 100%. The results shown in Fig. 7 are obtained on conditions that the size of population is 120, the iterations is100, 160, 220, 280, 340, 400. Figures 6 and 7 show that the value of C(HBA, Enu) will enhanced with the appropriate value of initial population size and number of iterations.

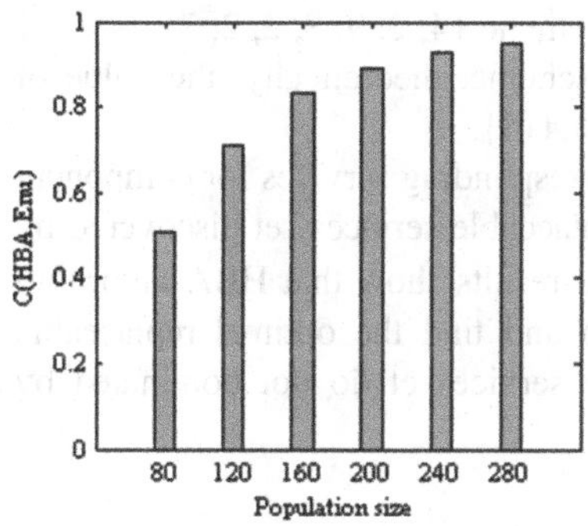

Fig. 6. Values with fixed iterations

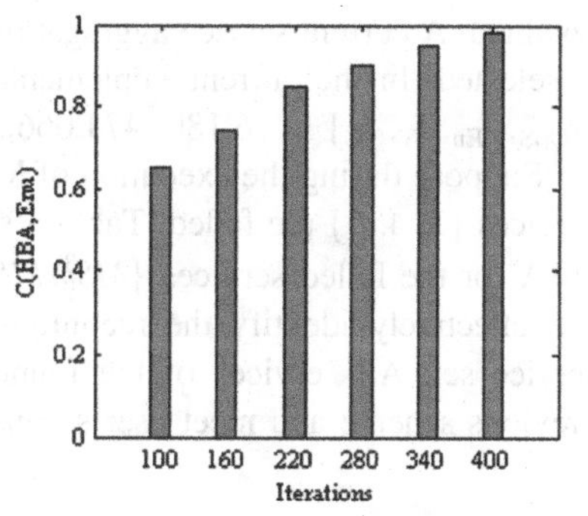

Fig. 7. Values with fixed population size

The performance of HBA is compared with DBA, DPSO, NSGA-II for the same model and experimental data. Figure 8 shows the running time of HBA compared to DBA, DPSO, NSGA-II when the population size is 120, the iterations is 120, 200, 280, 360. The results show that the average running time of HBA is less than DBA by taking advantage of DPSO, the running efficiency of HBA is improved. And the efficiency of HBA is far superior to NSGA-II. When the population is 120, the iterations is 360, the average running time is about 6.314 s. When the population is 160, the iterations is 220, the Pareto-optimal front obtained by HBA compared to DBA, DPSO,

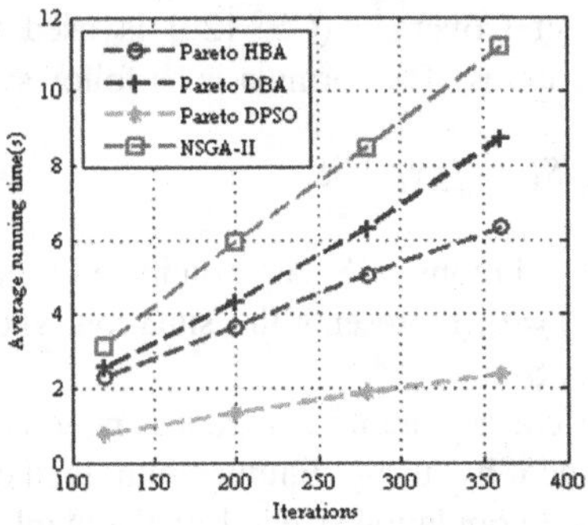

Fig. 8. Comparison of average running time

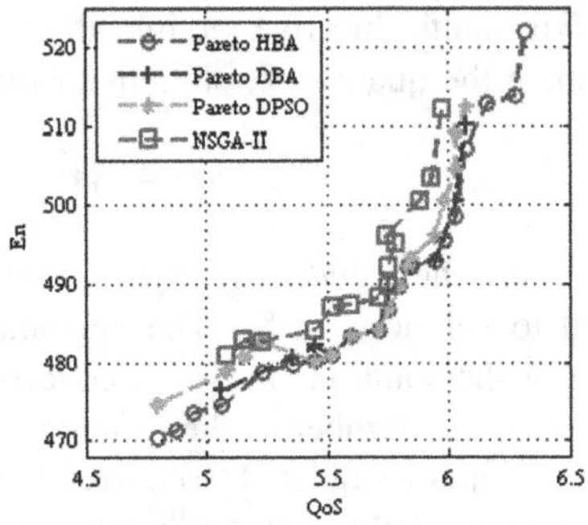

Fig. 9. Comparison of Pareto-optimal front

NSGA-II is shown in Fig. 9. The results show that by combining DBA and DPSO, the global search ability of HBA is increased with a rich diversity of population.

In summary, running efficiency and optimization capabilities of HBA algorithm are superior to DBA, DPSO, NSGA-II. The HBA has better performance for solving multi-objective aggregation problems.

- The process of manufacturing service reconfiguration optimization

When the number of Candidate service is 10, the population size is 200, the iterations is 240. A set of non-dominated solutions provided by HBA algorithm is obtained. A current service aggregation execution scheme {4, 2, 9, 8, 2, 2, 7, 10, 4, 4} is selected. In the current implementation of the scheme, theoretically, the value of $\{f_{QoS}, f_{En}, f_T, f_C\}$ is {6.180, 474.066, 165.818, 876.414}.

Suppose during the execution of MSAP, the corresponding services for component services {3, 4, 5} are failed. Table 3 shows the replaceable services set discovered by HBA for the failed services $\{MS_9^3, MS_8^4, MS_2^5\}$. The results show that HBA algorithm can effectively identify the reconfiguration region and find the optimal replaceable service set. All services of the found replaceable service set do not dominated by previous scheme and meet user's constraints.

Table 3. The replaceable service set of reconfiguration region

	$\{MS^1, MS^2, MS^3, MS^4, MS^5, MS^6, MS^7, MS^8, MS^9, MS^{10}\}$	$\{f_{QoS}, f_{En}, f_T, f_C\}$
cur	{ 4, 2, 9, 8, 2, 2, 7, 10, 4, 4}	{6.180, 474.066, 165.818, 876.414}
S_i	{ 4, 2, 5, 1, 10, 2, 7, 10, 4, 4}	{6.274, 509.505, 168.505, 866.907}
S_i	⋮	⋮
S_i	{ 4, 2, 3, 1, 10, 2, 7, 10, 4, 4}	{6.279, 513.780, 168.214, 867.659}
S_i	{ 4, 2, 7, 1, 10, 2, 7, 10, 4, 4}	{6.318, 521.986, 168.803, 864.797}

Table 4. The comparison of the reconfiguration performance

Parameter	HBA	DBA	DPSO	NSGA-II
Reconfiguration region	{3, 4, 5}	{3, 4, 5}	{3, 4, 5, 7}	Fail
The average number of S_r	6.234	3.454	2.128	NA
Reconfiguration time	0.945 s	1.256 s	2.660 s	NA

As HBA is more efficient in finding the reconfiguration region compared to DPSO and DBA. Table 4 shows that the reconfiguration time of HBA is much shorter than DBA and DPSO. And the average number of the replaceable set S_r is more than DBA and DPSO. However, NSGA-II cannot find the S_r in above reconfiguration region. The whole service process will be recomposed.

Therefore, the faulty can be restored by the HBA quickly and more choices can be provided for the user to replace the failed manufacture service. Besides, the services outside of the reconfiguration region are not affected. The proposed region-based reconfiguration algorithm can handle multiple faulty services.

7 Conclusion and Future Work

Considering both QoS and energy consumption issues, the region-based reconfiguration strategy is introduced and hybrid bees algorithm is proposed to solve the multi-objective manufacturing service reconfiguration problem. Experiment results show that the performance of the proposed hybrid bees algorithm is more effective than the other three algorithms in the discovery of replaceable services. The manufacturing service faults can be quickly and efficiently recovered during the service reconfiguration execution. Multiple faulty services can be handled.

In future work, high percentage of the service failures will be made to test the performance of the proposed algorithm in complex service aggregation execution path. In addition, more experiments using real-world CMfg Platform data will be conducted to testify the proposed approach and further improve its performance.

Acknowledgments. This research is supported by National Natural Science Foundation of China (Grant No. 51305319), the National High Technology Research and Development Program of China (863 Program) (Grant No. 2015AA042101), and the Fundamental Research Funds for the Central Universities (Grant No. 2015III003).

References

1. Li, B., Zhang, L., Wang, S., Tao, F., Cao, J., Jiang, X., Song, X., Chai, X.: Cloud manufacturing: a new service-oriented networked manufacturing model. Comput. Integr. Manuf. Syst. **16**(1), 1–7 (2010)
2. Xun, X.: From cloud computing to cloud manufacturing. Robot. Comput.-Integr. Manuf. **28**(1), 75–86 (2012)
3. Ren, L., Zhang, L., Tao, F., Zhao, C., Chai, X., Zhao, X.: Cloud manufacturing: From concept to practice. Enterp. Inf. Syst. **9**(2), 186–209 (2015). Taylor & Francis

4. Tao, F., Laili, Y., Lida, X., Zhang, L.: FC-PACO-RM: a parallel method for service composition optimal-selection in cloud manufacturing system. IEEE Trans. Ind. Inform. **9**(4), 2023–2033 (2013)
5. Jayashree, K., Anand, S.: Policy based distributed run time fault diagnoser model for web services. In: Meghanathan, N., Chaki, N., Nagamalai, D. (eds.) CCSIT 2012. LNICSSITE, vol. 86, pp. 9–16. Springer, Heidelberg (2012). doi:10.1007/978-3-642-27317-9_2
6. Yu, X., Luo, X., Chen, H., Hu, D.: Dynamic adaption in composite web services using expiration times. In: International Conference on Computer Engineering and Technology, pp. 47–50. IEEE (2009)
7. Ramacher, R, Monch, L.: Reliable service reconfiguration for time-critical service compositions. In: IEEE International Conference on Services Computing, pp. 184–191 (2013)
8. Lin, K.-J., Zhang, J., Zhai, Y.: An efficient approach for service process reconfiguration in SOA with end-to-end QoS constraints. In: IEEE Conference on Commerce and Enterprise Computing, pp. 597–600 (2009)
9. Li, J., Ma, D., Mei, X.: Sun, H., Zheng, Z.: Adaptive QoS-Aware service process reconfiguration. In: IEEE International Conference on Services Computing, pp. 282–289. IEEE (2011)
10. Pham, D.T., Ghanbarzadeh, A., Koç, E., Otri, S., Rahim, S., Zaidi, M.: The bees algorithm a novel tool for complex optimisation problems. In: Proceedings of IPROMS 2006 Conference, Intelligent Production Machines & Systems, pp. 454–461, July 2006
11. Coello, C.A.C., Lechuga, M.S.: MOPSO: a proposal for multiple objective particle swarm optimization. In: Proceedings of the 2002 Congress on Evolutionary Computation, pp. 1051–1056 (2002)
12. Zhang, W., Chang, C.K., Feng, T., Jiang, H.: QoS-based dynamic web service composition with ant colony optimization. In: IEEE 34th Annual Computer Software and Applications Conference (COMPSAC), pp. 493–502 (2010)
13. Deb, K., Agrawal, S., Pratap, A., Meyarivan, T.: A fast elitist non-dominated sorting genetic algorithm for multi-objective optimization: NSGA-II. In: Schoenauer, M., Deb, K., Rudolph, G., Yao, X., Lutton, E., Merelo, J.J., Schwefel, H.-P. (eds.) PPSN 2000. LNCS, vol. 1917, pp. 849–858. Springer, Heidelberg (2000). doi:10.1007/3-540-45356-3_83
14. Castellani, M., Pham, Q.T., Pham, D.T.: Dynamic optimisation by a modified bees algorithm. Proc. Inst. Mech. Eng. Part I J. Syst. Control Eng. **226**(7), 956–971 (2012)
15. Tian, S., Liu, Q., Xu, W., Yan, J.: A discrete hybrid bees algorithm for service aggregation optimal selection in cloud manufacturing. In: Yin, H., Tang, K., Gao, Y., Klawonn, F., Lee, M., Weise, T., Li, B., Yao, X. (eds.) IDEAL 2013. LNCS, vol. 8206, pp. 110–117. Springer, Heidelberg (2013). doi:10.1007/978-3-642-41278-3_14
16. Paulraj, D., Swamynathan, S., Madhaiyan, M.: Process model-based atomic service discovery and composition of composite semantic web services using web ontology language for services OWL-S. Enterp. Inf. Syst. **6**(4), 445–471 (2012)
17. Xiang, F., Hu, Y., Tao, F., Zhang, L.: Energy consumption evaluation and application of cloud manufacturing resource service. Comput. Integr. Manuf. Syst. Cims **18**(9), 2109–2116 (2012)
18. Hansen, P., Mladenović, N.: Variable neighborhood search: principles and applications. Eur. J. Oper. Res. **130**(3), 449–467 (2001)
19. Ratnaweera, A., Halgamuge, S.K., Watson, H.C.: Self-organizing hierarchical particle swarm optimizer with time-varying acceleration coefficients. IEEE Trans. Evol. Comput. **8**(3), 240–255 (2004)
20. Zitzler, E., Deb, K., Thiele, L.: Comparison of multiobjective evolutionary algorithms: empirical results. Evol. Comput. **8**(2), 173–195 (2000)

MyTrace: A Mobile Phone-Based Tourist Spatial-Temporal Behavior Record and Analysis System

Lei Dou[1,2], Haitao Qu[3], Xiaoqiang Bi[4], Yu Zhang[5], Chongsheng Yu[5], Jian Qin[5], Xiaoting Huang[6], and Xin Li[5(✉)]

[1] School of Economics, Shandong Normal University, Jinan, China
dl0531@hotmail.com

[2] Department of Tourism, Jinan Vocational College, Jinan, China

[3] Ji'nan Research Institute of Geotechnical Investigation & Surveying, Jinan, China

[4] Electronic Information Product Inspection Institute of Shandong Province, Jinan, China

[5] School of Computer Science and Technology, Shandong University, Jinan, China
lx@sdu.edu.cn

[6] School of Management, Shandong University, Jinan, China

Abstract. Motivated by the needs of personalized travel position logging and interest recommendation, an open research-oriented system to collect and analyze tourist spatial-temporal behavior has been developed. In this paper, we introduce the architecture and internal structure of the system, which not only provides a communication platform to tourists, but also as a medium of data collection for related researchers and administrators. The system includes three key components: mobile phone application, data receiver, and data management and analysis platform. An application user can record his travel traces with interesting activity points in map, which are consist of pictures, videos, user's feelings, comments, and companions, etc., and can be shared in his social network. Uploaded position logs and activity points of users can be used to analyze the characteristics of spatial-temporal behavior by researchers and administrators and infer the interesting insights that are useful in tourist behavior research and tourist attraction planning. Main functions of each component and key techniques inside the system are described briefly. The system has been tested openly since April, 2016 and promoted in two tourist destinations in July, 2016. Consequently, an available dataset including 188,944 GPS locations, 285 activity points and 251 questionnaire responses from 659 registered users is constructed. The initial experiment results show the system is effective and worth promoting. We hope that more users not only tourists and researchers join this research system.

Keywords: Mobile network application · Spatial-temporal behavior · Position log · GPS · Tourist

L. Zhang et al. (Eds.): Monterey Workshop 2016, LNCS 10228, pp. 99–108, 2017.
DOI: 10.1007/978-3-319-61994-1_10

1 Introduction

To forecast future travel demands and better guide the investment of tourist attraction planning projects, researchers have been committing to understand the significance of tourist spatial-temporal behavior, thus to explore the driven-factors that influencing their decision making. Previous tourist behavior analysis tends to rely on surveys and questionnaires [1–4]. Data information is collected when respondents are asked to report their activities and travels via paper, web, or phone interviews.

Recently, with huge development in information and communications technology (ICT), digital trace as a novel type of virtual data has helped researchers develop new methods to observe, record, and analyze human's spatial-temporal behavior. Applying these new methods, we can uncover the presence of crowds and the patterns of movement over time as well as compare human behavior to generate new hypotheses [5]. Gonzalez *et al.* [6] presented the digital traces of human daily performance was intentionally or unintentionally uncovered in the virtual space, for example, the positioning data when the users expose by mobile phone network can help reveal interesting characteristics of human mobility.

With the pervasiveness of smart phones with GPS and camera, many persons would like to record their outdoor movements and share the photos with location marked in their social networks. Meanwhile, we want to know different types of interesting places such as popular restaurants or tourist attractions in a geospatial region, especially when traveling in a strange place.

To analyze tourist spatial-temporal behavior, we have implemented an open tourist spatial-temporal behavior record and analysis system. In this system, a special mobile application (with Android and iOS versions) is used to collect location and behavior data of registered user and thus upload to a centralized database center automatically, meanwhile a website-based management system is developed to display user's trajectory histories, behaviors and related statistic results for researchers. The system has 1,133 users with total 311,729 collected GPS location records for now. We calculate the distribution of registered users, and give an analysis according to the response of questionnaires.

The rest of the paper is organized as follows. In Sect. 2, we present previous related work; Sect. 3 introduces mathematical models including some basic terms definition; we describe the architecture of our prototype system and its three key components in Sect. 4; initial experimental results are demonstrated in Sect. 5. Finally, Sect. 6 concludes this study.

2 Related Work

The rapid rise and prevalence of mobile network technologies have made it possible to collect spatial-temporal big data, and thus the individual digital traces have been used in tourist dynamics research gradually. Girardin *et al.* [5] studied the Flickr users who left along their digital traces by photos over a period of two years, to reveal tourist concentration and spatial-temporal flows based on the density of tourists, the points of interests they visited as well as the most common routes they followed; in the subsequent case study, he considered two types of digital traces from Rome: geo-referenced photos and aggregate records of wireless network events, which could map and visualize the presence and movement of tourists by user-generated spatial-temporal data [7]. Vaccari *et al.* [8] proposed a holistic framework to study urban digital traces including tourists' mobility, using a case study in New York City, which focused on how technology and information changed the way human movement and behavior in cities. In this sense, more researchers analyzed tourist spatial-temporal behavior as well as network patterns of tourism flow by geo-referenced photos, messages, and travel notes made publicly available on the photo-sharing Website [9–12].

To obtain spatial-temporal big data by GPS tracking technology has been applied in the study of tourist behavior [13–16]. Chen, *et al.* [13] presented tourist behavior survey was conducted coupled with GPS loggers during which respondents were asked to carry GPS loggers. Furthermore, Zheng *et al.* [15] collected digital traces from tourists using GPS tracking technology, and predicted tourist's next location within a given tourist attraction by a case study in Beijing, China. Phithakkitnukoon *et al.* [17] explained people's traveling patterns were influenced by the geography of their social ties, and described the digital traces by massive mobile phone GPS location records to study tourist spatial-temporal behavior [18].

In this study, spatial-temporal big data of tourist are collected by a mobile application (named "MyTrace"). Mobile phones with GPS sensor can be used as a location tracker [18], because mobile phone positioning is required when a user communicates with the network [19]. Consequently, tourist personal information, travel digital traces, real-time tourist activities and subjective feelings, suspending time at interesting points, travel expenditure, etc. are recorded to analyze tourist behavior characteristics as well as its driven-factors, which will be useful both for the tourist attractions administration and city planning.

3 Mathematical Model

In this section, we introduce three basic data models used to represent location log and activity log (Fig. 1).

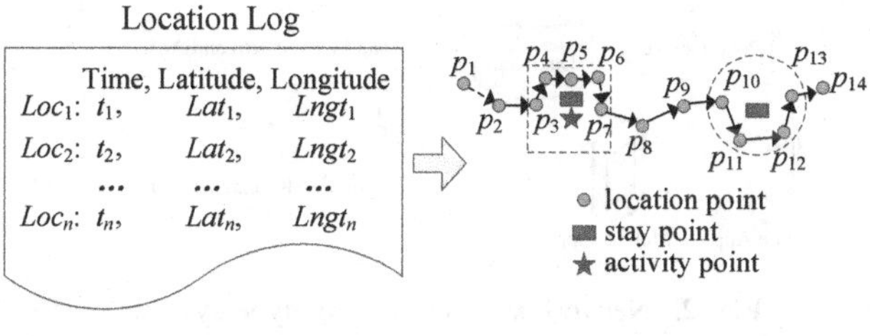

Fig. 1. An example of location point, location log, stop point, and activity point

Definition 1. Location log: A location log is a time sequence of GPS points $P = \{<t_i, p_i>| \ 1 \leq i \leq n\}$. The *i-th* time t_i means the timestamp when the GPS point p_i is collected. Each GPS point p_i contains latitude ($p_i.Lat$) and longitude ($p_i.Lngt$).

Definition 2. Stop point: A stop point *s* is a geographic region where a person stopped over a certain period of time Δt ($\Delta t > 0$). For simplification, a stop point *s* is described a segment of location log in a rectangle (*sr*) or a circle (*sc*) with a timespan, i.e., $sr = \{<t_i, p_i>| \ j \leq i \leq k, \ t_k - t_j \geq \Delta t, \ |p_k.Lat - p_j.Lat| \leq \Delta d, \ |p_k.Lngt - p_j.Lngt| \leq \Delta d\}$, and $sc = \{<t_i, \ p_i>| \ j \leq i \leq k, \ t_k - t_j \geq \Delta t, \ |p_k.Lat - p_j.Lat|^2 + |p_k.Lngt - p_j.Lngt|^2 \leq \Delta r^2\}$.

Obviously, a stop point depends on three parameters: a time threshold Δt, a distance threshold Δd and a radius threshold Δr. In our system, we can adjust these two parameters dynamically according to building shape and size found in map.

Definition 3. Activity point: An activity point *a* is a GPS point with user-labeled activity information including remarks, photos, feeling level, activity type, duration, partner and its relation, etc., i.e. $a = <t, p, labels>$. Using activity labels, we can know where, when, what and with who a user activity happed.

4 Construction of Prototype System

This section introduces the architecture of our system and its key components.

4.1 Architecture of Prototype System

The prototype system includes three key components: mobile phone application, data receiver and web-based platform for data management & analysis. Figures 2 and 3 show the network structure and main functions of each component in the system, respectively. The mobile phone application is used to record user's location, activity information, questionnaire responses, and thus upload them to a data receiver periodically. The data receiver receives different types of data and stores them into database. A web-based platform for data management & analysis supports interfaces to three types of roles: administrator, researcher and ordinary user. Their functions are discussed respectively in the following section.

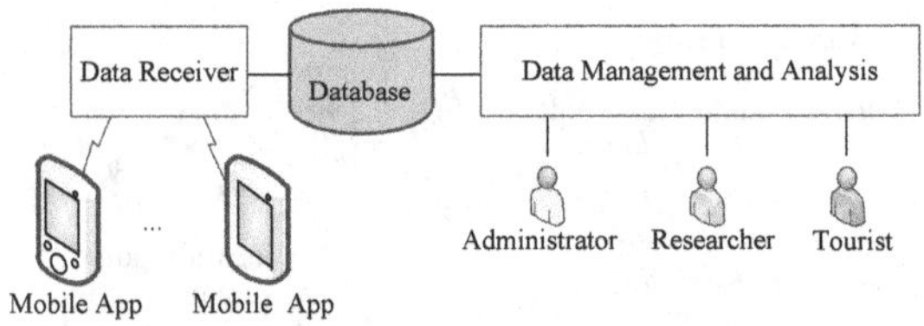

Fig. 2. Network structure of prototype system

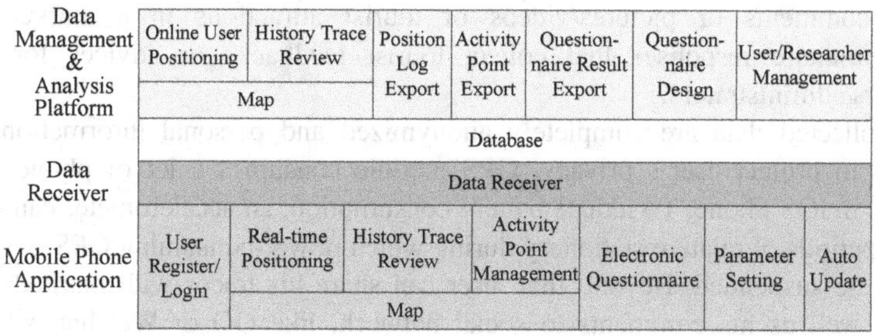

Fig. 3. Functional block diagram of prototype system

4.2 App in Mobile Device

As a GPS receiver chip is integrated in almost every smartphone. We develop a mobile application (App name: MyTrace, http://fir.im/MyTrace) for Android or iOS phones. Figure 4 shows the real UIs of our application. The main functions include user register/login, real-time positioning and trace recording, history traces review, activity points marking, electronic questionnaire delivering, related parameter setting (GPS signal access interval), and auto-updating.

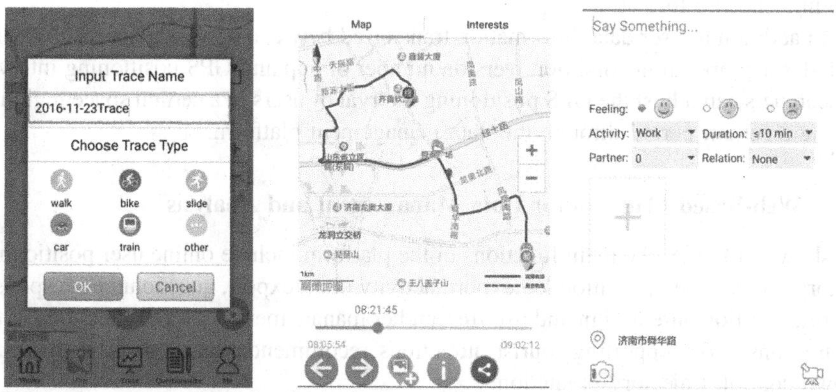

a) Begin a new trace (position log) b) Trace review c) Add a new activity point

Fig. 4. Main interfaces of mobile application

User's positioning data are passively generated through the network after user begins a new trace. Positioning data are automatically recorded in a certain interval or when user's location changes. At the same time, behavior information can be recorded in real time when user posts a geo-referenced new activity. In this study, the positioning interval is defined as 10 s to collect accurate behavior information of tourist. The collected dataset includes four types of data: (1) trace data that include position (latitude, longitude, and altitude), speed, and timestamp; (2) behavior data that explain tourist's feelings and activities in an activity point; (3) text and image data that show tourist's comments or pictures/videos of tourist attractions in a marked point; (4) questionnaire responses that collect tourist feedbacks or advices for related researchers/administrators.

All collected data are completely anonymized and personal information is not displayed to protect user's privacy. GPS module consumes a lot of phone energy, especially in iOS phone. To reduce battery consumption, an accelerometer can be used to detect periods of relative stationary during which power-consuming GPS acquisition functions be suspended. Beyond that, user can share his traces with marked activity points as well as his comments to social network, like QQ or WeChat, which are surprisingly popular in China.

4.3 Data Receiver

Data receiver realizes the data interaction (create/retrieve/update/delete operation) between mobile applications and the database. Data receiver will receive all data uploaded by mobile application and store them into database or file system (for images or videos). These data include user personal information, location logs, activity points and questionnaire responses. After a user posts an activity point, data receiver need accept and handle the comments, pictures or videos contained in the point. In the other hand, when a user reviews his own historical data in the mobile application, the receiver will retrieve the appropriate data from database and then reply them to mobile app in a specific format.

In addition to user data, information transferred between app and data receiver also includes app operation condition, version number of app and GPS positioning interval. Researchers can adjust the GPS positioning interval of users in a certain space region or during a certain period through the data management platform.

4.4 Web-Based Platform for Data Management and Analysis

As shown in Fig. 3, the main functions in the platform include online user positioning, history traces review, position log export, activity point export, questionnaire responses export, questionnaire design and user/researcher management. Possible functions in the future consist of supporting tourist attractions recommendation, landscape planning, crowd control, trajectory prediction.

It is difficult to infer and recommend a personalized interest only depending on one person's past location information because his interested places are not only related to the number of his visiting this place but also varied with his travel experience increment and some personal information like age, marriage status, and even the number of his children. In this context, our prototype system can provide personalized service by synthetically analyzing tourist spatial-temporal behavior data associated with personal information.

Web-based platform for data management & analysis is mainly used by ordinary user, researcher, or tourist attraction administrators. An ordinary user can review his history traces and other information posted. Researchers can design questionnaires, deliver them to users, or export position log, activity points or questionnaire responses of users. For easy management and private protection, we separate users into different groups, thus system administrator can create groups and appoint group managers.

5 Experiments

In this section, GPS locations and user property data collected are analyzed. We firstly present the outcomes of our platform briefly; and then we discuss the statistics of registered users. Finally, we give an analysis to the responses of questionnaires.

5.1 Trial Operation of Prototype System

Our system has gone into trial operation since April 2016. So far, we have 659 registered users with totally collected 188,944 valid GPS locations. We have promoted the mobile app in Shenzhen Overseas Chinese Town and Huizhou Xunliao Bay in July, 2017, through providing coupons and gifts for tourists to attract tourist registration and ensure completeness of the traces. As we expected, the number of new registrants reaches 447 and new GPS locations collected are closed to 140k in July.

5.2 The Statistics of User Information

Personal information is filled out voluntarily at the beginning of user registration, which includes age, gender, job, education level, marriage status, and the size and composition of household. Figure 5 shows the statistics of users based on demographic information. It is not difficult to see that nearly two thirds of registered users are students, which might because the promotion period is in summer vacation. Approximately 59.10% of users are in the ages of 16–29. It is assumed that retirees have more advantages to travel, whereas observed results display 60+ years old users only account to 3.28%, probably due to the property characteristics of elders. An overwhelming proportion of users have higher education background. The majority is unmarried, while a half of married users have not child up to now. Our results confirm students with higher education background are primary users of our app, with a trend towards younger in the future. This is probable because the young are inclined to adopt new technology and prefer to record and thus post travel traces in social networks.

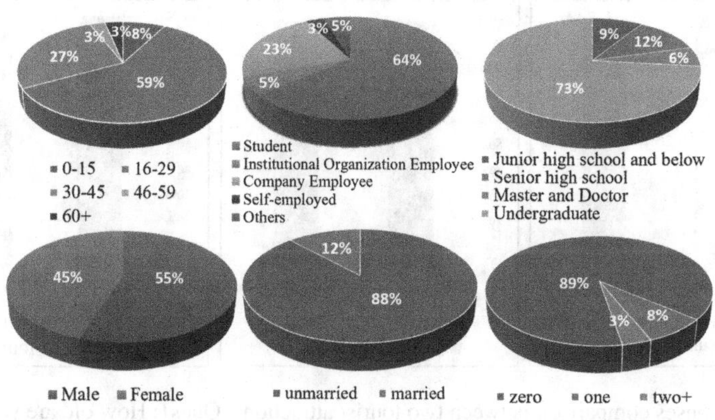

Fig. 5. Proportion distribution diagram based on users demographics

Given prior consent to the use of personal information, app can acquire the information of time events of phone calls, text messages, and taking pictures. We make a preliminary analysis according to these data, and the results are shown in Fig. 6. Observed results presented that users tend to take pictures around noon while make phone calls or text messages in the morning and afternoon.

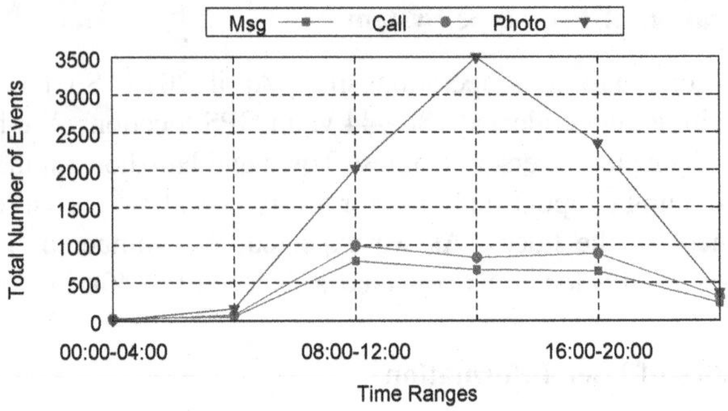

Fig. 6. The distribution diagram of three types of time events

5.3 Questionnaire Responses Analysis

During the period of mobile app promotion, we conduct a questionnaire survey in two tourist destinations respectively. Approximately 63.68% and 55.95% of users respectively in the two destinations submitted available questionnaire, which could be explained by that some users are not familiar with the use of this app and hence don't log in or fill in, or their mobile phones are not connect to the Wi-Fi at that time. Figure 7 shows the statistics of these responses. As we have seen, tourists in destination I are mostly younger; Tourists in destination II want longer duration of stay, and one more interesting insight is that they have visited destination II more than once, in the sense destination II maybe more attractive to tourists who like leisure travel products.

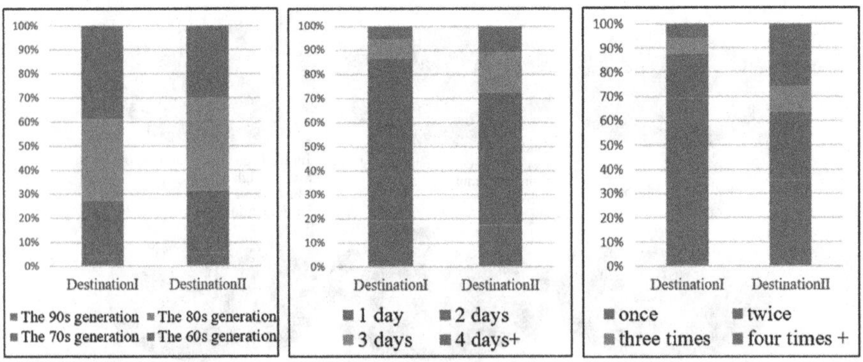

Fig. 7. Responses comparison between two tourist attractions. Ques1: How old are you? Ques2: How many days do you plan to stay here? Ques3: How many times have you been here?

6 Conclusions

In this paper, we introduce a prototype system for tourist spatial-temporal behavior record and analysis that is designed for outdoor tourists, researchers and tourist attraction administrators. The system includes three key components: mobile phone application, data receiver, and web-based platform for data management & analysis. Main functions of each component and key techniques are described briefly. The initial experiment results show the system is effective and worth promoting in the future commercial operation. In the further research, we would like to exploit big data of spatial-temporal behavior, in the perspective of personalized recommendation of tourist attractions and prediction of travel trajectory. Moreover, we hope that more tourists and researchers use this app and join our spatial-temporal behavior research.

Acknowledgements. This research is sponsored by the National Science Foundation of China (No. 41301142), Natural Science Foundation of Shandong Province (No. ZR2014FM014), the Key Program of Shandong Province (No. 2015GGX106002) and Research Fund for the Doctoral Program of Higher Education of China (No. 20120131120033).

References

1. Huang, X., Wu, B.: Intra-attraction tourist spatial-temporal behavior patterns. Tour. Geographies **14**, 625–645 (2012)
2. Huang, X.: Quality comparison between spaces-time data of tourists' behavior captured using GPS tracking technology and activity diaries. Tour. Tribune **29**(3), 100–106 (2014)
3. Juvan, E., Dolnicar, S.: Measuring environmentally sustainable tourist behavior. Ann. Tour. Res. **59**, 30–44 (2016)
4. Mahika, E.C., Rădulescu, R., Aluculesei, A.C.: The behavior of Romanian tourists regarding the attendance at festivals. Procedia Econ. Fin. **23**, 1239–1244 (2015)
5. Girardin, F., Blat, J., Calabrese, F., Fiore, F.D., Ratti, C.: Digital footprinting: uncovering tourists with user-generated content. IEEE CS (2008). Print ISSN 1536-1268
6. Gonzalez, M.C., Hidalgo, C.A., Barabasi, A.-L.: Understanding individual human mobility patterns. Nature **453**(5), 779–782 (2008)
7. Girardin, F., Fiore, F.D., Ratti, C., Blat, J.: Leveraging explicitly disclosed location information to understand tourist dynamics: a case study. J. Locat. Based Serv. **2**(1), 41–56 (2008)
8. Vaccari, A., Liu, L., Biderman, A., et al.: A holistic framework for the study of urban traces and the profiling of urban processes and dynamics. In: The 12th International IEEE Conference on Intelligent Transportation Systems (2009)
9. Li, J.Y.: Tourism digital footprint: online revealing spatiotemporal track of tourists. Ideol. Front **39**(3), 103–107 (2013)
10. Li, C., Wang, Y.J., Liu, Y., Dong, R.C., Zhao, J.Z.: A study of the temporal-spatial behavior of tourists based on geo referenced photos. Tour. Tribune **28**(10), 30–36 (2013)
11. Yang, M., Li, J.Y., Yang, L.: The study on spatiotemporal behaviors of inbound tourists based on tourists' digital footprints: a case study of Chengdu. Tour. Sci. **29**(3), 59–68 (2015)
12. Zhan, Y.Y., Li, J.Y., Yang, M.: The tourism flow network structure of Xi'an based on tourism digital footprint. Hum. Geogr. **129**(4), 111–118 (2014)

13. Chen, C., Ma, J., Susilo, Y., Liu, Y., Wang, M.: The promises of big data and small data for travel behavior (aka human mobility) analysis. Transp. Res. Part C **68**, 285–299 (2016)
14. Huang, X., Chai, Y., Zhao, Y.: The application of mobile positioning data source in tourism study. Tour. Tribune **25**(8), 39–45 (2010)
15. Zheng, W.M., Huang, X.T., Li, Y.: Understanding the tourist mobility using GPS: where is the next place? Tour. Manag. **59**, 267–280 (2017)
16. Zheng, Y., Zhang, L., Xie, X., Ma, W.Y.: Mining interesting locations and travel sequences from GPS trajectories. In: International Conference on World Wide Web, pp. 791–800 (2009)
17. Phithakkitnukoon, S., Smoreda, Z., Olivier, P.: Socio-geography of human mobility: a study using longitudinal mobile phone data. PLoS ONE **7**(6), 1–9 (2012)
18. Phithakkitnukoon, S., Horanont, T., Witayangkurn, A., Siri, R., Sekimoto, Y., Shibasaki, R.: Understanding tourist behavior using large-scale mobile sensing approach: a case study of mobile phone users in Japan. Pervasive Mob. Comput. **18**, 18–39 (2015)
19. Ficek, M., Kencl, L.: Inter-call mobility model: a spatio-temporal refinement of call data records using a Gaussian mixture model. In: Proceedings of INFOCOM. IEEE (2012)

Big Data Simulation

Multi-source Information Intelligent Collection and Monitoring of CNC Machine Tools Based on Multi-agent

Yun Yang[1], Chao Yin[1], Xiao-bin Li[2(✉)], and Liang Li[3]

[1] State Key Laboratory of Mechanical Transmission, Chongqing University, Chongqing, China

[2] School of Economics and Business Administration, Chongqing University, Chongqing, China
xiaobin_lee@cqu.edu.cn

[3] Chongqing HITECH Information-Based Manufacturing Productivity Promotion Center Co. Ltd., Chongqing, China

Abstract. Currently, CNC machine tools in manufacturing system are no longer effective in Multi-source data acquisition, real-time interaction and remote monitoring due to the poor ability of compatibility, cross-platform performance, and remote service. An information model and index system for multilayer operation situation considering the information's multi-source characteristics of CNC machine tools in the intelligent manufacturing environment are built in this paper, and a new approach to realize the multi-source data intelligent acquisition and monitoring based upon Multi-Agent is proposed. Especially, it focuses on the key technologies of intelligent multi-source data acquisition and visualized dynamic monitoring based on OPC and multi-agent. Finally, these analyses are illustrated in a real CNC machine tool VMC1060L and the result shows that it's an effective approach which has a better performance in practical application.

Keywords: CNC machine tools · Multi-source information · Multi-agent · MTConnect

1 Introduction

With the development and the increasing widely use of information technology, the manufacturing system is becoming more and more intelligent, service-oriented and green direction. New manufacturing methods, for example, networked collaborative manufacturing, cloud manufacturing and customer-oriented customization, have come into being in recent years [1, 2]. Hence, the manufacturing floor, as the production unit, also need to be agile, flexible, intelligent, collaborative and green transformation to adapt this new trend. As the core resources of the modern manufacturing enterprise, CNC machine tools play an important role in achieving the agility, flexibility and intelligent production in manufacturing. And because the real-time collection, transmission, processing and analysis of data for CNC machine tools provide the fundamental information for enterprises in efficient decision-making and rapid response for

L. Zhang et al. (Eds.): Monterey Workshop 2016, LNCS 10228, pp. 111–121, 2017.
DOI: 10.1007/978-3-319-61994-1_11

enterprises, the machine data acquisition is particularly important besides the system control, management and other related technology in intelligent manufacturing.

In recent years, many studies on CNC equipment information collection have been done by domestic scholars. For instance, aimed at the Heterogeneity of CNC machine tools and the difficulty of workshop information collection, a universal CNC machine intelligence gathering and rapid production of information collection system were proposed in [3]. To improve the transparency of workshop management, the framework and operation mode of workshop operation dashboard were proposed in [4] and its key enabled technologies were researched from the perspective of operation situation monitoring in workshop. To realize remote monitoring and manufacturing equipment management, a method of information integration of Numerical Control (NC) equipment in [5] was proposed, which included interconnection architecture, information model for devices and workflow of information interchange.

As for the studies abroad, a universal data access server using OPC and XML technologies proposed to realize the modern distributed data acquisition and monitoring system in [9]. A data acquisition language by analyzing the information requirements of active data acquisition and effective data acquisition system architecture was proposed in [10]. To deal with the diversity of interface and communication protocol of modern workshop, [11] proposed a kind of monitoring system based on MTConnect technology; [12] presented a control-monitoring-simulation architecture built around the use of "custom-made" machines models working with the actual "custom-made" control system.

As we can see from the existing studies, existing digital equipment information collection method mostly base on CNC machine communication interface, resulting in various disadvantages such as develop difficulties, poor abilities of compatibility, scalability, cross-platform performance, remote service etc. To solve these problems, we proposed a method of CNC machine tools intelligent information collection and monitoring based on Multi-Agent and established a CNC machine tools multilayer operation index system and information model. Finally, the related key technologies are researched.

2 The Index System for Multilayer Operation Situation and Information Model of CNC Machine Tools

As the core unit of intelligent manufacturing, the CNC machine tool's devices information and related production information are multi-sourced. The multi-source information of CNC machine tools is shown in Fig. 1. According to the structure of multi-source information, the CNC machine tools information is divided into two types: static data and dynamic data.

According to the comprehensive analysis of static and dynamic information for CNC machine tools, we can conclude the characteristics of the information are magnanimity, heterogeneity, dynamic, knowledgeability, cooperativity and service.

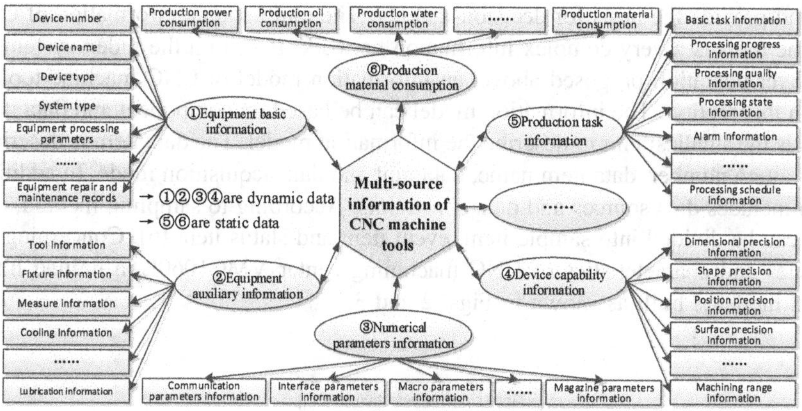

Fig. 1. The multi-source information of CNC machine tools

2.1 The Index System for Multilayer Operation Situation of CNC Machine Tools

Concerning the characteristics of multi-source information of CNC machine tools, this paper analyses the multilayer operation index of devices. The operation index is divided into three layers: the real-time operation index, the process operation index and the comprehensive operation index.

The real-time operation index is used to indicate the operating state at a given moment for CNC machine tools such as the real-time information of spindle speed, spindle feed rate, real-time coordinate of servo axis, instruction of controller etc., which can reflect the real-time conditions of CNC machine tools directly.

The process operation index is used to indicate the operating state during a specific time period of CNC machine tools, e.g. the spindle operation record, the trajectory of servo axis, the program segment of controller, equipment effective operation time, equipment repair and maintenance records, which can reflect the condition of CNC machine tools during the certain times.

The comprehensive operation index is used to indicate the production of statistical index of CNC machine tools, including quality, cost, time, energy consumption, and knowledge, for example, the product qualification ratio, product cost Information, comprehensive energy consumption information, equipment utilization ratio and equipment maintenance knowledge etc. [4].

2.2 The Information Model of CNC Machine Tools

The multi-layer operation index system of CNC machine tools can reflect the running state of different time spans. It can not only reflect the bottom information of CNC machine tools directly and promote the transparency of production process, but also give a thorough statistical analysis of the operation state based on historical operation data and provide the basis for decision-making. The multi-source information of CNC machine tools is a very complex information network. Based on the index system for multilayer operation proposed above, an information model of CNC machine tools is built in this section. The information model can be based on component and data item, which is the smallest unit to describe the information model. The data item is described by data item number, data item name, data unit and data acquisition mode. In addition, it also includes data sources and data constraints. According to sampling method, data items can be divided into sample item, event item and status item [6]. Concerning the attributes and characteristics of CNC machining center VMC1060L, a unified information model is built as shown in Figs. 2 and 3.

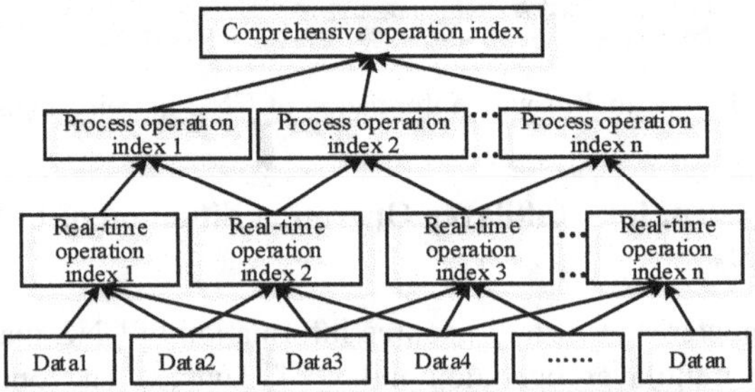

Fig. 2. The index system for multilayer operation situation of CNC machine tools

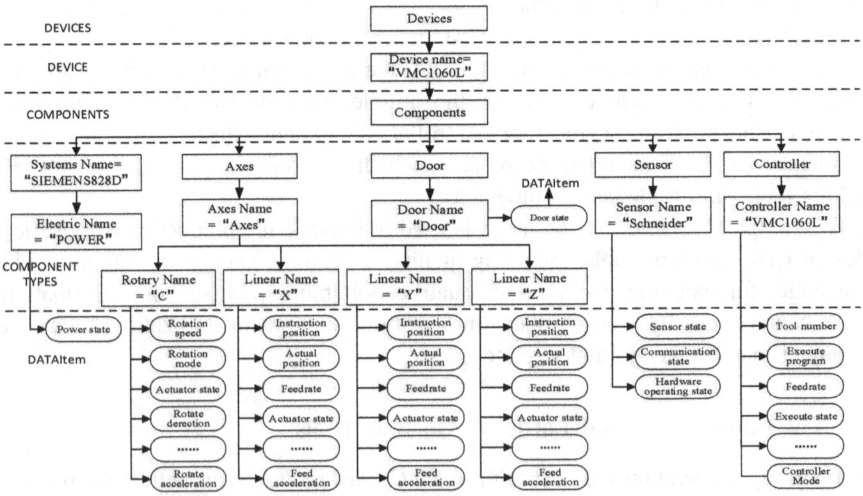

Fig. 3. The information model of VMC1060L

3 The Research on Multi-source Information Intelligent Collection and Monitoring Technologies of CNC Machine Tools Based on Multi-agent

3.1 General Implementation Idea

The general implementation idea based upon the index system for multilayer operation situation and the information model is proposed in Fig. 4.

The multilayer operation index system of CNC machine tools can reflect the operational status from time dimension and business dimension, and provide the users' individual needs by nesting, combination and calling among different components. The multi-source information is collected by the real-time information exchange of OPC servers and clients, and the information is passed to adapter which connects the OPC Agent and MTConnect Agent. As a bridge for information passing and conversion, the adapter consists of hardware system, operating system and application software, parsing the data from OPC Agent and converting the data into standardized XML message based on MTConnect protocol. The data will be dealt by MTConnect Agent according to users' needs, including data encapsulation, data association and data fusion, and then send to end users, which includes workshop management, mobile office terminals, remote access and monitoring terminals.

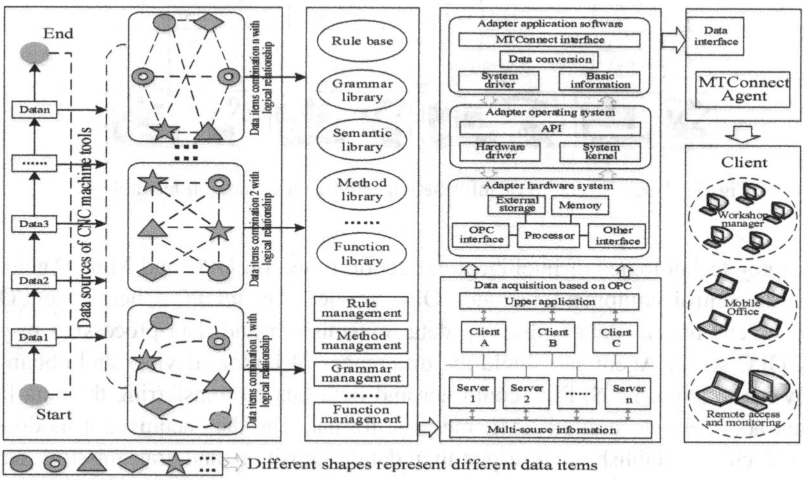

Fig. 4. The general implementation idea

3.2 The Information Extraction Technology of CNC Machine Tools Based on OPC and Multi-agent

Devices' information flow generalizes the interaction process between MES and field devices. Firstly, the MES system send requests to OPC agent communicator by smart interactive terminal to get the devices' information. Then the devices' information is dealt by data processing module based on OPC standards and sent to OPC client Agent. Finally, the information interaction between OPC client and OPC server can be realized by transmitting the information from OPC client Agent to OPC server Agent. Especially, the OPC Service Agent provides data exchange services as SOAP message formats. According to OPC interface standard, XML specification, and SOAP protocol, the heterogeneous information from field devices is shielded and transferred in a unified XML standard. The logic structure of information intelligent extraction technology is shown in Fig. 5.

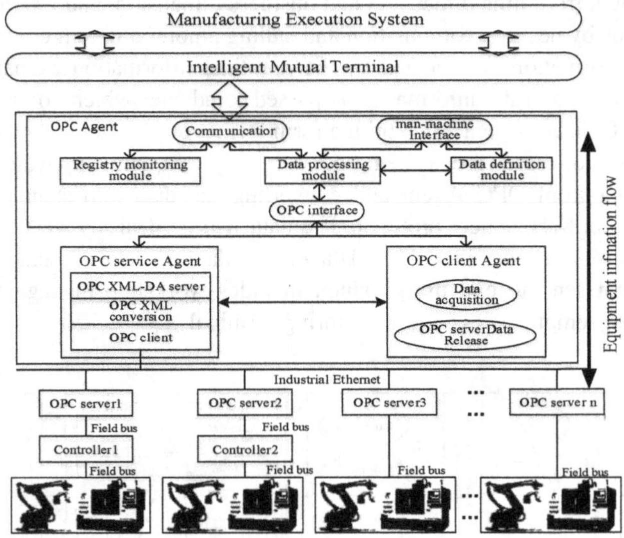

Fig. 5. Logic structure of information intelligent extraction technology

The key technologies of intelligent extraction based on OPC and Multi-Agent for numerical control equipment includes OPC service Agent/OPC Client Agent/OPC Agent, functioning as data collection, data transmission and data processing respectively. OPC server Agent can shield the differences of bottom devices and obtain the data by the different DCS, PLC controller and field bus by transferring the data from different accesses into unified XML message format. The data acquisition module of the OPC client establishes corresponding data acquisition and transmission access according to data type and configuration requirements of the host interface. The OPC Agent data processing module deals with the data by comprehending, analyzing, processing and clustering to simplify the function and development of Adapter. The data definition module configures the operating environment of Multi-Agent and defines the categories and types of collected device information. The registry detection module detects the dynamic information of Agent registration center in real time and informs related management modules to make corresponding adjustments when registration service changing.

In order to achieve the information interaction between agents, the KQML interface must be defined so that users can build the web service between the server and the client by KQML language in .NET framework and implement the information interaction between Agents by using SOA technology [7]. A part of code is shown below.

```
ModuleAgent
interface Tasktendering
{ Excedtion reject{longErrorNum};
Void buildToComponent(outstring Task_no,outstring SubTask_no, outstring Task_detail, outstring
Parteenumber, outstring Start_time,outstring End_time, outstring Reply_with):
Void tenderFromComponent(instringTask_no, instringSubTask_no, instringSubTend_value,
instringFinish_time, instringEnd_time,instringReply_with, instring Reply_with);
Void awardToTender(outstring request_no,   outstring SubTask_no,   Reply_with_to); };
interface reqPlanning
{ Excedtion reject{longErrorNum};
Void Preselected TenderList(outstring Tender_Path, outstring flash_1);
Void winnerList(instring Plan_path, instring flash_2);
Outstring;}
```

3.3 The Visualized Dynamic Monitoring Technology of CNC Machine Tools Based on MTConnect

MTConnect is an open, loyalty free industry communication protocol that intends to connect manufacturing equipment together. The MTConnect specification provides an open and extensible channel of communication for interconnectivity among devices, equipment, and systems. This common communication is facilitated by XML and HTTP technology. MTConnect empowers software developers to implement applications aimed at providing more efficient operations, improved production optimization, and increased productivity [11].

The working mode of MTConnect is based on Req/Res (requirement/response) method, including the request packet types as probe, current, sample and asset. The XML messages of CNC machine tools can be obtained by visiting the URL which includes Header and Body. As shown in the following code, the data type, data unit, sub-data type, data meaning and data range of the rotation axis A are described in detail [8].

```
<Rotaty id="A1" name="A">
  <DataItems>
    <DataItem category="SAMPLE" id="A2" name="Aactual" nativeUnites="Rpm"
subType="ACTUAL" type="ANGLE" units="Rpm" from= "1"  count= "50" />
    <DataItem category="SAMPLE" id="A3" name="Acommand"
nativeUnites="Rpm" subType="COMMANDED" type="ANGLE" units="Rpm"
from= "1"  count= "50" />
  </DataItems>
</Rotaty>
```

As the code shown, rotaty identifies rotating shaft; item is uniquely identified by id; data name is identified by name; data type is identified by category; local units and units of data are identified by nativeUnits/units; data type and sub type are identified by type/sub type; the beginning of data is identified by from; the length of data is identified by count. For example, < DataItem category = "SAMPLE" id = "A2" name = "Aactual" nativeUnites = "Rpm" subType = "ACTUAL" type = "ANGLE" units = "Rpm" from = "1" count = "50"/> means that the actual angle of axis A. Its unit is Rpm, ranging from 1 to 50.

OPC is the most wildly used in current market, but not free, that limits its further expansion. Based on the current OPC technologies, a new approach to realize visualized monitoring and transparent management for CNC machine tools is presented combined with MTConnect in this paper. The remote monitoring model for CNC machine tools based on MTConnect in shown in Fig. 6. MTConnect Agent and OPC Agent are linked in network by intelligent manufacturing execution system (i-MES). When the i-MES system sends a request to the MTConnect Agent, the corresponding will parse the data obtained from OPC Agent and convert the data into standardized XML message based on MTConnect, where the Adapter and MTConnect Agent are deployed in the intelligent interactive terminal.

According to the requirement of information acquisition, different items comprise the related service information for CNC machine tools based on component calling.

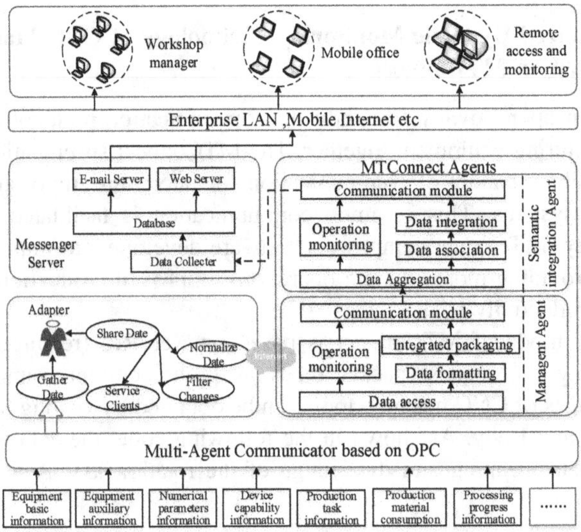

Fig. 6. Remote monitoring model for CNC machine tools based on MTConnect

The multi-source information of CNC machine tools is passed to Adapter by OPC Agent, where the Adapter connects OPC Agent information collection module downward and MTConnect Agent information processing module upward. MTConnect Agent is developed by MTConnect.NET and Agent SDK which is characterized by good compatibility, easily development, quickly data transmission and high efficiency in responding to customers' requests. In order to fulfill the requirement of data processing, a management and semantic integration Agent is designed in this paper. The data from Adapter will be converted into a unified format by the data formatting module of management Agent and then encapsulated by XML and ontology technologies. The data from multiple data sources will be associated by the data association module of semantic integration so that the multi-source information can be processed as redundancy reducing, data cleaning and merging by semantic integration module and save the storage space of Agent. Finally, the data processed by MTConnect Agent will be stored in the database by the data collector and passed to the host computer in i-MES system by E-mail Server and Web Server.

4 Application Verification

Based on our researches, a further development of original MES system is implemented based on SOA architecture combining with advanced information technologies as cloud computing, big data and so on. The new i-MES system is integrated into our previous machine tools manufacturing cloud service platform and applied in an experimental shop floor Chongqing University.

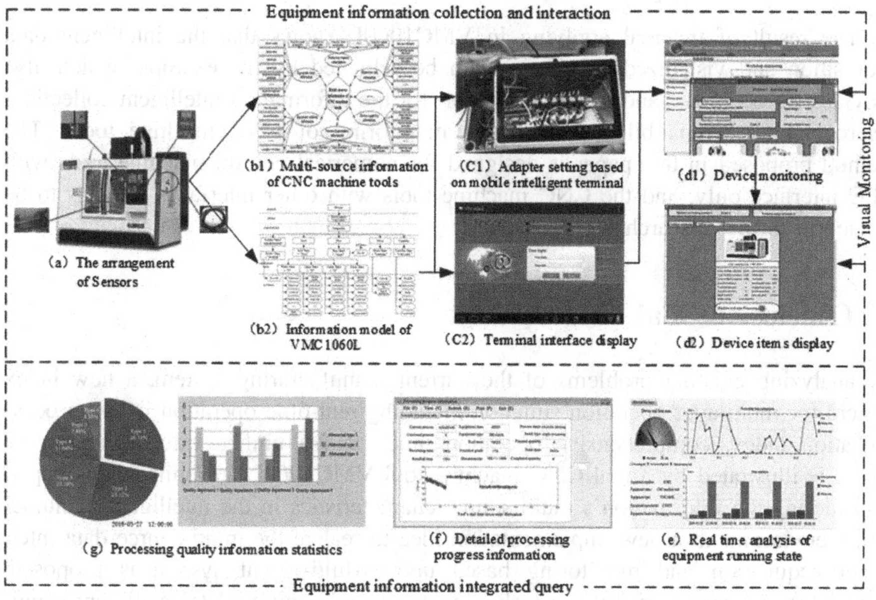

Fig. 7. The legend of experimental verification

(1) The arrangement of Sensors. The sensors are arranged as shown in Fig. 7a. Concerning the data collection requirements and the original numerical control system (①, ②, ③, ④ in the position of the FBG sensors, the CNC information collection, production quality detector and tool detector, respectively). Following the operation state of CNC machine tool, the sensor can collect the data in real-time and then the machine interfaces and mobile intelligent terminal (embedded adapter) will be connected to achieve the conversion of data and real-time interaction.

(2) Adapter setting based on mobile intelligent terminal. Mobile intelligent terminal software is developed in Android platform and the Android mobile intelligent interactive terminal can be connected with the LAN of enterprise by the wireless network. In the paper, the adapter is embedded in the intelligent interactive terminal to provide the "one stop" service for the information collection and conversion.
(3) The display of Multi-source data item of device. The information of CNC machining center is visible by i-MES system in our case. The items of the CNC machining center VMC1060L are shown in Fig. 7d.
(4) Information visualization of device. Based on i-MES personalized configuration module, multi-source information can be displayed in an easy-to-understand way to achieve visual monitoring of device information, as shown in Fig. 7e–g. Users can use the terminal to achieve the remote access and remote monitoring of i-MES system by entering the unique IP address of the server system.

The result of the real applying in VMC1060L shows that the intelligent data acquisition and visualized monitoring can be achieved by the example which also provides the academic and technical support for the information intelligent collection, heterogeneous compatibility and remote monitoring of CNC machine tools. The method proposed in this paper is designed for numerical control machine tools with OPC interface only, and the CNC machine tools with other interfaces remains to be studied in further research.

5 Conclusions and Future Work

By analyzing existing problems of the current manufacturing system, a new index system for multilayer operation situation including real-time operation index, process operation index, comprehensive operation index and a unified information model which is illustrated by a real CNC machine tool VMC1060L are built in this paper. Considering the information's multi-source characteristics in the intelligent manufacturing environment, a new implementation idea to realize the multi-source data intelligent acquisition and monitoring based upon Multi-Agent system is proposed. Especially, it focuses on the key technologies of multi-source data intelligent acquisition and visualized dynamic monitoring based on OPC and multi-agent. Finally, the practical application value of the method is verified by the test case.

Based on the results of this paper, further research will be focused on the intelligent transformation for CNC machine tools with different interface and realize the connection with MTConnect.

Acknowledgement. This work was supported by the National High-Tech. R&D Program, China. (No. 2015AA043801), and the Science and Technology Program of Guangdong Province (No. 2015A010103022).

References

1. Li, B.-H., Zhang, L., Ren, L., et al.: Typical characteristics, technologies and applications of cloud manufacturing. Comput. Integr. Manuf. Syst. **18**(7), 1345–1356 (2012)
2. Wu, D., Greer, M.J., Reson, D.W., et al.: Cloud manufacturing: strategic vision and state-of-the-art. J. Manuf. Syst. **19**(5), 1078–1084 (2013)
3. Liu, Z.-K.: Design research on CNC machine tools status and production information collection system. Dalian University of Technology (2014)
4. Liu, M.-Z., Wang, Q., Ling, L.: Research and implementation of workshop operation dashboard based on real-time information driven. Comput. Integr. Manuf. Syst. **08**, 2052–2062 (2015)
5. Lu, X.-H., Yu, D., Hu, Y., Yao, Z.: Numerical control system information integration method based on agent. J. Jilin Univ. **06**, 1980–1986 (2015)
6. Ri-Liang, L., Cheng-Rui, Z., Jiang, Y., Ke, W.: Networked monitoring technology of numerical control machine tools based on MTConnect. Comput. Integr. Manuf. Syst. **05**, 1078–1084 (2013)
7. Jie, Z.: Agent based production scheduling and controlling system. National Defense Industry Press, Beijing (2013)
8. Lu, L., Yu, D., Hu, Y., et al.: Research of the open CNC controller network interface technology. J. Chin. Comput. Syst. **03**, 621–626 (2015)
9. Yoo, D.-S., Van Tan, V., Yi, M.-J.: A universal data access server for distributed data acquisition and monitoring systems. ICIC **5754**, 762–773 (2009)
10. Kim, K., Choi, I.: Active data acquisition for proactive exception handling in manufacturing. Adv. Manuf. Technol. **43**, 365–378 (2009)
11. Edrington, B., Zhao, B., Hansel, A., et al.: Machine monitoring system based on MTConnect technology. In: Proceedings of the 3rd International Conference in Through-life Engineering Services, Procedia CIRP, vol. 22, pp. 92–97 (2014)
12. Garrido, C.J., Marin, M.R.: Remote maintenance and fault analysis system for custom-made machine. World Congr. **18**(1), 14976–14981 (2011)

Ontology Management and Ontology Reuse in Web Environment

Yapeng Cui[1,2], Lihong Qiao[1,2(✉)], and Yifan Qie[1,2]

[1] School of Mechanical Engineering and Automation, Beihang University, Beijing, China
lhqiao@buaa.edu.cn
[2] Engineering Research Center of Complex Product Advanced Manufacturing System, Ministry of Education, Beijing, China

Abstract. As a kind of knowledge representation method, ontology describes knowledge and information semantically in various fields and it has been widely used in Web environment. Ontology management and ontology reuse can solve the problems of knowledge confusion and inefficient knowledge base construction when applying ontology. This paper builds an ontology management framework and presents the system data storage model, ontology maintenance method and role-based ontology collaborative definition method. On this basis, an ontology reuse method based on Semantic Web Rule Language (SWRL) rule is proposed.

Keywords: Ontology management · Collaborative definition · Ontology reuse · SWRL

1 Introduction

Currently, the Internet has become an important way for people to obtain information. With the rapid development of intelligent equipment and information technology, the amount of information is growing exponentially, traditional data processing methods can only verify the huge data from the format level, but the problem of knowledge level verification remains a bottleneck.

As a kind of knowledge representation method, ontology describes knowledge and information semantically in various fields which can be identified and processed by the computer, so that integration and sharing of the data from different applications become possible. In the medical domain, Chmielewski et al. realized the integration and migration of medical data based on ontology [1]. In the manufacturing field, Qiao et al. proposed a process modeling method based on ontology and process specification language [2], Huang et al. built the ontology model of assembly process planning based on ontology [3]. Therefore, ontology has been widely used in the semantic Web. But with the continuous expansion of ontology needs in various fields, the number of Web ontologies has also grown substantially. On one hand a concept in the same field of different ontologies may be described differently. On the other hand, the same field has more than one ontology to repeatedly describe the same concept, which leads to knowledge confusion and redundancy as well as the lack of standardized management.

L. Zhang et al. (Eds.): Monterey Workshop 2016, LNCS 10228, pp. 122–130, 2017.
DOI: 10.1007/978-3-319-61994-1_12

In addition, manual creation of domain ontology poses a high requirement for the proficiency of the creator in ontology technology and domain knowledge, and the creation process is dull and inefficient. Reusing existing ontologies can reduce the system cost, improve efficiency of knowledge base construction, and reduce the workload and the cost structure. Therefore, how to build and standardize the domain ontology and realize the reuse of ontology in Web environment becomes a hot research topic.

In ontology management, Domingue et al. developed the WebOnto system to support the creation and editing of ontology in Web environment. After the installation of the WebOnto client, users can learn and edit ontology, view ontology relations, classes and rules, etc. [4]. Walisadeera et al. developed an agricultural field of user-centered ontology management system. Users and developers can edit ontology in the system, modify the structure of the ontology, search information in the context of ontology, share and reuse knowledge, and achieve large-scale ontology based Web development and maintenance purposes [5]. Buranarach et al. described an ontology application management (OAM) framework that aims to simplify creation and adoption of ontology-based application which is based on the Sematic Web technology. The framework focuses on providing reusable and configurable data and application templates, which allows users to create ontology without required programming skills [6].

In ontology reuse, Pan et al. proposed a brand new way for partial ontology reuse. It supports Tbox reasoning in simple ontology spaces, where an ontology semantically imports vocabulary from another ontology [7]. Xiang et al. developed OntoFox system, which supports ontology reuse and expansion. Users can dynamically extract ontology without the proficiency in any SPARQL Protocol, RDF Query Language (SPARQL) or other programming techniques [8]. Caldarola et al. put forward the technology for ontology reuse method based on matching of heterogeneous, which improves and simplifies the process of ontology constrain by automating the selection and reuses existing data models to support the creation of digital ecosystems [9].

Considering the two problems above, this paper builds a framework of ontology management system, and puts forward a mechanism based on the definition of role collaboration. On this basis, a new idea of ontology reuse based on SWRL rule is provided.

2 Ontology Management in Web Environment

Ontology management not only collects ontologies in a large variety of fields under the semantic Web. It takes into account the correctness, extensibility, interoperability and reusability of ontology. According to the need for sharing and exchanging information in each domain, the ontology management framework is built as shown in Fig. 1.

The system framework consists of data layer, application layer and presentation layer. The data layer comprises a relational database and an ontology document library, and provides data support for the management system. The application layer includes domain ontology partition, ontology file upload analysis as well as ontology building and maintenance mode. In this way, it ensures the correctness of the logic relationship between the ontology classes and object properties and data properties. The presentation

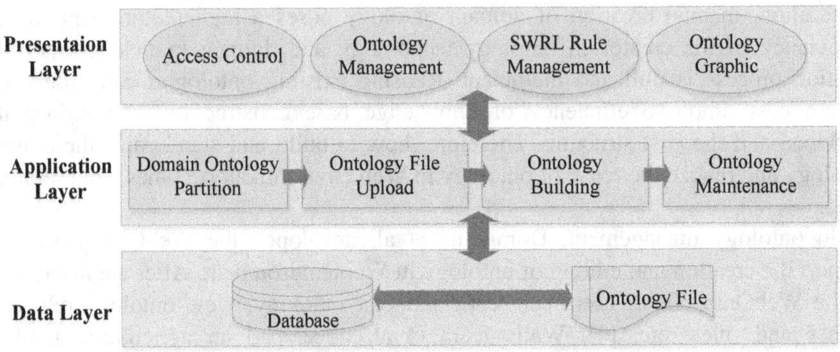

Fig. 1. Framework of ontology management system

layer consists of ontology and rule management, ontology visualization and authority control. Users can realize the learning of ontology and the reuse of ontology by reasonable human-computer interaction interface.

2.1 The Mapping Mode of Ontology and Database

Under the premise of satisfying the traditional pattern design principle, this paper parses the ontology by using Web Ontology Language (OWL) API. The OWL ontology storage mode is designed as shown in Fig. 2.

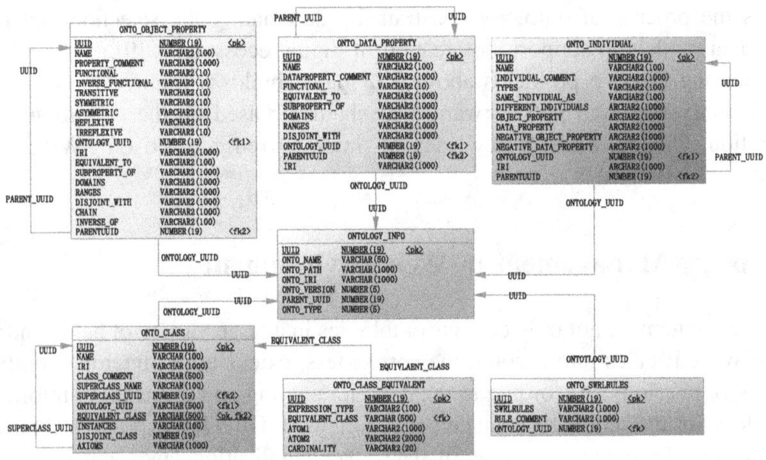

Fig. 2. Ontology storage mode

- Table ONTOLOGY_INFO stores the basic information of the ontology, including the name of ontology, ontology storage path, ontology Uniform Resource Identifier (URI), ontology version and other information.
- Table ONTO_CLASS_EQUIVALENT and table ONTO_CLASS store the information of ontology categories, including the name of the class, URI, annotation, disjoint classes, equivalent classes and other similar information.
- Table ONTO_DATA_PROPERTY and table ONTO_OBJECT_PROPERTY store the object property information and the data property information respectively. Including the basic property description such as the name of property, URI, annotation, equivalent property and domains etc. as well as the feature description such as functional, inverse functional, transitive, etc.
- Table ONTO_INDIVIDUAL stores individuals of ontology, including name, annotation, URI, class assertions, same individuals, object property declarations and data property declarations.
- Table ONTO_SWRLRULES stores the SWRL rules of ontology, including the rules and rules of the annotation itself.

It can be seen from the description above that the mode is simple in structure and easy to understand. It can clearly describe the relationship between the concepts. The mode structure is stable, so that when domain changes, there is no need to modify the table structure, the mode can be stored in various fields of ontology.

2.2 Ontology Maintenance Method

Ontology resources, such as classes, object properties, data properties and individuals in Ontology, all have their own URI. Describing the rule declaration to an ontology by using SWRL also can be regarded as a kind of resource of Ontology. When modifying or deleting five kinds of resources mentioned before, it is important to note that modifying or deleting a resource is not just a simple single resource modification or deletion, but all the resources that are related to the resources or resources properties to be modified or deleted in the ontology would be changed.

Therefore, resource attribute of five resources may be associated with the change, as shown in Fig. 3. The upper or the right side of the arrow are the properties that point to the possible change of the associated resource.

For instance, deleting a class may involve the parent class property, equivalent class property and disjoint class property of other classes in the ontology information change. It also may be associated with the properties of the object domain and range information, data properties domain information, individual class assertion information and related SWRL rules changes.

2.3 Role Based Ontology Collaborative Definition

There are ordinary users, system administrators and domain experts as three kinds of roles in the system. Role based ontology collaboration definition is shown in Fig. 4. Ordinary users can learn or reuse ontology from the system. A new domain ontology

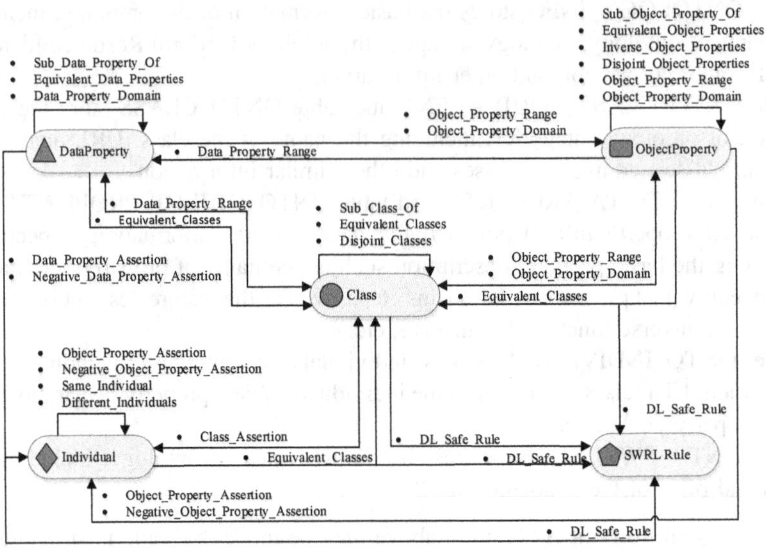

Fig. 3. The relationship of resources in ontology

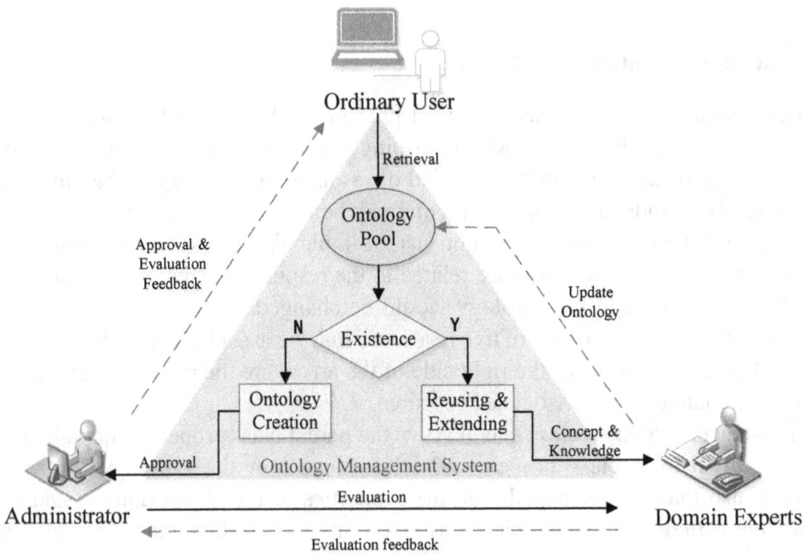

Fig. 4. Role based collaborative definition

can be created by ordinary users and then evaluated by the domain experts. After being audited by field experts, the created domain ontology will be incorporated into the system. The system administrator is a business maintenance person who is responsible for handling the response from the user or domain expert in the system. Domain experts are the defenders of ontology knowledge, who is responsible for the evaluation of the domain knowledge of user expansion.

- Ordinary users can search each domain ontology in the ontology pool of the system. Otherwise, they can create a new field in the system, and wait for the feedback of the rationality of this ontology by system administrators and experts in the field; if a domain ontology can be queried, it can be directly reused in the system. But the user has no authority to modify the ontology in the system.
- The system administrator is responsible for the approval of ordinary users because they do not search the desired ontology and create their own ontology information. After being approved through examination, the approval information will be fed back to users. At the same time, the ontology will be transferred to experts in the field to be evaluated. Finally the administrator receives the experts' feedback on the rationality of new domain ontology and accordingly gives feedback to ordinary users.
- Domain experts are responsible for the control of the correctness of the system ontology concepts and rules. On one hand, they receive the concepts and rules of the extension of the user in a certain field, and verify its reasonableness after determining whether to update the domain ontology. On the other hand, experts evaluate users' newly created ontology that not exist in the system, and give the evaluation feedback to determine whether the ontology should be added to the system ontology pool.

Role based ontology collaboration definition can ensure the correctness of the ontology description of the knowledge in the system. Ordinary users, system administrators and experts in the field use ontology management system based on Web, collaboratively maintain ontology which makes the ontology expression knowledge richer and it is conducive to the development of each domain ontology.

3 Ontology Reuse in Web Environment

Ontology is a kind of method used to describe knowledge. Rule can be used as a means to express knowledge when the concept of ontology is unified. Being a language which presents rules in the semantic way, SWRL provides the expression ability which is not allowable by OWL while maintaining compatibility with syntax, semantics, and theoretical model of OWL. Therefore, an ontology reuse method based on SWRL rule is proposed by the concept unification in this paper.

3.1 Unification of Ontology Concept

The concept of ontology refers to the class, object property and data property of it. If the name of the concept and its properties are in conformity with the things that are described in the field of application, then the existing concepts can be considered to be completely consistent with the concept of application domain description.

There are four kinds of situations in the process of the unification of ontology concept:

(1) The described concept exists in the existing ontology, and it is completely consistent with the concept described in application domain.
(2) There are similar concepts in the existing ontology, only its name is inconsistent with the description of the application domain. Other properties are exactly the same.
(3) There are similar concepts in the existing ontology, its name is consistent with the description of the application domain. But its properties are not.
(4) The described concept does not exist in the existing ontology, both its name and properties cannot match the description of application domain.

For case (1), new concepts do not need to be given to original ontology while it is applied. For case (2), different nouns are used to describe the same thing in different domains. So owl: euquivalentClass, owl: equivalentObjectPropert or owl: equivalentDataProperty will be used to declare that the new concept is equivalent to the existing concept description when new concepts are added. For case (3), the name of new concept adopts the naming rules of "similar concept name + suffix" to add the properties of application domain described concept. For case (4), a new concept has to be added.

3.2 Rule Based Ontology Reuse

SWRL rules specify a conjunction of facts. If the rules are met, another collection of facts is contained. SWRL rules are mainly composed of two parts: Head and Body. Head represents the conclusion of the rule while Body represents the premise. Head and Body are made up of zero or more atoms. The type of atom might be: class element, relationship element between class and class, relationship element between class and data, type element of variable, equivalent element, non-equivalent element and built-in element.

The type of atoms is defined as follows:

- Class element - C($?c$), which represents an individual variable c that belongs to class C.
- Relationship element between class and class - P($?c_1, ?c_2$), which denotes that the individual c_1 and the individual c_2 that has a relation, that is, property P.
- Relationship element between class and data - R($?c, ?v$), which denotes that individual c has relation of property R with the literal value V.
- Type element of variable - D($?t, ?v$), which denotes that the data type of literal variable V is t.
- Equivalent element - SA ($?c_1, ?c_2$), which denotes that individual c_1 is equivalent to individual c_2.
- Non-equivalent element - DF ($?c_1, ?c_2$), which denotes that individual c_1 is not equivalent to individual c_2.

- Built-ins element - BI $(?x, ?y)$, which denotes that variable x and variable y have certain kind of function relation.

Based on the definition above, SWRL rule could contain zero or more atoms for each type of atoms. As a result, Head or Body can be expressed as:

$$\{C, P, R, D, SA, DF, BI\} \tag{1}$$

Ontology reuse based on SWRL rules is built on the basis of a unified understanding of described concept and sharing the same ontology to express new knowledge by rules. For example, a knowledge in the field of tolerance: A cylindrical feature is marked with a cylindrical tolerance, with a tolerance grade as "IT7" and diameter t of the cylinder. When $250\text{mm} < t \leq 400\text{mm}$, cylindrical tolerance value of this cylindrical feature is 0.014 mm. When the concepts, such as cylindrical feature, tolerance grade, tolerance type, etc. are unified, this piece of knowledge will be represented by the SWRL rule as: Cylinder_Feature (?x), Cylidrical_Tolerance (?y), has_ToleranceType (?x, ?y), has_ToleranceGrade (?x,"IT7"^^String), has_MainSize (?x, ?value), greaterThan (?value, 250.0f), lessThanOrEqual (?value, 400.0f) → has_ToleranceValue (?x,0.014f).

When various fields share one ontology from the beginning and concepts of this field are unified, domain knowledge can be expressed with SWRL rules. In the end, reuse of ontology can be achieved without information alignment process between two ontologies.

4 Conclusions

Ontology management and ontology reuse play a vital role in the ontology application. This paper builds an ontology management system based on role collaboration definition, and puts forward a SWRL-based ontology reuse method. Each domain ontology is constantly developed under the premise of cognitive unification of domain experts, and the efficiency of ontology construction is greatly improved.

Acknowledgments. This work is supported by the National High-Tech. R&D Program, China (No. 2015AA043702), the Graduate Student Innovation Fund of Beihang University and the key program of the Engineering Research Center of Complex Product Advanced Manufacturing System, Ministry of Education.

References

1. Chmielewski, M., Stąpor, P.: Medical data unification using ontology-based semantic model structural analysis. In: Świątek, J., Borzemski, L., Grzech, A., Wilimowska, Z. (eds.) Information Systems Architecture and Technology: Proceedings of 36th International Conference on Information Systems Architecture and Technology – ISAT 2015 – Part III. AISC, vol. 431, pp. 139–151. Springer, Cham (2016). doi:10.1007/978-3-319-28564-1_12

2. Qiao, L., Kao, S., Zhang, Y.: Manufacturing process modelling using process specification language. Int. J. Adv. Manuf. Technol. **55**(5–8), 549–563 (2011)
3. Huang, Z., Qiao, L., Anwer, N., et al.: Ontology model for assembly process planning knowledge. In: Proceedings of the 21st International Conference on Industrial Engineering and Engineering Management, pp. 419–423 (2014)
4. Domingue, J.: Tadzebao and Webonto: Discussing, Browsing, Editing Ontologies on the Web. In: Proceedings of the 11th Knowledge Acquisition for Knowledge-Based Systems Workshop, pp. 686–689 (1998)
5. Walisadeera, A.I., Ginige, A., Wikramanayake, G.N., Pamuditha Madushanka, A.L., Shanika Udeshini, A.A.: A framework for end-to-end ontology management system. In: Gervasi, O., et al. (eds.) ICCSA 2015. LNCS, vol. 9155, pp. 529–544. Springer, Cham (2015). doi:10.1007/978-3-319-21404-7_39
6. Buranarach, M., Supnithi, T., Thein, Y.M., et al.: OAM: an ontology application management framework for simplifying ontology-based semantic web application development. Int. J. Softw. Eng. Knowl. Eng. **26**(01), 115–145 (2016)
7. Pan, J.Z., Serafini, L., Zhao, Y.: Semantic import: an approach for partial ontology reuse. In: Proceedings of the 1st International Conference on Modular Ontologies, vol. 232, CEUR-WS.org, pp. 71–84 (2006)
8. Xiang, Z., Courtot, M., Brinkman, R.R., et al.: Ontofox: web-based support for ontology reuse. BMC Res. Notes **3**(1), 1 (2010)
9. Caldarola, E.G., Picariello, A., Rinaldi, A.M.: An approach to ontology integration for ontology reuse in knowledge based digital ecosystems. In: International Conference on Management of Computational and Collective Intelligence in Digital Ecosystems. ACM (2015)

Research on the Shortest Path of Two Places in Urban Based on Improved Ant Colony Algorithm

Yanjuan Hu[1,2](✉), Luquan Ren[1], Hongwei Zhao[1], and Yao Wang[3]

[1] College of Biological and Agricultural Engineering, Jilin University, Changchun, China
yanjuan_hu@126.com

[2] Mechatronic Engineering, Changchun University of Technology, Changchun, China

[3] College of Mechanical Engineering, Beihua University, Jilin City, China

Abstract. Based on the GIS electronic map and traffic control information database, a shortest path algorithm based on GIS technology is proposed, the A and B geographic information of the monitoring points are extracted, and the shortest path algorithm is used to solve the shortest path between A and B. Using the improved ant colony algorithm to calculate the shortest distance from the start node to the target node. In view of the phenomenon of ant colony algorithm convergence speed is slow and easy to fall into premature defects, and the effective measures for improvement was put forward, and take the simplifying road network as an example, a simulation of the algorithm was conducted. The satisfactory results of the simulation verify the effectiveness of the algorithm.

Keywords: Ant colony algorithm · Simulation · Path · Convergence speed

1 Introduction

Network is abstracted as a form of picture expression in the fields of mathematics and computer. In the calculation of the shortest path in GIS, it must first be expressed in the form of nodes and edges, and construct the topology of the network. Topological structure is used to express the spatial relationship of geographic information, and it is the high generalization of geographical elements. Network topology [1, 2] can describe the connection of road network nodes and main roads, by extracting the coordinates of each node in the network and the attribute data of each link, the topology structure of the road network is constructed by using the network topology information.

2 Road Network Topology

The specific implementation method, according to the information extracted from the vector map, generates the node table and arc segment table. The node table and arc segment table form are as shown in Tables 1 and 2.

L. Zhang et al. (Eds.): Monterey Workshop 2016, LNCS 10228, pp. 131–138, 2017.
DOI: 10.1007/978-3-319-61994-1_13

Table 1. Attribute table of nodes

Field name	Field type
Node ID	Integer
Longitude	Float
Latitude	Float

Table 2. Attribute table of arc segment

Field name	Field type
Arc segment ID	Integer
Starting point ID	Integer
End ID	Integer
Weight	Float
Other	Float

Road network storage usually has adjacency matrix and adjacency list two forms, both have their own strengths, through specific application to determine what kind of storage method to use. The comparison of the two forms of storage is shown in Table 3.

Table 3. Comparison of two kinds of storage forms of road network

	Adjacency matrix	Adjacency list
Storage representation	Only	Not unique
Space complexity S(n, e)	$O(n^2)$ suitable for dense graphs	$O(n + e)$ sparse graph
Seek the degree of the vertex	Easily	It is difficult to solve the directed graph
Number of edges	It must detect the entire matrix, time consuming $O(n^2)$	It only need to count the number of nodes per side table, time consuming $O(n + e)$

Traffic network is characterized by a lot of nodes, very few edges, for the network adjacency matrix which contains a large number of nodes, its storage space utilization rate is very low, and the adjacency list structure has been proved to be the most effective data structure in sparse network. So this article uses the adjacency list to store the network topology.

3 Rectangle Restricted Searching Area Algorithm

Figure 1 is a small part of a city map after the simplified schematic.

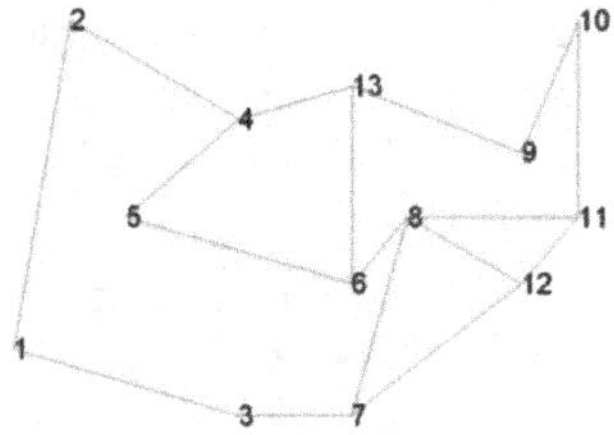

Fig. 1. Schematic diagram of a city network

Assuming that in Fig. 1, the No. 5 node is the starting node S, and No. 9 node is the target node E, according to the ellipse limit search area algorithm [3, 4], the limited search area is shown as Fig. 2.

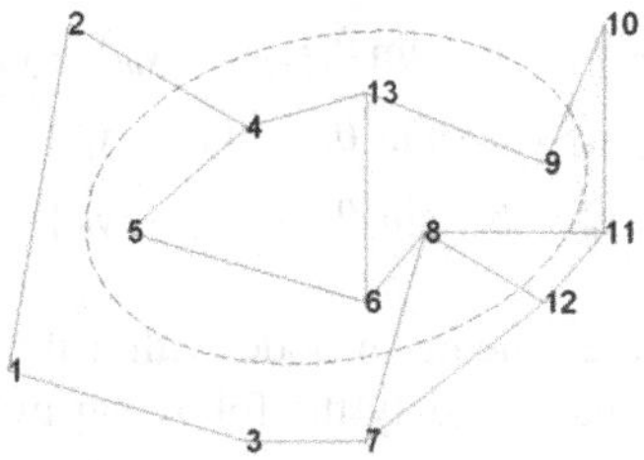

Fig. 2. Elliptic restricted search area map

As shown in Fig. 2, the dotted line shows an effective search area within the ellipse region. It can be seen that the algorithm can greatly reduce the search scale of the shortest path algorithm, but the algorithm shortcomings are to determine the expansion of the each node whether in the elliptic region and need a lot of product and square root operations and the running time is longer.

For the operation time of ellipse limit search is longer, Lu Feng et al. put forward an improved rectangle limit search area algorithm [5]. This algorithm is used to find the minimum rectangle that contains the ellipse, and the four sides (horizontal and vertical direction) are the boundary line of the search area in, so as to reduce the search scope. The rectangle searching area algorithm combines the rationality of ellipse searching area algorithm, at the same time, it avoids a large number of root operations of the ellipse regional search algorithm. However, when the long axis of the ellipse is not in the horizontal direction, the minimum enclosing rectangle obtained by the method, is not parallel to the long axis of the rectangle, and the directivity of ellipse is not well used. On this basis, this paper presents an improved algorithm of rectangular search area, which is based on coordinate transformation, so that the edge of the rectangle is parallel to the long axis of the ellipse, as shown in Fig. 3.

In Fig. 3, the black rectangle is the improved restricted area. Compared with the red rectangle without improvement, the shortest path direction formed by the ellipse focus line is fully utilized, which is more closed to the idea of the ellipse restricted area.

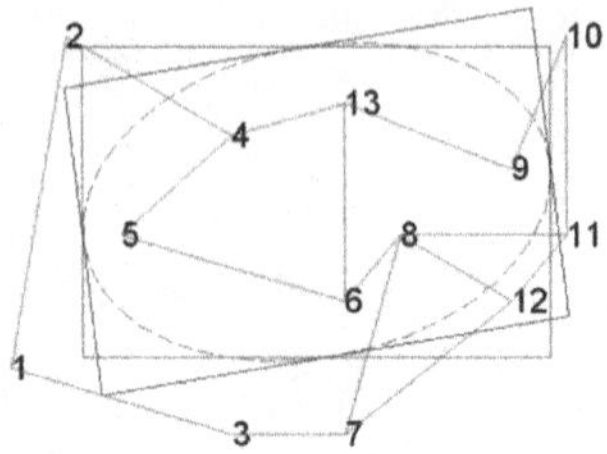

Fig. 3. The improved rectangular restricted search area (Color figure online)

By the coordinate transformation formula, the four vertices coordinates of the improved rectangular can be respectively introduced:

$$\begin{cases} \frac{1}{e}(x_e - x_m) + x_m + b \cdot \sin\theta, \frac{1}{e}(y_e - y_m) + y_m - b \cdot \cos\theta \\ \frac{1}{e}(x_e - x_m) + x_m - b \cdot \sin\theta, \frac{1}{e}(y_e - y_m) + y_m + b \cdot \cos\theta \\ -\frac{1}{e}(x_e - x_m) + x_m + b \cdot \sin\theta, -\frac{1}{e}(y_e - y_m) + y_m + b \cdot \cos\theta \\ -\frac{1}{e}(x_e - x_m) + x_m + b \cdot \sin\theta, -\frac{1}{e}(y_e - y_m) + y_m - b \cdot \cos\theta \end{cases} \tag{1}$$

On this basis, to determine whether a node within the restricted areas, it is only needed to let the node coordinates satisfy the following two conditions:

$$x_m - a \leq x_d + l \cdot \sin\theta \leq x_m + a \tag{2}$$

$$y_m - b \leq y_d + l - l \cdot \cos\theta \leq y_m + b \tag{3}$$

4 The Improved Ant Colony Algorithm

Basic ant colony algorithm [6–8] for the pheromone update adopts Eqs. (4), (5) and (6), parameters that affect the function of the pheromone areρ, Q and L_k, among them, the volatilization coefficient ρ and pheromone concentration Q are given by the program, however the path length L_k of the ant k walked in this cycle is variation. For the AS_{elite} system, the pheromone [9, 10] updating only considers the optimal path length L^* of this iteration.

$$\tau_{ij}(t+n) = (1-\rho) \cdot \tau_{ij}(t) + \Delta\tau_{ij}(t) \tag{4}$$

$$\Delta\tau_{ij}(t) = \sum_{k=1}^{m} \Delta\tau_{ij}^{k}(t) \tag{5}$$

$$\Delta\tau_{ij}^{k}(t) = \begin{cases} \frac{Q}{L_k}, & \text{If the ant K in this cycle passes the path}(i,j) \\ 0, & \text{Otherwise} \end{cases} \tag{6}$$

This paper, by judging whether the ant colony is dispersed in different paths or concentrated in a certain one or only a few more optimal paths to dynamically adjusts the pheromone update rules, and combines the MMAS system to limit the amount of information in the range $[\tau_{\min}, \tau_{\max}]$, which makes the convergence rate and avoiding premature convergence to achieve a more ideal balance. The L^i_{avg} indicates the average length of the ith iteration of the ant colony, there is:

$$L^i_{avg} = \frac{1}{m}\sum_{k=1}^{m} L_k \tag{7}$$

The L^i_{best} indicates the optimal path of the ith iteration of the ant colony. In the ith iteration, by comparing the difference between the optimal path and the average path of ant colony, we can determine that the path of the ant colony is relatively aggregate or relatively scattered. When the difference between the two is very large, it is explained that most of the ants in the ant colony are scattered far away from the path of the optimal solution; When the difference between the two is not large, it is explained that most of the ants in the ant colony are aggregated in the path of the optimal solution or the optimal solution. The τ^i indicates the polymerization degree of ant colony in the ith iteration, there is:

$$\tau^i = \frac{L^i_{best}}{L^i_{ava}} \tag{8}$$

Assuming that in each iteration, the ant colony is not all caught in a dead end, there is $\tau^i \in (0,1)$, where $0 < i \leq NC$, NC is the maximum number of iterations. When the ant colony relative aggregation, the probability of premature phenomenon is relatively large, at this time, it is necessary to reduce the attraction to ants of pheromone; On the contrary, when the ant colony is relatively dispersed, it is needed to increase the concentration of pheromone on one or some of the best path, and speed up the convergence rate of ant colony. It is reflected in the degree of ant colony aggregation τ^i, when the τ^i is more close to 1, the ant colony is relative aggregation, when the τ^i is away from 1, the ant colony is relative dispersion. So we need to find a threshold λ^τ for the degree of aggregation of ant colony, when $\tau^i \leq \lambda^\tau$, the amount of information is increased; when $\tau^i > \lambda^\tau$, the amount of information is reduced. Through a large number of experimental analysis, we take $\lambda^\tau = 0.4$. To improve the update rules of the information mentioned above, the Eq. (6) is changed to Eq. (9).

$$\Delta\tau^k_{ij}(t) = \begin{cases} \frac{\varepsilon_k Q}{L_k}, & \text{If the ant K in this cycle passes the path } (i,j) \\ 0, & \text{Otherwise} \end{cases} \tag{9}$$

$$\varepsilon_k(t) = \begin{cases} \frac{L_{avg} - L_k}{L_{avg} - L_B}, & \tau^i \leq \lambda^\tau \\ 0, & \tau^i > \lambda^\tau \end{cases} \tag{10}$$

In Eqs. 9 and 10, L_k represents the path walked through by the superior elite ant K previous cycle, take the shorter two different paths, and the ant who walks through the two paths is defined as the elite ants; L_B represents the optimal solution found at the present. From the above equation be seen, the more close to the optimal path L_k is, the more close to 1 the weight $\varepsilon_k(t)$ is. In this way, it can not only speed up the convergence rate, but also improve the global search ability of ant colony, and it is very advantageous to solve large-scale optimization problems.

The program flow chart is shown in Fig. 4.

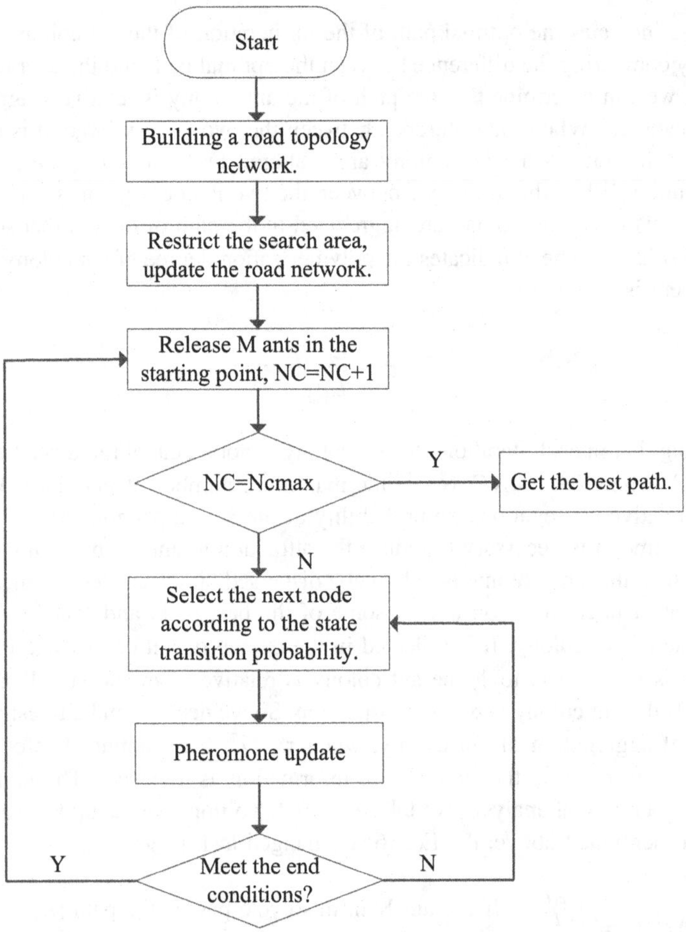

Fig. 4. Program flow chart of improved ant colony algorithm

5 Simulation Results and Analysis

Take the simplified road network Fig. 5 as an example, the network map contains 20 nodes, the shortest distance between node 5 and node 10 needs to be solved. In the ant colony algorithm, $\alpha = 1.2$, $\beta = 0.9$, $Q = 200$, $\rho = 0.5$, $M = 34$, $NC_{\max} = 35$, $\tau_{\max} = 2.5$, $\tau_{\min} = 0.4$. Program is written in Matlab7 and simulation results are shown in Fig. 6.

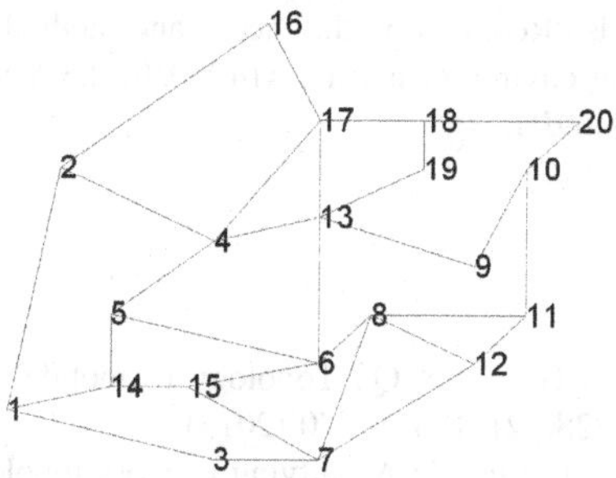

Fig. 5. Simplified road network of simulation

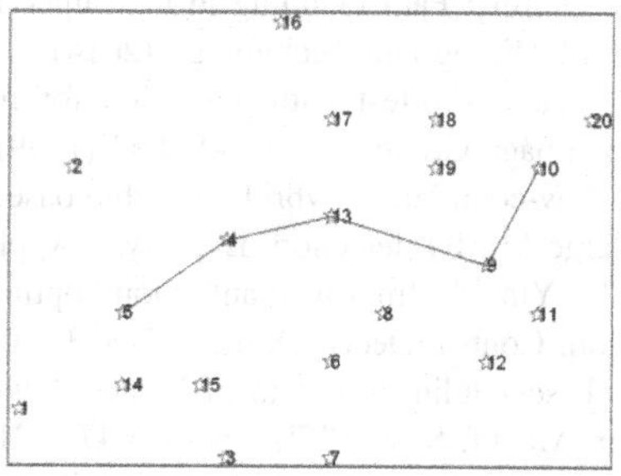

Fig. 6. Simulation results

In Fig. 6, the pointed star represents the 20 city nodes, The path which is connected by a straight line represents the shortest path between No. 5 node and No. 10 node solved by the improved ant colony algorithm proposed in this paper. The path is 5-4-13-9-10, and its length is 995.99 m.

6 Conclusions

This paper aims to solve the shortest path between the two places in the city, according to the defects of the slow convergence rate and easy to fall into local optimal solution of the ant colony algorithm, a method is proposed to determine the status of the ant colony by calculating the degree of polymerization, so as to increase or reduce the attraction of pheromone to the ant colony. At the same time, in order to prevent the amount of information is too large, the amount of information for all the paths is set the maximum amount of information and the minimum amount of information, which is used to limit the amount of information. In this paper, an improved algorithm of rectangle restricted search area is proposed, which reduces the search area and avoids unnecessary traversal of the ant colony algorithm. The simulation results show that the algorithm is effective. The results of the study are of great significance.

Acknowledgment. This research work was supported by the Nature Science Foundation of China, and the project name is "Research on the theory and method of manufacturability evaluation in cloud manufacturing environment", no. 51405030; the Youth Science Foundation of Jilin Province, no. 20160520069JH.

References

1. He, M., Liang, W., Chen, G., Chen, Q.: Topology of mobile underwater wireless sensor networks. Control Decis. **28**(12), 1761–1770 (2013)
2. Cai, W., Zhao, H., Wang, J., Lin, C.: A unifying network topological model of the energy internet macro-scope structure. Proc. CSEE **35**(14), 3503–3510 (2015)
3. Wang, S., Xing, J., Zhang, Y., Bai, B.: Ellipse-based shortest path algorithm for typical urban road networks. Syst. Eng. Theory Prac. **31**(6), 1158–1164 (2011)
4. Bi, F.: Application of the Optimal Path Planning in the Supervision of Land Enforcement System. China University of Mining and Technology (2014)
5. Lu, F., Lu, D., Cui, W.: Time shortest path algorithm for restricted searching area in transportation networks. J. Image Graph. **4**(10), 849–853 (1999)
6. Manish, M., Vimal, B.: A low-complexity hybrid algorithm based on particle swarm and ant colony optimization for large-MIMO detection. Exp. Syst. Appl. **50**, 66–74 (2016)
7. Li, Q., Zhang, C., Chen, P., Yin, Y.: Improved ant colony optimization algorithm based on particle swarm optimization. Control Decis. **28**(6), 873–883 (2013)
8. Song, D., Zhang, J.: Batch scheduling problem of hybrid flow shop based on ant colony algorithm. Comput. Integr. Manuf. Syst. **19**(7), 1640–1647 (2013)
9. Zhang, J., Zhang, P., Liu, G.: Two-stage ant colony algorithm based job shop scheduling with unrelated parallel machines. J. Mech. Eng. **49**(6), 136–144 (2013)
10. Enxiu, S., Minmin, C., Jun, L., Yumei, H.: Research on method of global path-planning for mobile robot based on ant-colony algorithm. Trans. Chin. Soc. Agric. Mach. **45**(6), 53–57 (2014)

RUL Prediction of Bearings Based on Mixture of Gaussians Bayesian Belief Network and Support Vector Data Description

Qianhui Wu, Yu Feng, and Biqing Huang(✉)

Department of Automation, Tsinghua University, Beijing 100084, China
hbq@tsinghua.edu.cn

Abstract. This paper presents a method to predict the Remaining Useful Life (RUL) of bearings based on theories of Mixture of Gaussians Bayesian Belief Network (MoG-BBN) and Support Vector Data Description (SVDD). In this method, the feature vectors, which are used to train the corresponding MoG-BBN and SVDD model, are extracted from raw sensor data by using wavelet packet decomposition (WPD). Genetic algorithm is employed to determine the initial value of the variables in MoG-BBN training algorithm so that the stability of MoG-BBN can be enhanced. The two models are combined to acquire a good generalization ability. We demonstrate the effectiveness of the proposed method by using actual bearing datasets from the NASA prognostic data repository.

Keywords: Wavelet packet decomposition · Mixture of gaussians bayesian belief network · Genetic algorithm · Support vector data description · Remaining useful life

1 Introduction

Bearings are one of the most commonly used and the most easily damaged components in mechanical equipment. As a key part of condition based maintenance (CBM) [1], RUL prediction of bearings make it possible to effectively anticipate bearings' failure, reduce the maintenance cost as well as increase the productivity.

Since the condition monitoring data is available, this paper focuses on the data-driven methods [2]. Under this framework, a variety of previous researches about bearing prognostic and RUL prediction has been conducted, including artificial networks [3–5], hidden Markov models (HMM) [6, 7], support vector machines [8–10], etc. By using the MQE indicator obtained from SOM, Huang *et al.* [5] trained back propagation neural networks, which focus on ball bearings' degradation periods, and then applied WAFT technology to predict RUL. Tobon-Mejia *et al.* [6] proposed a method based on the Mixture of Gaussian Hidden Markov Models. In this method, hidden states of the model represent the failure modes of bearings, and the RUL can be estimated straightly by the stay duration of each state. With the consideration of the fuzziness of degradation process, Shen *et al.* [8] proposed a damage severity index (DSI) based on fuzzy support vector data description (FSVDD). And the growth of degradation with running time was indicated by the DSI.

L. Zhang et al. (Eds.): Monterey Workshop 2016, LNCS 10228, pp. 139–151, 2017.
DOI: 10.1007/978-3-319-61994-1_14

In addition, Xinghui Zhang *et al.* [11] constructed the Mixture of Gaussians Bayesian Belief Network (MoG-BBN) to characterize degradation states by using the condition monitoring data from sensors. However, the initial values of the parameters used in the training algorithm have a great impact on the accuracy of the RUL prediction. Hence, the stability and generalization of the model are reduced. To overcome this deficiency, this paper proposed a RUL prediction method based on the MoG-BBN and SVDD. The novelty of this method lies in two respects. First, genetic algorithm is employed to find the optimal initial values of the parameters used when training the MoG-BBN model so that the stability of the MoG-BBN model enhances significantly. Second, a method based on SVDD are presented to estimate the RUL when the MoG-BBN model does not work well, aiming at improving the generalization capability and the prediction accuracy at the same time.

The remainder of this paper is organized as follows: Sect. 2 introduces the methodology proposed for remaining useful life prediction of bearings. Section 3 carries out experiments on actual bearing data from NASA to examine the effectiveness of the proposed method. Section 4 concludes the work.

2 Methodology

Figure 1 shows the framework of our methodology. It can be divided into two phases. One is the off-line phase, where features are extracted from raw data set, and then are used to train the MoG-BBN model and the SVDD model. The other is the on-line phase: First of all, we adopt the same approach as that in the off-line phase to extract features from the real-time vibration signal. Next, these features are fed into the MoG-BBN model to characterize the degradation state. Some measures will be taken to determine whether the trained MoG-BBN model matches current component well. If matching well, it comes to the RUL prediction step directly. Otherwise, the features will be fed into the SVDD model to get better performance and robustness. Finally, the RUL estimation will be implemented.

2.1 Feature Extraction

Wavelet packet decomposition (WPD) is an effective technique in signal analysis. Its result has sufficient high-frequency resolution, and contains the most useful fault information of bearings [12]. WPD can be considered as a tree, of which the original signal is the root. By recursively applying the wavelet transform, WPD can automatically choose the appropriate frequency scale according to the characteristics of the analyzed signal, further decompose the high and low frequency data, and divide the spectrum band into several levels [7].

Due to the excellent properties mentioned above, this paper uses WPD to extract features from the raw vibration data of bearings. Assume that the decomposition level is l, then there will be $L = 2^l$ nodes on the last level. The feature vector at time t can be described as follows, where f_{it} denotes the energy coefficient of the ith node of the last level.

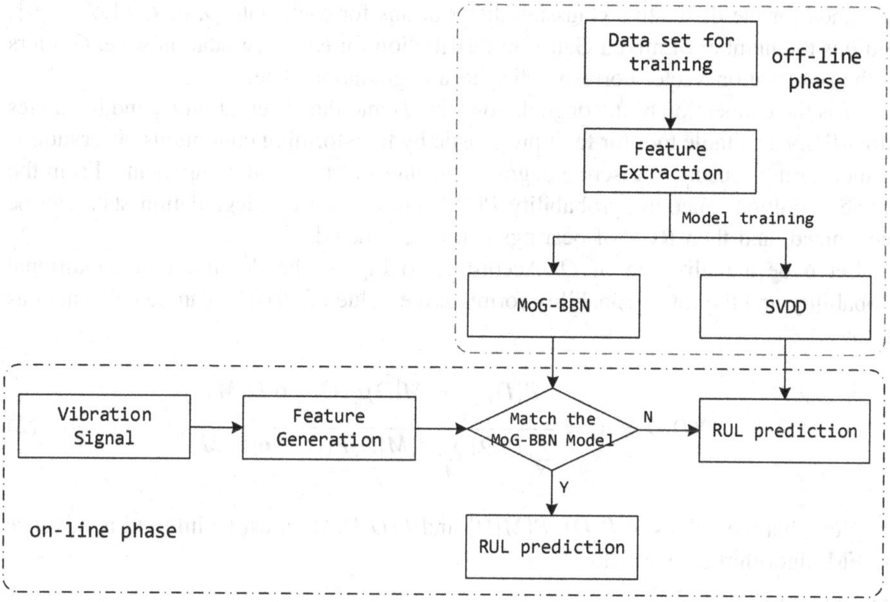

Fig. 1. Framework of the proposed method

$$\mathbf{f} = (f_{1t}, f_{2t}, \cdots, f_{Lt})^T \tag{1}$$

Note that a normalization processing based on the mean and standard deviation should be applied to the result of WPD before training the model, in order to improve the generalization capability.

2.2 The Mixture of Gaussians Bayesian Belief Network

Structure

Figure 2 illustrates the MoG-BBN structure, where D and M are discrete variables, and O is a continuous variable. To be specific, D denotes the degradation states that cannot be directly observed. $D \in \{1, 2, \cdots a\}$, and a is the maximum degradation state number. In this paper, a is set to 3, representing healthy, sub-healthy, and faulty states.

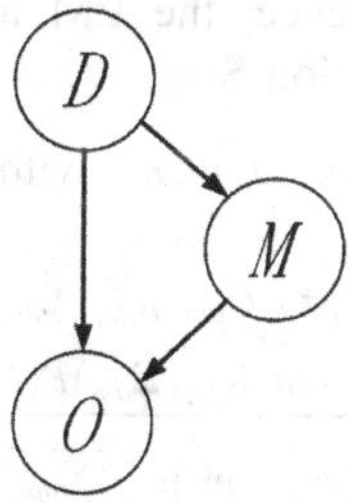

Fig. 2. Mixture of Gaussian Bayesian belief network.

M stands for the distinctive Gaussian distributions for each state D. $M \in \{1, 2, \cdots b\}$, and b is the number of mixed Gaussian distribution for each degradation state. O refers to the observation vector corresponding to a degradation state.

M is the connection of the degradation state D and the observation O, and it enables MoG-BBN a suitable tool for fault prognostic by transforming continuous observations of monitoring sensors to discrete degradation states of physical components. From the above definition, once the probability $P(D|O)$ is known, the degradation state can be recognized, and then RUL of bearings can be estimated.

Let $\mathbf{o}$ be a realization of O. According to Fig. 2, the definition of conditional probability and the total probability formula, the value of $P(D|O)$ can be calculated as follows.

$$P(D|O=\mathbf{o}) = \frac{P(D)\sum_{M} P(M|D)P(O=\mathbf{o}|D,M)}{\sum_{X} P(D)\sum_{M} P(M|D)P(O=\mathbf{o}|D,M)} \quad (2)$$

Note that the values of $P(D)$, $P(M|D)$ and $P(O|D,M)$ must be inferred in advance by EM algorithm shown below.

EM Algorithm

A declaration of the variables used in the estimation procedure is given first.

- π_d: the initial distribution of degradation state D, and $\pi_d = P(D=d)$ for $d \in \{1, 2, \cdots, a\}$.
- C_{dm}: mixture coefficient of the mth Gaussian distribution for degradation state d, where $C_{dm} = P(M=m|D=d)$, for $d \in \{1, 2, \cdots, a\}$ and $m \in \{1, 2, \cdots, b\}$.
- $\boldsymbol{\mu}_{dm}$: mean vector of the mth Gaussian distribution for degradation state d.
- $\boldsymbol{\Sigma}_{dm}$: covariance matrix of the mth Gaussian distribution for degradation state d.

To compute $P(O|D,M)$, suppose O_d is the distribution of an observation O generated by degradation state d, then

$$O_d = \sum_{m=1}^{b} C_{dm} N(\mu_{dm}, \Sigma_{dm}), 1 \le d \le a \quad (3)$$

The statistical values of the above parameters can be inferred via training data sets and the EM algorithm. Given an observation sequence $\mathbf{o} = \{\mathbf{o}^{(1)}, \mathbf{o}^{(2)}, \cdots, \mathbf{o}^{(N)}\}$, where N denotes the length of the sequence, the EM algorithm is implemented by the Expectation-Step and the Maximization-Step.

- Expectation-Step: for each pair of (d, m, n), with $n \in \{1, 2, \cdots, N\}$,

$$\begin{aligned}\omega_{dm}^{(n)} &= P(D^{(n)} = d, M^{(n)} = m|\mathbf{o}^{(n)}, \pi_d, C_{dm}, \boldsymbol{\mu}_{dm}, \boldsymbol{\Sigma}_{dm}) \\ &= \frac{P(\mathbf{o}^{(n)}|D^{(n)} = d, M^{(n)} = m, \boldsymbol{\mu}_{dm}, \boldsymbol{\Sigma}_{dm})P(D^{(n)} = d, M^{(n)} = m, \pi_d, C_{dm})}{\sum_{d=1}^{a}\sum_{m=1}^{b} P(\mathbf{o}^{(n)}|D^{(n)} = d, M^{(n)} = m, \boldsymbol{\mu}_{dm}, \boldsymbol{\Sigma}_{dm})P(D^{(n)} = d, M^{(n)} = m, \pi_d, C_{dm})}\end{aligned} \quad (4)$$

- Maximization-Step: update the above parameters as follows:

$$\begin{aligned}
\pi_d &= \frac{1}{N}\sum_{n=1}^{N}\sum_{m=1}^{b}\omega_{dm}^{(n)} \\
C_{dm} &= \frac{1}{N\pi_d}\sum_{n=1}^{N}\omega_{dm}^{(n)} \\
\boldsymbol{\mu}_{dm} &= \frac{\sum_{n=1}^{N}\omega_{dm}^{(n)}\mathbf{o}^{(n)}}{\sum_{n=1}^{N}\omega_{dm}^{(n)}} \\
\boldsymbol{\Sigma}_{dm} &= \frac{\sum_{n=1}^{N}\omega_{dm}^{(n)}(\mathbf{o}^{(n)}-\boldsymbol{\mu}_{dm})(\mathbf{o}^{(n)}-\boldsymbol{\mu}_{dm})^T}{\sum_{n=1}^{N}\omega_{dm}^{(n)}}
\end{aligned} \tag{5}$$

Let $\lambda = (\boldsymbol{\pi}, \mathbf{C}, \boldsymbol{\mu}, \boldsymbol{\Sigma})$. The process is repeated until $\left|P(\mathbf{o}|\lambda^t) - P(\mathbf{o}|\lambda^{t-1})\right| < \xi$ or iteration number exceeds the maximum value set in advance. The threshold $\xi = 10^{-4}$ is used in the experiment section of this paper.

Initial Value Optimization Based on Genetic Algorithm
The initial value of $\boldsymbol{\pi}$ and $\mathbf{C}$ can be generated randomly from a uniform distribution, while $\boldsymbol{\mu}$ and $\boldsymbol{\Sigma}$ can be acquired through clustering methods by using training samples. Due to the fact that the initial values of $\boldsymbol{\pi}$ and $\mathbf{C}$ have a great impact on the model obtained by training, in this paper, an initial value optimization approach based on genetic algorithm is proposed.

Encoding. Encoding methods of GA can be classified into two main approaches [13]: binary encoding and float encoding. Considering the convenience and accuracy, this paper adopts floating encoding. Suppose that the maximum degradation state number of the MoG-BBN model is a, and the mixed Gaussian distribution number for each state is b. The numbers of total parameters to optimize related to $\boldsymbol{\pi}$ and $\mathbf{C}$ are a and $a \cdot b$, respectively. This means that an individual is constituted by $a \cdot (b + 1)$ decimal floating numbers.

Fitness Function. Similar to the fitness of each individual to the environment, the value of this function reflects the fitness of each individual to the measurement indicator. In this paper, the fitness function depicts the performance of the models, which are generated by different individuals, when identifying the degradation states.

Selection. According to each individual's fitness, the strategy of Roulette Wheel Selection (RWS) is to calculate the probability, with which the offspring will inherit genes from each individual. Based on that probability, the offspring population is randomly selected in the parent generation. The higher the fitness of the parent individual is, the greater the probability will be. Let f_i denote the fitness of the ith individual, and pop denote the population quantity. The probability with which this individual will be selected is

$$P_i = \frac{f_i}{\sum_{i=1}^{pop} f_i} \tag{6}$$

A method based on RWS is applied in this paper: first of all, sort the individuals according to the fitness (from large to small). Then, let the first to the kth individuals be a part of the next generation directly. Finally, generate the rest $pop - k$ individuals by genic recombination and mutation of the $pop - k$ pairs that are selected from the current population by RWS method.

Crossover. This paper employs Arithmetic crossover to produce a new individual. Assume that two parent individuals are X_A and X_B, then new individual will be generated as follows, where γ is the parameter, commonly set to 0.5.

$$\begin{cases} X_A' = \gamma X_B + (1-\gamma)X_A \\ X_B' = \gamma X_A + (1-\gamma)X_B \end{cases} \tag{7}$$

Mutation. Mutation is a genetic operator which is used to maintain genetic diversity. To ensure the convergence, the mutation operator is implemented by adding or subtracting a small random number, which is called step width, to the original floating number in this paper. Bigger step width leads to faster evolution speed at the beginning. However, it will be more difficult to converge at the end. In order to speed up the evolution and ensure the accuracy when converging to the optimal solution at the same time, the step width should be adjusted dynamically.

The steps of float coding genetic algorithm to optimize the initial values of $\boldsymbol{\pi}$ and $\mathbf{C}$ are summarized as follows.

(a) Randomly generate the initial population that consists of pop individuals.
(b) Calculate the fitness of each individual in the current population, then sort them from large to small.
(c) Based on the result of the fitness sorting, take the first to the kth individuals as a part of the next generation directly. Generate the rest $pop - k$ individuals by implementing genic crossover and mutation on the $pop - k$ pairs that are selected from the current population by RWS. Note that the step width in the mutation process should decrease gradually along with the iteration. Moreover, ensure that the values of genes are significant after crossover and mutation.
(d) Terminate iteration if the result converges or the number of iterations reaches the maximum value. Otherwise, turn to step (b).

2.3 Support Vector Data Description

Assume a training dataset containing n vectors of objects $\{\mathbf{x}_i, i = 1, 2, \cdots, N\}$. The objective of the SVDD method is to find the minimum-volume hypersphere containing all or most data points in feature space. It can be described as follows:

$$\begin{aligned} &\min_{R,\mathbf{c},\xi} R^2 + C\sum_{i=1}^{N} \xi_i \\ &s.t.(x_i - c)^T(x_i - c) \le R^2 + \xi_i,\ \xi_i \ge 0, i = 1, 2, \cdots, N \end{aligned} \tag{8}$$

where c is the center of the hypersphere, and ξ_i is slack variable, cooperating with the penalty constant C to make the trade-off between the radius R and the number of data points that lie out of the hypersphere [14]. Construct the Lagrangian:

$$L(R, c, \alpha_i, \xi_i) = R^2 + C\sum_{i=1}^{N} \xi_i - \sum_{i=1}^{N} \alpha_i\{R^2 + \xi_i - (x_i^2 - 2cx + c^2)\} - \sum_{i=1}^{N} \gamma_i\xi_i \tag{9}$$

Where $\alpha_i \ge 0$ and $\gamma_i \ge 0$. Set the partial derivatives of Eq. (9) to 0.

$$\begin{aligned} &\frac{\partial L}{\partial R} = 0, \therefore \sum_{i=1}^{N} \alpha_i = 1 \\ &\frac{\partial L}{\partial c} = 0, \therefore c = \sum_{i=1}^{N} \alpha_i x_i \\ &\frac{\partial L}{\partial \xi_i} = 0, \therefore C - \alpha_i - \gamma_i = 0 \end{aligned} \tag{10}$$

With Eqs. (9) and (10), the objective function can be reconstructed:

$$\begin{aligned} &\max L(\alpha) = \sum_{i=1}^{N} \alpha_i(x_i \cdot x_i) - \sum_{i=1,j=1}^{N} \alpha_i\alpha_j(x_i \cdot x_j) \\ &s.t. \sum_{i=1}^{N} \alpha_i = 1, 0 \le \alpha_i \le C \end{aligned} \tag{11}$$

In practice, the inner product $(x_i \cdot x_j)$ is replaced by a kernel function $K(x_i \cdot x_j)$ that satisfies Mercer's theorem. The RBF kernel function is opted in this paper. Then Eq. (11) is transformed to the following form:

$$\begin{aligned} &\max L(\alpha) = \sum_{i=1}^{N} \alpha_i K(x_i \cdot x_i) - \sum_{i=1, j=1}^{N} \alpha_i\alpha_j K(x_i \cdot x_j) \\ &s.t. \sum_{i=1}^{N} \alpha_i = 1, 0 < \alpha_i < C \end{aligned} \tag{12}$$

The value of α_i can be obtained by solving Eq. (12), and support vectors are the data points which correspond with $0 < \alpha_i < C$. With Eq. (13), where x_{sv} is a support vector, the radius R of the hypersphere can be acquired.

$$R^2 = K(x_{sv} \cdot x_{sv}) - 2\sum_{i=1}^{N} \alpha_i K(x_i \cdot x_{sv}) + \sum_{i=1,j=1}^{N} \alpha_i \alpha_j K(x_i \cdot x_j) \tag{13}$$

2.4 RUL Prediction

To predict the RUL in the on-line phase, two curves (the degradation state curve and the radius curve) must be obtained in advance in the off-line phase.

Degradation State Curve
After estimating the parameters $\boldsymbol{\pi}$, $\mathbf{C}$, $\boldsymbol{\mu}$ and $\boldsymbol{\Sigma}$ of the MoG-BBN using EM algorithm, through Eq. (2), we obtain the state sequence of the training data and the degradation state curve (Fig. 3). The time duration, for which the component in the off-line phase has been in each state, can be computed based on that curve, as Eq. (14),

$$T(S_d) = \sum_{\omega=1}^{\Omega} T(S_{d\omega}) \tag{14}$$

where $T(S_d)$ stands for the total time duration of the state d, and Ω denotes the number of consecutive visits.

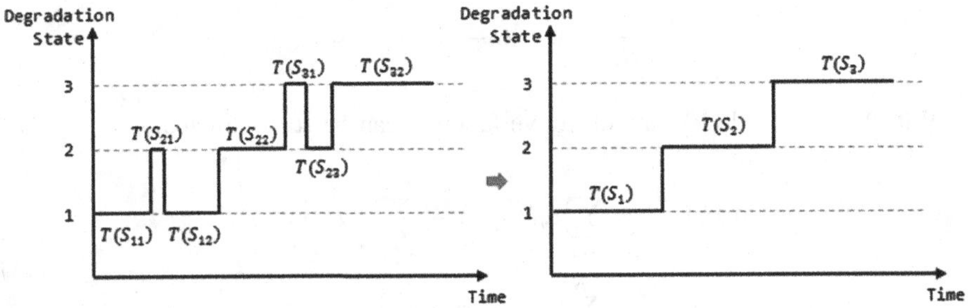

Fig. 3. The degradation state curve of the MoG-BBN.

Radius Curve
Suppose that training dataset contains N vectors of objects $\{\mathbf{x}_1, \mathbf{x}_2, \cdots, \mathbf{x}_N\}$, and the objects $\{\mathbf{x}_1, \mathbf{x}_2, \cdots, \mathbf{x}_{n_0}\}$ generated in the healthy state at the beginning. We sequentially train the SVDD models with each sub data set $\{\mathbf{x}_1, \mathbf{x}_2, \cdots, \mathbf{x}_n\}$, $n \in \{n_0, n_1, \cdots, N\}$, to get the corresponding SVDD hypersphere's radius R_n. Then we obtain the radius change $\mathbf{R} = \{R_{n_0}, R_{n_1}, \cdots, R_N\}$ with the time evolution, as shown in Fig. 4.

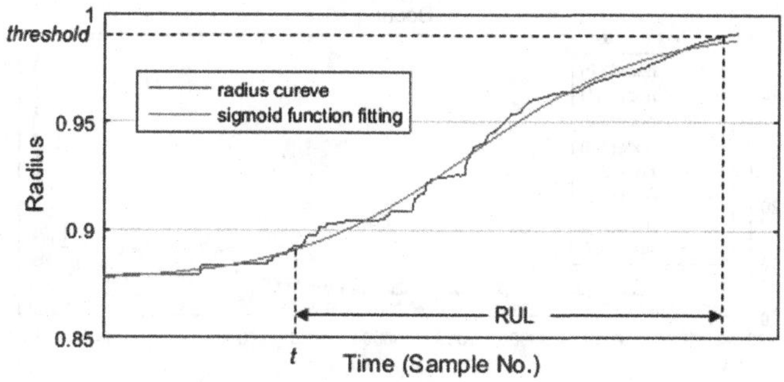

Fig. 4. Radius curve and the Sigmoid function fitting.

RUL Prediction

To predict the remaining useful life of the component in the on-line phase, according to each observation, we first characterize the degradation state by Eq. (2), then determine whether current state of the component match the trained MoG-BBN model: at time t, suppose that the characterized degradation state is s and the degradation state corresponding to the right part of Fig. 3 (obtained by training data) is $\bar{s}$. If s is equal to $\bar{s}$, it matches the model, otherwise it doesn't.

Denote $L(t)$ as the prediction of remaining useful life at time t. If s is equal to $\bar{s}$, $L(t)$ can be computed as follows.

$$\begin{aligned} L(t) &= \sum_{d=1}^{a} P(D=d)L_d(t) \\ &= \sum_{d=1}^{a} P(D=d)\left(\sum_{i=d}^{a} T(S_i) - \bar{T}_d(t)\right) \end{aligned} \tag{15}$$

In Eq. (15), $L_d(t)$ denotes the RUL corresponding to the degradation state d, and $\bar{T}_d(t)$ stands for the past time for which the component has been in the degradation state d.

If s is not equal to $\bar{s}$, we implement the Sigmoid function curve fitting on the radius curve obtained by SVDD. Figure 4 illustrates how to estimate the RUL at time t.

3 Experiments and Discussions

The bearing RUL prediction approach proposed previously is verified by the condition monitoring data from NASA's prognostics data repository [2]. Throughout the experiments, raw data of bearing 1 and bearing 4 in the test #2 is used, and the two bearings can be considered both failed at the end.

First of all, we employed wavelet packet decomposition (WPD) to the data, with the number of decomposition levels setting to 3 and the wavelet base being 'db4'. The result of WPD is shown in Fig. 5. After that, two experiments were implemented:

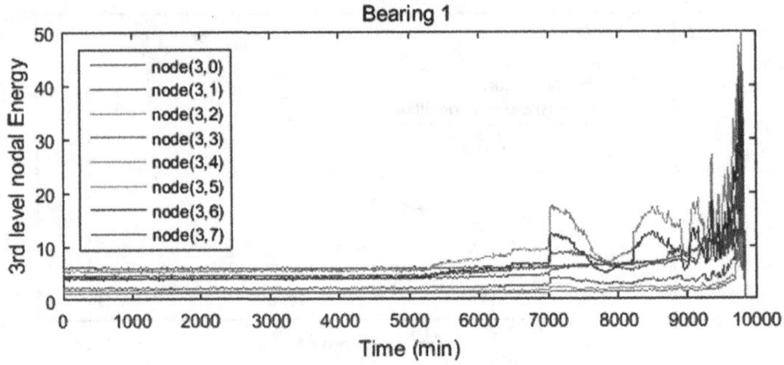

Fig. 5. WPD is applied to raw signal of bearing 1.

experiment #1, where the raw data collected from bearing 1 was divided into training data and test data, and experiment #2, where the dataset of bearing 1 was used as training data and the dataset of bearing 4 was used as test data. A detailed discussion of the experiment #1 and the results of both experiments are given as follows.

In the off-line phase, the sojourn time $T(S_d)$ of each degradation state of the trained MoG-BBN model is shown in Table 1, and the radius curve obtained by SVDD is shown in Fig. 6. The radius curve starts at time 4500 min since the former data was collected when the bearing was in the healthy state, and the SVDD model was first trained at time 4500 min with all the former data. Since the bearing has been in the healthy state (State 1) for a long time according to Table 1, and in this period, the radius of the hypersphere grew slowly, while at the end of bearings' life cycle, the radius grew slowly too because of the slack variable ξ_i in the objective function of SVDD, we chose Sigmoid function to implement the curve fitting on the radius curve. Figure 6 demonstrates that the radius curve fits well with the Sigmoid function.

Table 1. Sojourn time of each degradation state in Expt. #1

Degradation state	1	2	3
Sojourn time (min)	5090	1890	2870

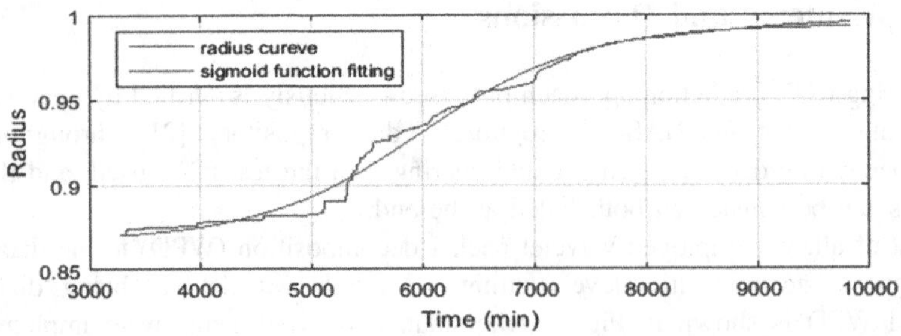

Fig. 6. Radius curve generated by the training data.

In the on-line phase, Fig. 7 depicts how the degradation states were characterized after the validate data was fed into the MoG-BBN model. According to Fig. 7, we can tell that the bearing had been in the healthy state for almost 50% of its whole lifetime and went into the third state after working for about 7000 min, having a good consistency with what is described in Table 1. This can be interpreted that the training data and the validate data is collected from the same bearing.

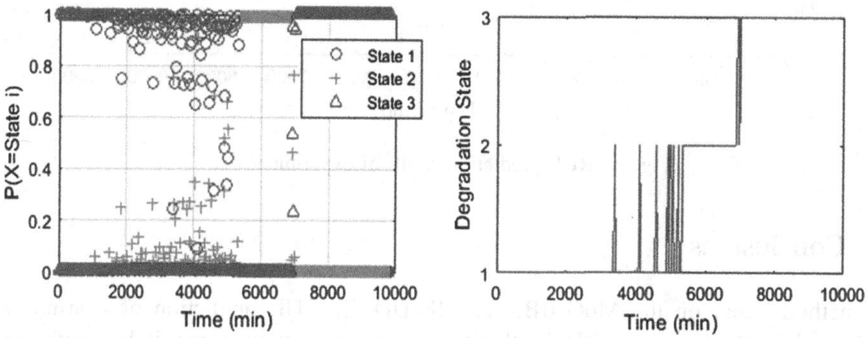

(a) Probability of each degradation state. (b) Degradation state characterization result.

Fig. 7. Degradation state characterization in Expt. #1.

The RUL prediction results of the method based on MoG-BBN without GA and the method proposed by this paper are compared in Figs. 8 and 9.

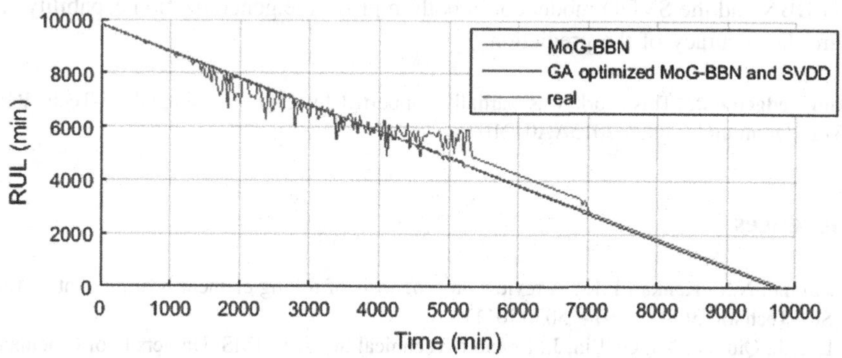

Fig. 8. RUL prediction result of experiment #1.

In the light of Figs. 8 and 9, we can figure out that the predicted remaining useful life converges at the end of the prediction. With the optimization of the initial value by genetic algorithms and the combination of the SVDD model, our method has an excellent performance on the RUL prediction of bearings since it has higher prediction accuracy, better generalization ability and stronger robustness.

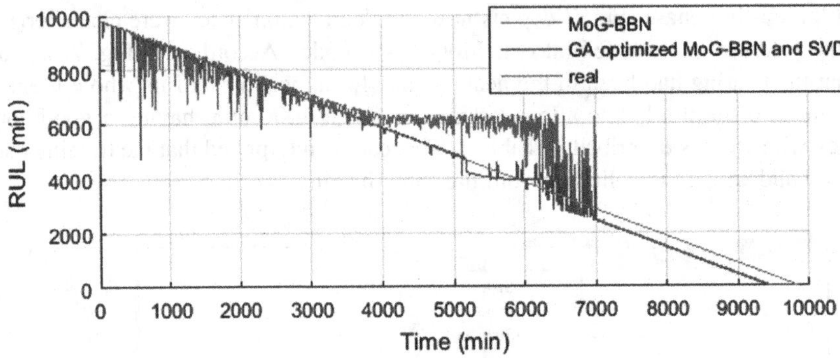

Fig. 9. RUL prediction result of experiment #2.

4 Conclusions

A method based on the MoG-BBN and SVDD for RUL prediction of bearings is proposed in this paper. WPD is chosen to extract features since it has sufficient high-frequency resolution, which contains the most useful fault information of bearings. The MoG-BBN model is a useful tool to predict the RUL with high accuracy when the work condition of bearings in on-line phase is very similar to the training data. However, different initial value may lead to different performance, the genetic algorithm is employed to overcome this deficiency of initial parameters generated randomly, and to acquire good stability. Moreover, an appropriate combination of the MoG-BBN and the SVDD model could both improve the generalization capability and ensure the accuracy of the prediction.

Acknowledgement. This work was partially supported by Chinese National Hi-Tech. R&D (863) Program under grant 2015AA042102.

References

1. Jammu, N.S., Kankar, P.K.: A review on prognosis of rolling element bearings. Int. J. Eng. Sci. Technol. **3**(10), 7497–7503 (2011)
2. Lee, J., Qiu, H., Yu, G., Lin, J.: Rexnord Technical Services, IMS, University of Cincinnati. Bearing Data Set, NASA Ames Prognostics Data Repository. NASA Ames Research Center, Moffett Field, CA (2007). http://ti.arc.nasa.gov/project/prognostic-data-repository
3. Gebraeel, N.Z., Lawley, M.A.: A neural network degradation model for computing and updating residual life distributions. IEEE Trans. Autom. Sci. Eng. **5**(1), 154–163 (2008)
4. Tian, Z., Wong, L., Safaei, N.: A neural network approach for remaining useful life prediction utilizing both failure and suspension histories. Mech. Syst. Signal Process. **24**(5), 1542–1555 (2010)
5. Huang, R., Xi, L., Li, X., et al.: Residual life predictions for ball bearings based on self-organizing map and back propagation neural network methods. Mech. Syst. Signal Process. **21**(1), 193–207 (2007)

6. Tobon-Mejia, D.A., Medjaher, K., Zerhouni, N., et al.: Hidden Markov models for failure diagnostic and prognostic. In: Prognostics and System Health Management Conference (PHM-Shenzhen), 2011, pp. 1–8. IEEE (2011)
7. Tobon-Mejia, D.A., Medjaher, K., Zerhouni, N., et al.: A data-driven failure prognostics method based on mixture of Gaussians hidden Markov models. IEEE Trans. Reliab. **61**(2), 491–503 (2012)
8. Shen, Z., He, Z., Chen, X., et al.: A monotonic degradation assessment index of rolling bearings using fuzzy support vector data description and running time. Sensors **12**(8), 10109–10135 (2012)
9. Wang, H., Chen, J.: Performance degradation assessment of rolling bearing based on bispectrum and support vector data description. J. Vibr. Control **20**(13), 2032–2041 (2014)
10. Sloukia, F., El Aroussi, M., Medromi, H., et al.: Bearings prognostic using mixture of gaussians hidden markov model and support vector machine. In: 2013 ACS International Conference on Computer Systems and Applications (AICCSA), pp. 1–4. IEEE (2013)
11. Zhang, X., Kang, J., Jin, T.: Degradation modeling and maintenance decisions based on Bayesian belief networks. IEEE Trans. Reliab. **63**(2), 620–633 (2014)
12. Wald, R., Khoshgoftaar, T.M., Sloan, J.C.: Using feature selection to determine optimal depth for wavelet packet decomposition of vibration signals for ocean system reliability. In: 2011 IEEE 13th International Symposium on High-Assurance Systems Engineering (HASE), pp. 236–243. IEEE (2011)
13. Zhang, T., Zhang, H., Wang, Z.: Float encoding genetic algorithm and its application. J. Harbin Inst. Technol. **32**(4), 59–61 (2000)
14. Tax, D.M.J., Duin, R.P.W.: Support vector data description[J]. Mach. Learn. **54**(1), 45–66 (2004)

Industrial Track of Big Data

Social Recommendation Terms: Probabilistic Explanation Optimization

Jie Liu[1,2], Lin Zhang[1,2(✉)], Victor S. Sheng[3], and Yuanjun Laili[1,2]

[1] School of Automation Science and Electrical Engineering, Beihang University, Beijing, China
zhanglin@buaa.edu.cn

[2] Engineering Research Center of Complex Product Advanced Manufacturing System, Ministry of Education, Beijing, China

[3] Department of Computer Science, University of Central Arkansas, Conway, USA

Abstract. The Probabilistic Matrix Factorization (PMF) model has been widely studied for recommender systems, which outperform previous models with a solid probabilistic explanation. To further improve its accuracy by using social information, researchers attempt to combine the PMF model with social network graphs by adding social terms. However, existing works on social terms do not provide theoretical explanations to make the models well understood. The lack of explanations limits further improvement of prediction accuracy. Hence, in this paper we provide our explanation and propose a unified covariance framework to solve this problem. Our explanation, including regularization terms, factorization terms and an ensemble of them, reveals how most social terms work from a probabilistic view. Our framework shows that those terms could be optimized in a direct way compatible to PMF. We find out that accuracy improvements for existing works on regularization terms rely more on personalized properties, and that social information for factorization terms is helpful but not always necessary.

Keywords: Probabilistic matrix factorization · Regularization terms · Factorization terms · Social networks

1 Introduction

Recommender systems have been widely studied for decades to increase company profits and provide users convenience. Researchers notice that additional information other than rating records could predict users' preferences [1]. For example, social links on social network sites could help model inter-dependent rating relations.

Social recommendation models usually apply social information to Probabilistic Matrix Factorization (PMF) [2], which finds the maximum a posteriori probability (MAP) estimate of each parameter of the model, using social terms [4–22]. The terms could be divided into two categories: regularization terms and factorization terms.

Some notable works on regularization terms, including SocialMF [4], SoReg [5] and SR [6], try to exploit the social network graph by regularizing user latent vectors [4–11].

L. Zhang et al. (Eds.): Monterey Workshop 2016, LNCS 10228, pp. 155–167, 2017.
DOI: 10.1007/978-3-319-61994-1_15

The regularization takes vectors' linear trust relations into consideration. However, these works adopt regularization terms without providing explicit explanation. Thus, the reason why these additional trust relations could take effect might not be clearly understood. According to the demonstration (See Eq. 16) in this paper, the regularization terms indirectly modify some properties of the PMF model, i.e. the combined effects of the additional regularization term and the prior term that personalizes user properties.

Works on factorization terms are introduced in ways different from regularization terms where a user-specific matrix, representing similarity or a social network graph, is to be factorized into user latent vectors and newborn vectors [12–16]. The factorization could also be item-specific. The idea is to integrate the social network graph and rating matrix into a consistent and compact feature representation, in order to reflect the phenomenon that a user's social connections affect his judgment of interest in items [12]. However, the idea is not closely related with accuracy improvement. This idea changes the goal of better predicting rating records into multiple goals. The original goal of factorizing the rating record matrix to gain prediction accuracy is clear, but the additional goal of factorizing another matrix is not well explained. According to the demonstration (See Eqs. 26 and 27) in this paper, some inherent restrictions of social network graphs could be removed.

For a more explicit explanation, we propose our Unified Covariance Framework (UCF), condensing all users' latent vectors into one single vector. Connections among elements in the reshaped single vector represent the inverse of a covariance matrix (ICM). UCF is composed of ICM, the reshaped vector and mean priors. We use UCF to replace Gaussian prior terms in PMF. UCF explains the accuracy improvement in the above social methods.

According to the philosophy of UCF, the key to accuracy improvement is the covariance matrix (ICM). For regularization terms, the covariance matrix serves as an important premise. This premise is directly considered and optimized for the first time. For factorization terms, we consider the newborn vectors as indicators of both personalized properties and correlations among vectors' elements. Based on this consideration, how the newborn vectors from additional factorization contribute to improved accuracy is probabilistically explained and the multiple goal problem is avoided. More importantly, existing works' restrictions could be removed.

In addition, UCF also contributes to the factorization terms: We consider the newborn vectors as indicators of personalized properties and correlations among vectors' elements, based on which, how the newborn vectors from additional factorization contribute to improved accuracy is probabilistically explained and the multi-goal problem is avoided.

Many works attempt to integrate regularization and factorization [17–22]. These works confuse ICM's representation of correlations of elements in the users' latent vectors. We show in Sect. 3 how two distinct forms of ICM work for regularization and factorization.

The remainder of this paper is organized as follows. Section 2 describes some classic methods for social recommendation. Section 3 introduces our proposed UCF and two forms of ICM. Section 4 explains the rationale behind existing works via UCF. In Sect. 5, we draw conclusions.

2 Related Work

Among all the social recommendation methods, the innovation of SocialMF [4], SoReg [5] and SoRec [12] has been widely investigated and referenced [4–12, 17–22]. We briefly review these methods here and analyze them in detail in Sect. 4.

In SocialMF, a regularization term is added as the last term in the PMF equation as follows.

$$L = \frac{1}{2}\sum_{u=1}^{N}\sum_{i=1}^{M} I_{ui}^{R}(r_{ui} - g(U_u^T V_i))^2 + \frac{\lambda_V}{2}\sum_{i=1}^{M} V_i^T V_i + \frac{\lambda_U}{2}\sum_{u=1}^{N} U_u^T U_u$$
$$+ \frac{\lambda_T}{2}\sum_{u=1}^{N}\left((U_u - \sum_{v\in N(u)} t_{u,v} U_v)^T (U_u - \sum_{v\in N(u)} t_{u,v} U_v) \right)$$

where U_u is a user latent vector and V_i is an item latent vector; R is the rating record matrix whose element is r_{ui}; $v \in N(u)$ means that user v is trusted by u; I_{ui}^{R} is 0 if user u does not rate item i, otherwise it is 1; λ_V, λ_U and λ_T are all weight parameters. If user u trusts user v, $t_{u,v}$ will be a constant value within (0, 1). Otherwise it will be zero. It is clear that each rating record denoted by r_{ui} is factorized into user latent vector U_u and item latent vector V_i. SocialMF assumes that the latent feature vector of a user is dependent on that of all his direct neighbors. As a result, the value of a user's vector should be linearly close to the weighted average of his trustees.

SoReg designs a different regularization term to impose constraints between a user and all his friends, but individually, in order to handle the potential information loss problem in SocialMF. SoReg equation is defined as follows.

$$L = \frac{1}{2}\sum_{i=1}^{N}\sum_{j=1}^{M} I_{ij}^{R}(r_{ij} - U_i^T V_j)^2 + \frac{\lambda_V}{2}\sum_{j=1}^{M} \|V_j\|_F^2 + \frac{\lambda_U}{2}\sum_{i=1}^{N} \|U_i\|_F^2$$
$$+ \frac{\lambda}{2}\sum_{i=1}^{N}\sum_{j\in N(i)} Sim(i,j)\|U_i - U_j\|_F^2$$

where *Sim* means similarity. Prior terms are written in the form of Frobenius norms.

SocialMF gives a probabilistic analysis. With Gaussian priors and the user's direct neighbors, we can get the conditional distribution of the expected user latent vector. With Gaussian priors, we can also get the conditional distribution of item latent vectors. Given the user latent vectors and item latent vectors, we get the conditional distribution of rating records. Since the rating records are known, we obtain the posterior probability of latent vectors through Bayesian inference. There is a problem that the explanation about the conditional distribution of its user's latent vector, given the vectors of his/her direct neighbors, could not be clearly understood, in that the neighbor vectors should have Gaussian priors. Hence it is more appropriate to consider the distributions from the global perspective, where all the trust relations and priors for neighbors are considered. In SoReg, the consideration of propagation of taste as its rationale is briefly discussed. SoReg has more intuitions than theoretical explanations. How the accuracy is improved is not quite clear.

In SoRec, the social network graph c is factorized into user latent vectors and newborn vectors as follows.

$$L = \frac{1}{2}\sum_{i=1}^{N}\sum_{j=1}^{M} I_{ij}^{R}\left(r_{ij} - g\left(U_i^T V_j\right)\right)^2 + \frac{\lambda_V}{2}\sum_{j=1}^{M} V_j^T V_j + \frac{\lambda_Z}{2}\sum_{k=1}^{N} Z_k^T Z_k$$
$$+ \frac{\lambda_C}{2}\sum_{i=1}^{N}\sum_{k=1}^{N} I_{ik}^{C}\left(c_{ik}^{*} - g\left(U_i^T Z_k\right)\right)^2 + \frac{\lambda_U}{2}\sum_{i=1}^{N} U_i^T U_i$$

where λ_V, λ_Z, λ_C and λ_U are all weight parameters, I_{ik}^{C} is an indicator function, which is equal to 1 if user i trusts user k, and equal to 0 otherwise, c_{ik}^{*} means how much user i trusts user k, and Z_k is the newborn vector.

SoRec has multiple goals of both gaining accuracy by factorizing the rating matrix and approximating the social network graph by factorization terms. As the final goal of those models is to gain accuracy instead of approximating the social network graph, a theoretical explanation on how the factorization goal affects the gaining accuracy goal is essential. However, such an explanation is not provided by SoRec, without which whether SoRec could be improved is unknown.

3 Proposed Method

In order to comprehensively explain existing works, we first present our UCF (unified covariance framework) in this section and then analyze existing works in more detail later.

In Subsect. 3.1, the latent vectors are reshaped, and a mean prior vector and a covariance matrix are adopted. In Subsect. 3.2, we show that the inverse of the covariance matrix (ICM) is able to describe different kinds of connections for regularization terms and factorization terms named "Each-diagonal form" and "Global-diagonal form".

3.1 Unified Covariance Framework

Via the UCF, user latent vectors are reshaped into one single vector. The reshaped vector could be used to reflect either the connections for vectors or connections for elements within a vector in UCF as follows.

$$U = \begin{pmatrix} U_1^T \\ U_2^T \\ \vdots \\ U_N^T \end{pmatrix} = \begin{pmatrix} u_{11} & u_{12} & \cdots & u_{1D} \\ u_{21} & u_{22} & \cdots & u_{2D} \\ \vdots & \vdots & \ddots & \vdots \\ u_{N1} & u_{N2} & \cdots & u_{ND} \end{pmatrix}. \quad (1)$$

$$U_{re} = \begin{bmatrix} u_{11} & u_{12} & \ldots & u_{1D} & \cdots & u_{N1} & u_{N2} & \ldots & u_{ND} \end{bmatrix}. \quad (2)$$

where U is the user latent matrix, U_i is the ith user latent vector, u_{ij} is the jth element for user I, and U_{re} is the reshaped single vector. There are N users, M items and D features. Each element in U_{re} obeys the Gaussian distribution [2] with a mean prior in the following form:

$$M_{re} = [\ \mu_{11} \quad \mu_{12} \quad \ldots \quad \mu_{1D} \quad \cdots \quad \mu_{N1} \quad \mu_{N2} \quad \ldots \quad \mu_{ND}\ ]. \tag{3}$$

where μ_{ij} is the corresponding mean prior for element u_{ij}. We assume that each element in U_{re} could be connected with others. If two different elements in U_{re} are connected, they are correlated. We use a covariance matrix Cov(U) to denote the connections. Cov (U) and ICM are defined as follows.

$$\mathrm{Cov}(U) = \begin{pmatrix} r^{11}_{11} & \cdots & r^{11}_{ND} \\ \vdots & \ddots & \vdots \\ r^{ND}_{11} & \cdots & r^{ND}_{ND} \end{pmatrix}. \tag{4}$$

$$\mathrm{ICM} = \mathrm{Cov}^{-1}(U) = \begin{pmatrix} r^{11}_{11} & \cdots & r^{11}_{ND} \\ \vdots & \ddots & \vdots \\ r^{ND}_{11} & \cdots & r^{ND}_{ND} \end{pmatrix}^{-1} = \begin{pmatrix} a^{11}_{11} & \cdots & a^{11}_{ND} \\ \vdots & \ddots & \vdots \\ a^{ND}_{11} & \cdots & a^{ND}_{ND} \end{pmatrix}. \tag{5}$$

where r denotes the element correlations in U_{re}. Then, our UCF is in the following form as Eq. 6.

$$\mathrm{UCF} = (U_{re} - M_{re})^T \cdot \mathrm{ICM} \cdot (U_{re} - M_{re}). \tag{6}$$

The above equation shows that we get the multivariate Gaussian distribution with the covariance matrix and mean priors. Figure 1 shows that UCF is to take place of Gaussian priors. The reshaped matrix has the advantage of making it possible for each element to have a personalized property and for any elements in any vectors to be connected.

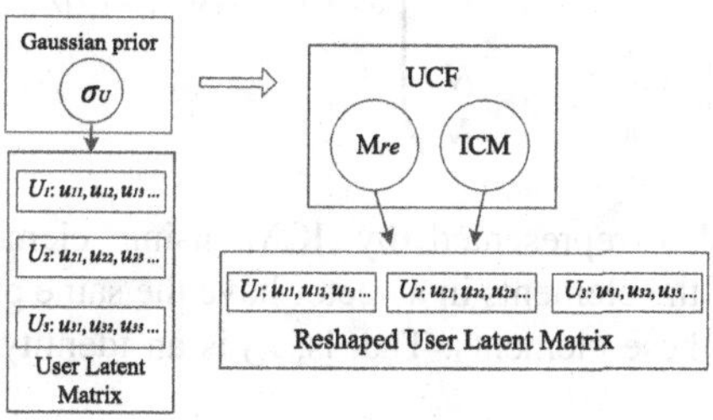

Fig. 1. Unified covariance framework

In Sect. 4, we will show that the ensemble of social terms (regularization terms or factorization terms) and Gaussian prior terms (Frobenius norm of user or item latent vectors) could be represented by UCF. In our optimization steps, we use UCF to replace social terms and Gaussian prior terms.

3.2 Two Forms in the Inverse of Covariance Matrix

It is the key to UCF that ICM has two forms, Each-diagonal form and Global-diagonal form.

In Each-diagonal, each vector has personalized properties, and there may exist correlations among vectors. Personalized properties are means (i.e., M_{re}) and variances (i.e., diagonal elements of ICM). Correlations are represented by non-diagonal elements of ICM. Elements in the same vector have the same properties, and they are not correlated. That is,

$$\begin{aligned} M_{re} &= [\mu_1 \quad \cdots \quad \mu_1 \quad \cdots \quad \mu_N \quad \cdots \quad \mu_N\,] \\ &= [\mu_1 \quad \cdots \quad \mu_N\,] \otimes [1 \quad \cdots \quad 1] \\ &= \mu_U \otimes [1 \quad \cdots \quad 1]. \end{aligned} \tag{7}$$

$$\mathrm{Cov}(U) = \begin{pmatrix} r_1^1 & \cdots & r_N^1 \\ \vdots & \ddots & \vdots \\ r_1^N & \cdots & r_N^N \end{pmatrix} \otimes I_D = \Sigma_{N\times N} \otimes I_D. \tag{8}$$

where r_j^i in the ith row and j^{th} column could represent the correlation of elements $u_{i,x}$ and $u_{j,x}$, $x \in [1, 2, \ldots, D]$. Each element in U_i has the same correlation coefficient with its counterpart in U_j. Thus r_j^i could represent the correlations of user latent vectors U_i and U_j.

Accordingly, ICM is in the following form (Also see Fig. 2a):

$$\mathrm{ICM} = \begin{pmatrix} a_1^1 & \cdots & a_N^1 \\ \vdots & \ddots & \vdots \\ a_1^N & \cdots & a_N^N \end{pmatrix} \otimes I_D = \Sigma_{N\times N}^{-1} \otimes I_D = \Lambda_U \otimes I_D. \tag{9}$$

Correlations are also represented by ICM using elements' connections. In Each-diagonal form, all the elements in a vector have the same properties, and there are no correlations among these elements. That is, I_D is an identity matrix.

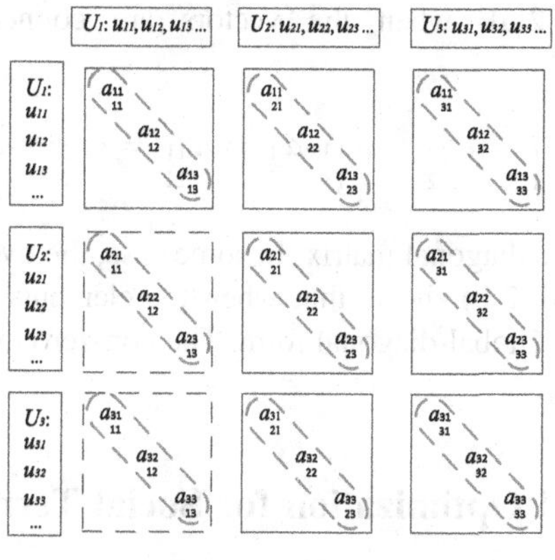

(a) Each-diagonal form for ICM

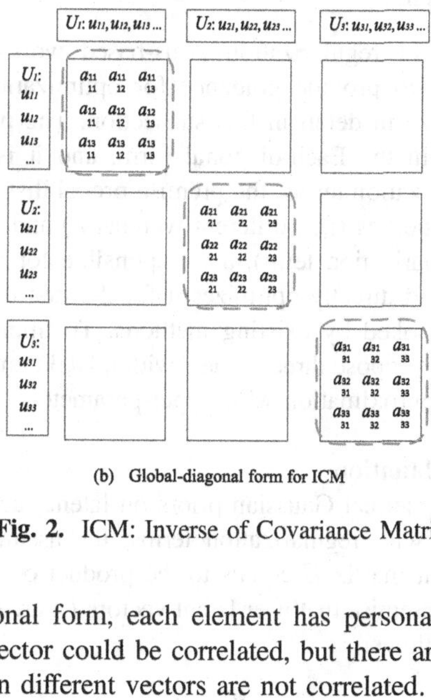

(b) Global-diagonal form for ICM

Fig. 2. ICM: Inverse of Covariance Matrix

In the Global-diagonal form, each element has personalized properties and the elements in the same vector could be correlated, but there are no correlations among vectors; i.e., elements in different vectors are not correlated. ICM is in the following form (Also see Fig. 2b).

$$\mathrm{ICM} = \begin{pmatrix} A_{\substack{1\\1}} & \cdots & 0 \\ \vdots & \ddots & \vdots \\ 0 & \cdots & A_{\substack{N\\N}} \end{pmatrix}. \tag{10}$$

where A is the D × D inverse of the covariance matrix denoting the connections and personalized properties of elements in each user.

As shown in Fig. 2(a), when the vectors are connected, ICM is in the Each-diagonal form.

$$a_{\substack{1\\1}} = a_{\substack{11\\11}} = a_{\substack{12\\12}} = a_{\substack{13\\13}} \; a_{\substack{1\\2}} = a_{\substack{11\\21}} = a_{\substack{12\\22}} = a_{\substack{13\\23}} \cdots$$

Each block matrix is a diagonal matrix. In some case, the overall ICM could also be a diagonal matrix. Figure 2(b) shows that when the elements in the same vector are connected, ICM is in the Global-diagonal form. The non-zero matrices are full matrices in the diagonal positions.

4 Explanation and Optimization for Social Terms

4.1 Regularization Terms

To give an explanation of regularization-terms-based works towards the goal of improving accuracy, and to provide guidance for optimization, a premise is to be considered that we analyze in detail in this subsection. The premise could be represented directly by ICM in the Each-diagonal form, and it is the key for accuracy improvement. For regularization terms, the premise probabilistically illustrates that the vectors' personalized properties (i.e., different weights λ) and correlations (i.e., linear relations within the regularization term), are responsible for accuracy improvement. UCF takes the premise and directly optimizes it for the first time, which is implicitly used but explicitly overlooked by existing methods. To improve the regularization-terms-based accuracy, we propose three models within UCF, employing Markov Chain Monte Carlo (MCMC) approximation with hyper-parameters.

4.1.1 Theoretical Explanation

PMF places zero-mean spherical Gaussian priors on latent vectors. However, we find that when integrating it with regularization terms, the assumption that the density function of the user latent matrix U equals to the product of vectors Ui is no longer holds, because there is a premise that user latent vectors Ui are dependent. This finding is shown in Eq. 11 as follows.

$$p\left(U|\sigma_U^2\right) \neq \prod_{i=1}^{N} \mathcal{N}\left(U_i|0, \sigma_U^2 I\right). \tag{11}$$

where N denotes the Gaussian distribution, and σ_U^2 is the variance. Considering the interdependency premise, it is more appropriate for the density function to be in the following form.

$$p(U) = \mathcal{N}\left(U|0, \sum\nolimits_{N\times N}\right). \tag{12}$$

where Σ is the covariance matrix. Correspondingly, the log of the prior distribution (also Gaussian prior term) is transformed to the following form.

$$\ln p\left(U|\sigma_U^2\right) = \frac{1}{2\sigma_U^2}\sum_{i=1}^{N} U_i^T U_i. \tag{13}$$

$$\begin{aligned}\ln p(U) &= \frac{1}{2}\left(U_1^T, U_2^T, \ldots, U_N^T\right) \cdot \sum\nolimits_{N\times N}^{-1} \otimes I_D \cdot \left(U_1^T, U_2^T, \ldots, U_N^T\right)^T \\ &= \frac{1}{2} U_{re}^T \cdot \mathrm{ICM} \cdot U_{re}.\end{aligned} \tag{14}$$

where ICM is in the Each-diagonal form. This new form of the Gaussian prior term could be represented by UCF (See Eq. 6).

According to Eqs. 9 and 14 could be transformed into the following form.

$$\ln p(U) = \tfrac{1}{2}\sum_{i=1}^{N}\sum_{j=1}^{N} a_{\,j\atop i}\, U_i^T U_j = \tfrac{1}{2}\sum_{i=1}^{N}\sum_{j=1}^{N} a_{\,j\atop i}\, U_i^T U_j (i \neq j) + \tfrac{1}{2}\sum_{i=1}^{N} a_{\,i\atop i}\, U_i^T U_i. \tag{15}$$

Since Eq. 15 is essentially the same as Eq. 14, it is also another form of UCF. We will demonstrate that the integration of regularization terms and Gaussian prior terms in existing works could be transformed to Eq. 15. According to Eq. 15, when user i and user j are different users, they are correlated. For each user, the variance (Gaussian variance prior) becomes personalized.

Works on regularization terms have implicitly used the interdependency premise represented by UCF in the Each-diagonal form. Regularization terms have similar forms to either SocialMF or SoReg, whose innovations have been widely investigated and referenced [4–11, 17–22].

The integration of regularization terms and Gaussian prior terms obeys UCF. Take SocialMF as an example.

$$\begin{aligned}
&\frac{\lambda_T}{2}\sum_{u=1}^{N}\left((U_u - \sum_{v\in N(u)} t_{u,v}U_v)^T (U_u - \sum_{v\in N(u)} t_{u,v}U_v)\right) + \frac{\lambda_U}{2}\sum_{u=1}^{N} U_u^T U_u \\
&= \frac{\lambda_T}{2} tr\left((I-T)^T(I-T)\begin{pmatrix} U_1^T \\ \vdots \\ U_N^T \end{pmatrix}(U_1, U_2, \cdots, U_N)\right) + \frac{\lambda_U}{2}\sum_{u=1}^{N} U_u^T U_u \\
&= \frac{\lambda_T}{2} tr\left((I - T^T - T + T^T T)\begin{pmatrix} U_1^T U_1 & \ldots & U_1^T U_N \\ \vdots & \ddots & \vdots \\ U_N^T U_1 & \ldots & U_N^T U_N \end{pmatrix}\right) + \frac{\lambda_U}{2}\sum_{u=1}^{N} U_u^T U_u \\
&= \frac{\lambda_T}{2}\sum_{u=1}^{N} U_u^T U_u + \frac{\lambda_T}{2}\sum_{u=1}^{N}\sum_{v=1}^{N} a_{u,v} U_v^T U_u + \frac{\lambda_U}{2}\sum_{u=1}^{N} U_u^T U_u \\
&= \left(\frac{\lambda_U}{2} + \frac{\lambda_T}{2} + \frac{\lambda_T}{2} a_{u,u}\right)\sum_{u=1}^{N} U_u^T U_u + \frac{\lambda_T}{2}\sum_{u=1}^{N}\sum_{v=1}^{N} a_{u,v} U_v^T U_u (v \neq u).
\end{aligned}$$

where $v \in N(u)$ means that user v is trusted by u, and λ is the weight parameter. If user u trusts user v, $t_{u,v}$ will be a constant value within (0, 1). Otherwise it will be zero. $T = (t_{u,v})_{N \times N}$. $A = (a_{i,j})_{N \times N} = -T - T^T + T^T T$. The above equation is in the same form as Eq. 15. The user latent vectors are correlated and have personalized properties.

Similarly, the SoReg integration could also be transformed to the following form:

$$
\begin{aligned}
&\frac{\lambda_U}{2}\sum_{i=1}^{N}\|U_i\|_F^2 + \frac{\lambda}{2}\sum_{i=1}^{N}\sum_{j\in N(i)} Sim(i,j)\|U_i - U_j\|_F^2 \\
&= \frac{\lambda_U}{2}\sum_{i=1}^{N}\|U_i\|_F^2 + \sum_{i=1}^{N}\frac{\lambda}{2}\left(\sum_{j\in N(i)} Sim(i,j) + \sum_{i\in N(j)} Sim(j,i)\right)U_i^T U_i \\
&- \lambda \sum_{i\in N(j)\cup j\in N(i)} Sim(i,j) U_i^T U_j. \\
&= \sum_{i=1}^{N}\left(\frac{\lambda_U}{2} + \frac{\lambda}{2}\left(\sum_{j\in N(i)} Sim(i,j) + \sum_{i\in N(j)} Sim(j,i)\right)\right)U_i^T U_i \\
&- \lambda \sum_{i\in N(j)\cup j\in N(i)} Sim(i,j) U_i^T U_j.
\end{aligned}
\tag{16}
$$

where *Sim* denotes Pearson similarity. $j \in N(i)$ means user j is trusted by user i. The above equation for SoReg could also be represented by UCF.

Although the integration of the regularization term and the Gaussian prior term is in the same form as Eq. 15, the usage of the social network graph does not necessarily guarantee optimal covariance matrix which is essential to improving prediction accuracy. Hence, we propose optimization methods in Sect. 4.1.2.

4.2 Factorization Terms

In ICM, each user latent vector has mean priors and a covariance matrix in Global-diagonal form, all of which are produced by the newborn vectors. We propose two models to improve factorization-terms-based methods using Stochastic Gradient Descent (SGD), where the social network graph is replaced with an indicator matrix suggesting how user vectors are connected with newborn vectors. If the vectors are not connected, the corresponding connection element in the indicator matrix is 0. Otherwise, the element is a non-zero parameter to be tuned. The number of rows in the indicator matrix is the same as the number of user latent vectors, while the number of columns is the same as the number of newborn vectors. The ensemble of the indicator matrix and newborn vectors are represented directly by ICM. Although we set the number of newborn vectors the same as the number of user latent vectors, the indicator matrix could work with any number of newborn vectors.

4.2.1 Theoretical Explanation

In the Global-diagonal form, UCF is in the following form:

$$\begin{aligned}
\mathrm{UCF} &= (U_{re} - M_{re})^T \cdot \mathrm{ICM} \cdot (U_{re} - M_{re}) \\
&= (U_{re} - M_{re})^T \cdot \begin{pmatrix} A_{\substack{1\\1}} & \cdots & 0 \\ \vdots & \ddots & \vdots \\ 0 & \cdots & A_{\substack{N\\N}} \end{pmatrix} \cdot (U_{re} - M_{re}) \\
&= U_1^T A_{\substack{1\\1}} U_1 + U_2^T A_{\substack{2\\2}} U_2 + \cdots U_N^T A_{\substack{N\\N}} U_N \\
&\quad - U_1^T A_{\substack{1\\1}} M_1 - U_2^T A_{\substack{2\\2}} M_2 - \cdots U_N^T A_{\substack{N\\N}} M_N \\
&\quad - M_1^T A_{\substack{1\\1}} U_1 - M_2^T A_{\substack{2\\2}} U_2 - \cdots M_N^T A_{\substack{N\\N}} U_N + C \\
&= \sum_{i=1}^{N} U_i^T A_{\substack{i\\i}} U_i - \sum_{i=1}^{N} M_i^T \left(A_{\substack{i\\i}} + A_{\substack{i\\i}}^T \right) U_i + C \\
&= \sum_{i=1}^{N} U_i^T A_{\substack{i\\i}} U_i - \sum_{i=1}^{N} Y_i^T U_i + C.
\end{aligned} \tag{17}$$

where Y is a constant vector denoting the effect of mean priors,and C is a constant matrix. It is obvious that each user latent vector has a covariance matrix and mean priors.

Works on factorization terms [12–22] have similar forms to SoRec [12]. We take SoRec as an example to show how factorization terms help improve accuracy. Its graphical model is shown in Fig. 3. We do not analyze the effect of the logistic function, which is only a non-linear transform, but we still adopt the logistic function in our corresponding UCF models. Integration of the prior term and the factorization term is as follows.

$$\begin{aligned}
&\frac{\lambda_c}{2} \sum_{i=1}^{N} \sum_{k=1}^{N} I_{ik}^C (c_{ik}^* - U_i^T Z_k)^2 + \frac{\lambda_U}{2} \sum_{i=1}^{N} U_i^T U_I \\
&= \sum_{i=1}^{N} U_i^T \left(\frac{\lambda_C}{2} \sum_{k=1}^{N} I_{ik}^C Z_k Z_k^T + \frac{\lambda_U}{2} I_{D\times D} \right) U_i \\
&\quad - \lambda_C \sum_{i=1}^{N} \sum_{k=1}^{N} I_{ik}^C c_{ik}^* Z_k^T U_i + \frac{\lambda_C}{2} \sum_{i=1}^{N} \sum_{k=1}^{N} I_{ik}^C c_{ik}^{*2}.
\end{aligned} \tag{18}$$

where λ_C and λ_U are all weight parameters, I_{ik}^C is the indicator function that is equal to 1 if user i trusts user k, and equal to 0 otherwise, c_{ik}^* denotes how much user i trusts user k, and Z_k is the newborn vector. Equation 27 has the same form as Eq. 26. The role of newborn vectors Z is considered to be adding covariance and mean priors for user latent vectors instead of achieving multiple goals. Such an explanation is probabilistically compatible with PMF and convenient for optimization.

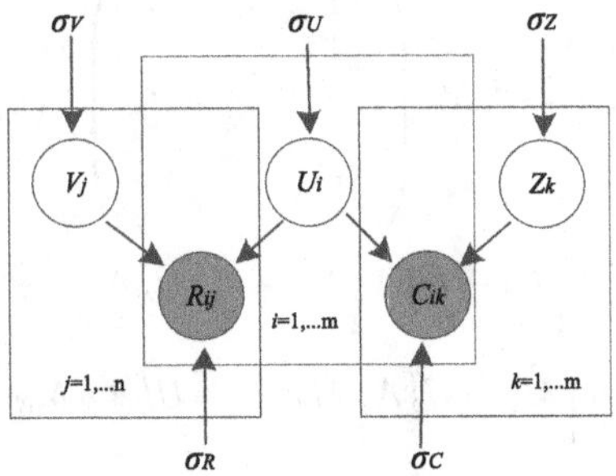

Fig. 3. Graphical model for SoRec

Many works attempt to integrate factorization terms with regularization terms [17–22]. This makes ICM's representation of correlations of elements in all vectors mix-up, because elements either in the same user latent vector or in different user latent vectors could be correlated. Some works further introduce biases to the integration.

5 Conclusions

In this paper, we analyze the rationale behind social terms in existing social recommendation methods, and illustrate how these terms help improve accuracy. Our explanation is different from existing works in two ways: First, there exists no clear explanation with a theoretical proof on regularization terms. Thus, whether the prediction accuracy could be improved is unknown. Second, existing explanations on factorization terms do not illustrate how the factorization terms help improve accuracy, and are based only on intuition. The problem is solved by our explanation that the factorization term is extrapolated into priors for accuracy improvement.

Acknowledgments. This work is partially supported by National Nature Science Foundation of China (No. 61374199, National High-tech R&D Program (No. 2015AA042101),) and Beijing Natural Science Foundation (No. 4142031).

References

1. Chua, F.C.T., Lauw, H.W., Lim, E.-P.: Generative models for item adoptions using social correlation. IEEE Trans. Knowl. Data Eng. **25**(9), 2036–2048 (2013)
2. Salakhutdinov, R., Mnih, A.: Probabilistic matrix factorization. In: Proceedings of the NIPS, pp. 1257–1264, 2007

3. Salakhutdinov, R. Mnih, A.: Bayesian probabilistic matrix factorization using Markov chain Monte Carlo. In: Proceedings of the ICML, pp. 880–887 (2008)
4. Jamali, M., Ester, M.: A matrix factorization technique with trust propagation for recommendation in social networks. In: Proceedings of the RecSys, pp. 135–142 (2010)
5. Ma, H., Zhou, D., Liu, C., Lyu, M.R., King, I.: Recommender systems with social regularization. In: Proceedings of the WSDM, pp. 287–296 (2011)
6. Ma, H.: An experimental study on implicit social recommendation. In: Proceedings of the SIGIR, pp. 73–82 (2013)
7. Yang, X., Steck, H., Liu, Y.: Circle-based recommendation in online social networks. In: Proceedings of the SIGKDD, pp. 1267–1275 (2012)
8. Forsati, R., Mahdavi, M., Shamsfard, M., Sarwat, M.: Matrix factorization with explicit trust and distrust side information for improved social recommendation. ACM Trans. Inform. Syst. **32**(4) (2014)
9. Ma, H., Lyu, Ml.R., King, I.: Learning to recommend with trust and distrust relationships. In: Proceedings of the RecSys, pp. 189–196 (2009)
10. Fazeli, S., Loni, B., Bellogin, A., Drachsler, H., Sloep, P.: Implicit vs. explicit trust in social matrix factorization. In: Proceedings of the RecSys, pp. 317–320 (2014)
11. Xia, F., Liu, H., Asabere, N.Y., Wang, W., Yang, Z.: Multi-category item recommendation using neighborhood associations in trust networks. In: Proceedings of the WWW, pp. 403–404 (2014)
12. Ma, H., Yang, H., Lyu, Ml.R., King, I.: SoRec: social recommendation using probabilistic matrix factorization. In: Proceedings of the CIKM, pp. 931–940 (2008)
13. Yang, B., Yu, L., Liu, D., Liu, J.: Social collaborative filtering by trust. In: Proceedings of the IJCAI, pp. 2747–2753 (2013)
14. Zhang, Y., Lai, G., Zhang, M., Zhang, Y., Liu, Y., Ma, S.: Explicit factor models for explainable recommendation based on phrase-level sentiment analysis. In: Proceedings of the SIGIR, pp. 83–92 (2014)
15. Jiang, M., Cui, P., Liu, R., Yang, Q., Wang, F., Zhu, W., Yang, S.: Social contextual recommendation. In: Proceedings of the CIKM, pp. 45–54 (2012)
16. Wang, T., Jin, X., Ding, X., Ye, X.: User interests imbalance exploration in social recommendation: a fitness adaptation. In: Proceedings of the CIKM, pp. 281–290 (2014)
17. Jiang, Y., Liu, J., Zhang, X., Li, Z., Lu. H.: TCRec: product recommendation via exploiting social-trust network and product category information. In: Proceedings of the WWW, pp. 233–234 (2013)
18. Yao, W., He, J., Huang, G., Zhang, Y.: Modeling dual role preferences for trust-aware recommendation. In: Proceedings of the SIGIR, pp. 975–978 (2014)
19. Zhao, T., Li, C., Li, M., Ding, Q., Li, L.: Social recommendation incorporating topic mining and social trust analysis. In: Proceedings of the CIKM, pp. 1643–1648 (2013)
20. Yuan, Q., Chen, L., Zhao, S.: Factorization vs. regularization: integrating heterogeneous social relationships in top-n recommendation. In: Proceedings of the RecSys, pp. 245–252 (2011)
21. Guo, L., Ma, J., Chen, Z.: Learning to recommend with multi-faceted trust in social networks. In: Proceedings of the WWW, pp. 205–206 (2013)
22. Feng, H., Qian, X.: Recommendation via user's personality and social contextual. In: Proceedings of the CIKM, pp. 1521–1524 (2013)
23. Tang, J., Hu, X., Gao, H., Liu, H.: Exploiting local and global social context for recommendation. In: Proceedings of the AAAI, pp. 2712–2718 (2013)

Towards a Holistic Method for Business Process Analytics

Gianna Reggio, Maurizio Leotta(✉), Filippo Ricca, and Egidio Astesiano

Dipartimento di Informatica Bioingegneria,
Robotica e Ingegneria dei Sistemi (DIBRIS), Università di Genova,
Genoa, Italy
{gianna.reggio,maurizio.leotta,filippo.ricca,
egidio.astesiano}@unige.it

Abstract. In this paper, we propose a holistic approach aimed at combining business process modelling and data-driven business process improvement. The first step requires to develop a "precise" model of the processes of the organization using the UML. Precise means that all business entities involved in the process are determined as well as all the tasks composing the process executions, and all relevant data about them are modelled. Then, a model of the data space of the process will be derived taking into account also the quantitative aspects of each process (e.g. how many instances of the process will run each day?, how many possible instances of some business entities will be around or have ever been created?). In this way it is possible to conceive and design various analyses and improvements of the process based on its data, since all the aspects related to each business process have been explicitly modelled, and in a sufficiently formal way. We will introduce our approach using a small case study: the Buying process having as participants manufacturers, dealers, shippers, and payment systems.

1 Introduction

In the last decade, the availability of massive storage systems, large amounts of data and the advances in several disciplines related to data science such as data mining, data analytics, business intelligence, and machine learning provided powerful tools for potentially improving the business activities of the organizations. Indeed, the management can leverage the large amounts of data for extracting, by means of different techniques, useful information with the aim of improving the business processes and related activities.

To this end a variety of Business Process Management Systems (BPMS) have been investigated and proposed, that usually include a component dealing with Process Business Analytics (BPA), for collecting and analysing the process-related data to answer some process-centric questions (see, e.g. [16] and [2]).

Anderson [1] hints at the assumed canonical steps to be followed for a data analytics task: "*(a) developing questions to be answered, (b) curating the potential data sources, (c) collecting data from these sources, (d) cleaning the collected*

L. Zhang et al. (Eds.): Monterey Workshop 2016, LNCS 10228, pp. 168–183, 2017.
DOI: 10.1007/978-3-319-61994-1_16

data, (e) storing it, (f) processing/analysing the data, and then (g) displaying and visualizing the data in response to queries.".

Most often, organizations start introducing "analytics" from bottom, i.e. by trying to do some analysis on data that they have already at hand and found inside the many different systems and storage means available. However there has been a lot of work for organizing process data in a way suitable to answer the questions relevant to BPA (see for references Ch. 5 in [2]). As a notable example, in [3] a process data warehouse schema is presented that is derived as an abstraction from the experimental analysis of a variety of effectively running business processes, together with their related BPA questions. That work "makes possible a unified approach to reporting and analysis, so that the effort for setting up the analysis for a new process or customer consists mostly of customization rather than development". From a different angle, the decision-making viewpoint, in [7] a goal-oriented approach is pursued addressing the first point raised by Anderson "developing questions to be answered". We are looking at the problem, in particular, from still a different perspective, trying to see whether the level of abstraction can be raised further. We have in mind what happens in the software engineering field where best practices require structured development processes composed of various steps such as domain modelling, capture and specify requirements, design the software, and then implementation, made using high-level programming languages, reusing design patterns, and putting together large pieces of software, such as components and services, when not just by transforming models into running code (e.g. when following a model-driven approach [13]).

The lack of a well-defined engineered approach can lead to various problems:

- the collected data could be inadequate or excessive for useful analysis; in the first case it is not possible to answer the relevant questions, while, in the latter case, the organizations sustain unnecessary storage costs;
- connections between business processes, stakeholder's goals, and stored data could be ill-defined;
- the right questions for improving the business activities could be difficult to find.

In this paper, we propose a first step towards a holistic approach aimed at combining business process modelling and data-driven business process improvement and able to overcame the problems mentioned above.

The remainder of the paper is organized as follows. Section 2 provides an overview of the method while the subsequent Sects. 3, 4 and 5 sketch the first steps of our method (i.e. respectively the creation of the Precise Business Process Model, of the Business Process Data Space Model, and definition of the relevant questions). Finally, Sect. 6 concludes the paper.

2 Method Overview

An attempt at analysing an already running business process may start just by (a) looking at the available, more or less raw, data, (b) discussing with the stakeholders relying on their know-how, (c) examining the existing documentation of the process (e.g. a model of the process itself). The first point (a) may lead to concentrate on analysing aspects of the process expressed at a low-level (e.g. the mean time between two low-level messages, or expressing relationships between the codes classifying different categories of clients). The second point (b) may generate the classical problems associated with ambiguous terminology, hidden assumptions and misunderstandings between stakeholders and the analyst. The third point (c), if the documentation (e.g. a process model expressed using some notation) is of good quality and quite extensive, may provide a mean to conceive the relevant questions on the process and communicate them to the analyst, and in the meantime could also help present the results of the analysis in a way suitable for the stakeholders.

For the above reasons and as well-recognized in the literature (see e.g. [2]), we think that a good starting point for the analysis of a process may be its model (i.e. not limiting only to the (a), (b), (c) activities). Nowadays there are many different proposals for business process modelling, mainly based on graphical notations, e.g. BPMN [5], EPC [14,15], and UML [6]. UML is widely known and used [10,12], and provides many different diagrams suitable to cover all aspects of a business process such as data and participant features (in contrast, e.g. to BPMN, whose specification [5] explicitly states "*Therefore, the following are aspects that are out of the scope of this specification: ...Data and information models ...*"); furthermore, by means of the profile mechanism, UML provides a way to define its own variants, thus it may be easily tailored for this specific modelling task. The above considerations lead us to prefer the UML, which allows to model any aspect of a business process.

Any business process modelling notation, or better modelling method [8] represents the process dynamics as a workflow of basic chunks of activity, that may be either actions (not better qualified) or message exchanges, or events either instantaneous or having a duration. The granularity level of these chunks will be reflected in the granularity of the elicited questions, and thus of the designed process analysis. If the chosen modelling method allows to decompose and/or compose these chunks, it will be possible to arrange their granularity.

In some previous papers, we have developed some modelling methods for business processes based on the precise use of the UML, following the service oriented paradigm [9], where the basic unit of activity was the message exchange between two business entities [11], and another one based instead on tasks to which various entities may cooperate that we will briefly sketch in Sect. 3.

Figure 1 summarizes the activities required by our method to enhance a business process using analytics technique on its data (here, for the sake of simplicity, we consider only a business process but usually there are many of them sharing participants and data).

The first step is to produce a precise UML model of the process itself (and this can be done either on a process "to-be" or an existing one). Precise means that all business entities involved in the process are defined, as well as all the basic actions composing the process executions, and all relevant data about them are modelled.

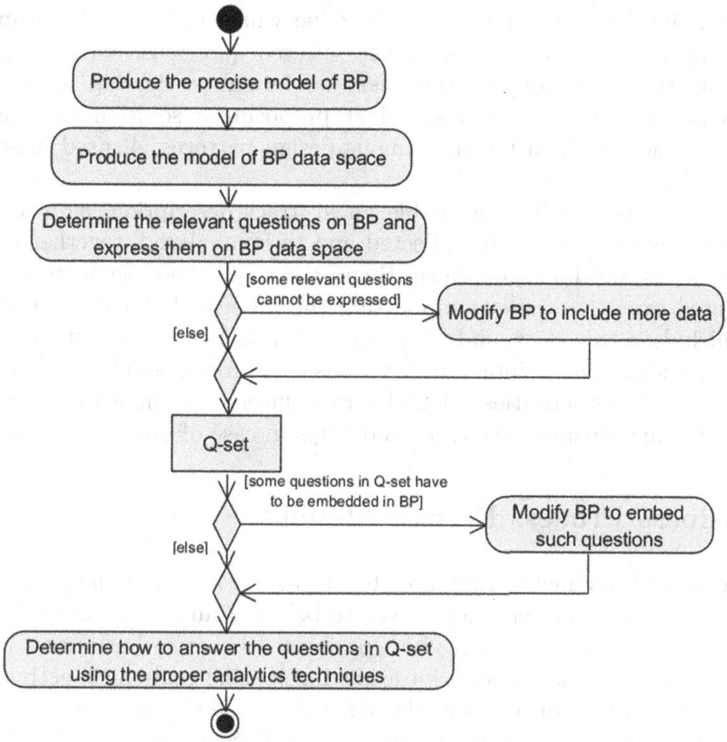

Fig. 1. Our method proposal for business process analytics

Then, a model of the *data space of the process* [2] will be derived taking into account also the quantitative aspects of each process (e.g. how many instances of the process will be run each day?, how many possible instances of some business entities will be around or have ever been created?). The data space is related to all possible data that can be generated by the executions of the process, as defined by its model, i.e. by its instances. Moreover, it is described at the same abstraction level, following the same style, and using the same terminology of the business process model. Thus it is suitable to express all possible questions on the process itself in a way understandable by the business process model's stakeholders.

Subsequently, it is required to determine the relevant questions on the business process expressed using the process data space and following one of the two strategies provided by our approach ("Bottom-up" and "Top-down").

Once the list of questions to answer is produced, we may modify the process to be sure to collect and store all the relevant data, and these modifications will be reflected on its model. Moreover, the activity of generating the relevant questions can be considered also a kind of inspection of the process model. This could lead to discover, already at this point, some problems in the process, before to start the analytics job.

Finally, the method requires to determine which theories, algorithms and analytic approaches allow to answer the selected questions, and to select the best among them. To support this task, we intend to develop what we call *analytics patterns*, i.e. patterns aimed at proposing a solution to a business process analytics problem (as the famous design patterns [4] used in software development).

At the end there will be available an abstract description, akin a kind of specification, of the data to be collected and to be analysed, together with the needed analyses and how to perform them. Later, all these elements should be implemented over the systems supporting the process, but having a guide to select which data to collect, and which kind of analytics tool to integrate.

Having modelled in an integrated way business process and their data spaces, defined the analytics activities, allows to trace the changes among them and thus simplifies the maintenance activities and helps in case of business evolution.

3 Business Process Precise Model

The first step of our method requires to produce a model of the process itself (and this can be done either of a process "to-be" or of an existing one). The term *business process* denotes the activities performed by some businesses, or more in general by some organizations, for achieving specific goals; such activities will be structured in terms of basic chunks of activity (*tasks*) related by the classical control flow operators, such as sequencing, parallelism, and conditional choice. In a business process there are a number of entities that perform activities or are manipulated by such activities, that we call *business entities*. We classify the business entities in *workers*, *systems*, and *business objects* (they will be detailed in Sect. 3.1). A business is usually structured in several processes, which may be mutually interfering since they may involve the same business entities, here for simplicity we consider the modelling of a single process in isolation.

The structure of the models of the business processes is defined in Fig. 2 by means of a UML class diagram[1].

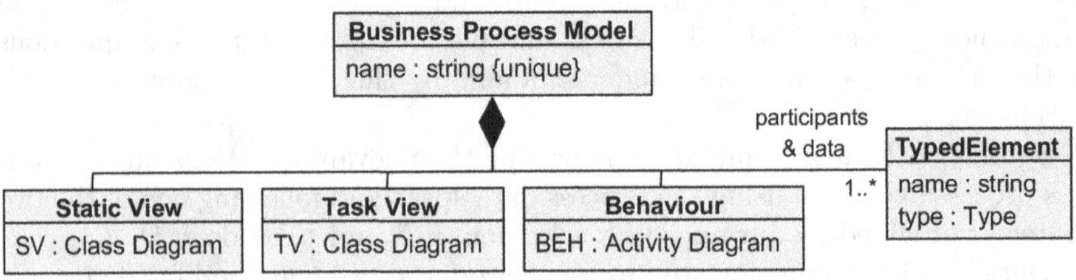

Fig. 2. Business process model structure

[1] In this paper, we follow the convention that in a UML class diagram the multiplicity of an association will be omitted whenever it is equal to 1.

In the following, we will detail the various parts of a business process model, exemplifying them on the business process Buying. The Buying business process concerns a business community including three primary kinds of parties: the dealers, the manufacturers and the shippers. They are independent parties, but they want to work together. All the manufacturers sell a unique kind of product (e.g. gasoline), the dealers buy that product from the manufacturers, and the shippers deliver it to the dealers. When a dealer wants to buy a certain quantity of the product from a manufacturer, it may before ask to the manufacturer for the current price, and decides if it is convenient. In the case of an affirmative answer, it will place an order to that manufacturer to buy some quantity of the product. When a manufacturer receives an order, it will check the product availability. If the ordered amount of product is available, the order will be accepted, otherwise, the order will be rejected. The dealer will pay for the order. If the payment ends successfully, the manufacturer will send a confirmation to the dealer, and will ask a shipper to deliver the product to the dealer; otherwise, i.e. if the payment failed, the manufacturer will cancel the order. When a shipper receives a shipping request from a manufacturer, it may refuse, otherwise it will inform the manufacturer of the date for picking up the shipment. Once the shipment is delivered to the dealer, the shipper will send a confirmation to the manufacturer.

3.1 Static View

The static view is a UML class diagram defining the classes typing the business entities (i.e. they will be modelled by objects typed by such classes), and their mutual relationships (modelled by associations among the corresponding classes).

In the static view, we use the following class stereotypes to classify the business entities in the three categories:

- ≪worker≫: (human) entities that perform the basic actions of the business;
- ≪system≫: entities corresponding to hardware or software systems taking part in the business;
- ≪object≫: those entities over which the basic actions of the business are performed;

The three stereotypes defined above are mutually exclusive. We name *entity class* any class stereotyped with either ≪worker≫ or ≪system≫ or ≪object≫.

The business entities (types) relative to our running example Buying are modelled by means of the classes appearing in the static view shown in Fig. 3. More in detail:

- Manufacturer, those that provide the product sold in the network (remind that a unique kind of product is commercialized, e.g. gasoline);
- Dealer, those that buy the product from the manufacturers;
- Shipper, those able to move the product from the manufacturers to the dealers;
- Payment not further detailed system supporting the handling of payments between two parties, e.g. by means of credit card or Paypal;

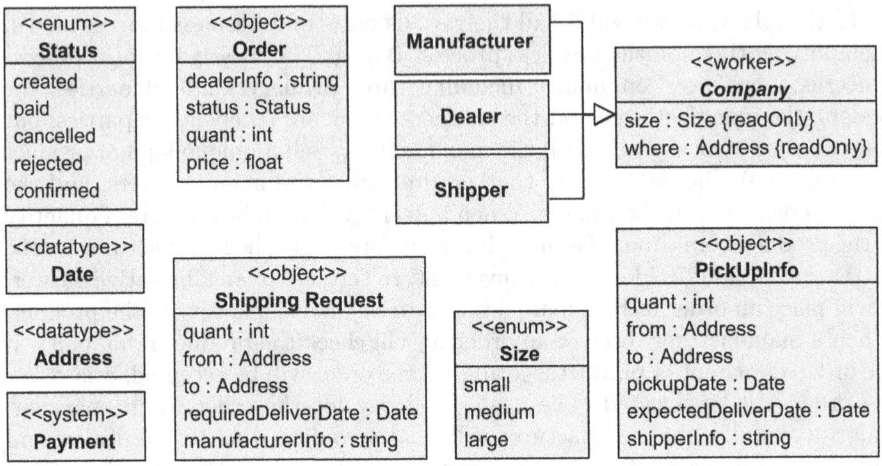

Fig. 3. Business process Buying model: Static view

- Order the orders sent by the dealers to the manufacturers;
- ShippingRequest the documents sent by the manufacturers to the shippers for asking the transportation of products to the dealers;
- PickUpInfo the info sent back by a shipper when accepts a request.

Notice that only the relevant info about the various entities is considered in the model, that reflects the view of the stakeholders, and will influence the subsequent analytics activities.

3.2 TaskView

The task view is a class diagram containing classes stereotyped by ≪task≫ modelling the basic activities of the process, and any other class/datatype needed to define them, but the latter must have been already introduced in the static view.

The participants of a task, that are roles typed by entity classes and not specific instances, are represented by means of associations connecting the task class with participant classes, and the association end attached to the entity class should be the participant name.

If a task participant should be instantiated before the task may start (whereas others may be determined by the task activities, e.g. when an order is created or a shipper selected), then it will be stereotyped by ≪in≫ (short for input). A task class may have any number of attributes typed by datatypes; they represent the data used by the task; similarly to the participants they may be stereotyped with ≪in≫. A task class may be characterized by means of pre/post/invariant constraints concerning its participants and used data (expressed using the OCL).

The task view of the process Buying is shown in Fig. 4. For instance, both Dealer and Manufacturer take part in the RequestQuote task given that Dealer may

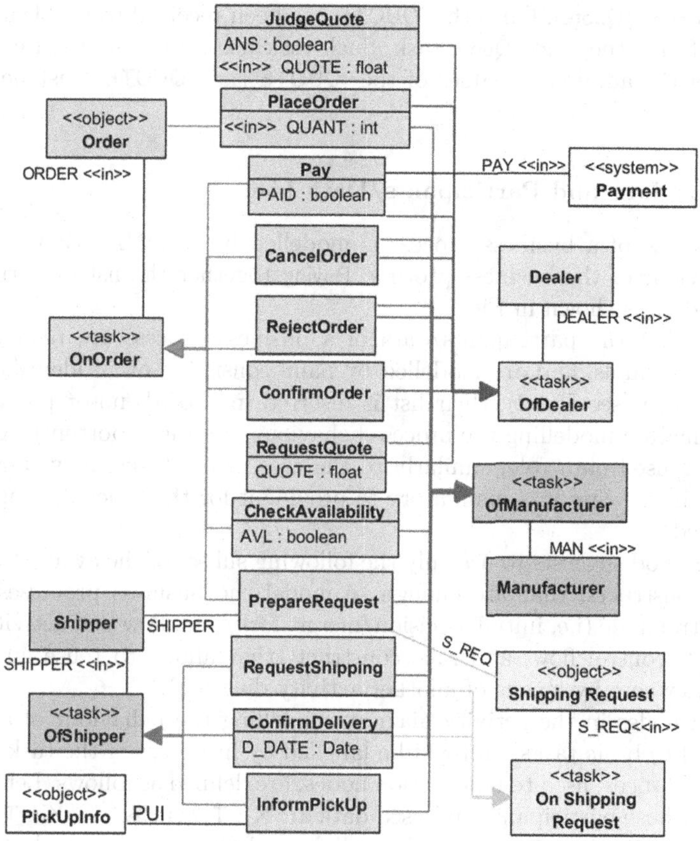


```
context JudgeQuote
 pre: QUOTE>0
context PlaceOrder
 pre: QUANT>0 and PRICE>0
 post: ORDER.status=created and ORDER.price=PRICE and ORDER.quantity=QUANT
context CancelOrder
 pre: ORDER.status = created     post: ORDER.status = cancelled
context RejectOrder
 pre: ORDER.status = created     post: ORDER.status = rejected
context ConfirmOrder
 pre: ORDER.status = created     post: ORDER.status = confirmed
context RequestQuote
 post: QUOTE>0
context RequestShipping
 pre: ORDER.status = confirmed
```

Fig. 4. Process Buying model: Task view

before ask to Manufacturer for the current price of the product (i.e. executing the task RequestQuote). Once the QUOTE has been received from Manufacturer, Dealer performs the JudgeQuote task. Such task has a pre-condition constraint concerning the admissible values of the QUOTE (i.e. QUOTE must be greater than 0).

3.3 Behaviour and Participants/Data List

The behaviour of a business process is modelled by a UML activity diagram. The behaviour of the business process Buying together the list of participants and used data is shown in Fig. 5.

Notice that the participants/data of a business process are roles and not specific individuals, and are modelled by pairs consisting of an identifier and a class/datatype (see Fig. 2); their list is inserted in a UML note[2] put near the activity diagram modelling the process behaviour (see Fig. 5 bottom). A process participant/used data role, similarly to the case of the tasks, may stereotyped by ≪in≫ in the case it is mandatory to provide it for the process being able to be executed.

Our method suggests to use only the following subset of the available activity diagram constructs, that are enough to model the business processes: action node, control node (i.e. initial, decision/merge, fork/join, flow and activity final), time event, control flow, and rake construct (that allows to reuse an activity defined elsewhere by means of another activity diagram).

Action nodes in the activity diagram modelling the behaviour of a process correspond to basic tasks, and will be labelled by instances of the task classes.

Task instances, used to label action nodes, are defined as follows. Let TC be a task class whose participants and used data are X_1: T_1≪in≫, ..., X_n: T_n≪in≫, X_{n+1}: T_1, ..., X_m: T_n, E_1, ..., E_n be well-formed OCL expressions having type $T_1, \ldots, T_n$ respectively, and Y_{n+1}: $T_{n+1}, \ldots, Y_m$: T_m be participants/used data of the process, then

$$Y_{n+1}, \ldots, Y_m = TC<E_1, \ldots, E_n>$$

represents the instance of TC determined by E_1, ..., E_n whose outputs will be assigned to Y_{n+1}, ..., Y_m respectively.

A name must be assigned to each final node, to discriminate between successful and failed process terminations, and among the different reasons for terminating or failing.

Furthermore, business processes require often non-deterministic choices among several alternatives and, since the UML activity diagram does not offer a specific construct to represent it, but it may be obtained by a choice where all the guards of the alternatives are true, we introduce the black diamond to represent such construct (see for instance the black diamond near the initial state in Fig. 5).

[2] Represented by the icon of the paper leaf with a bended corner.

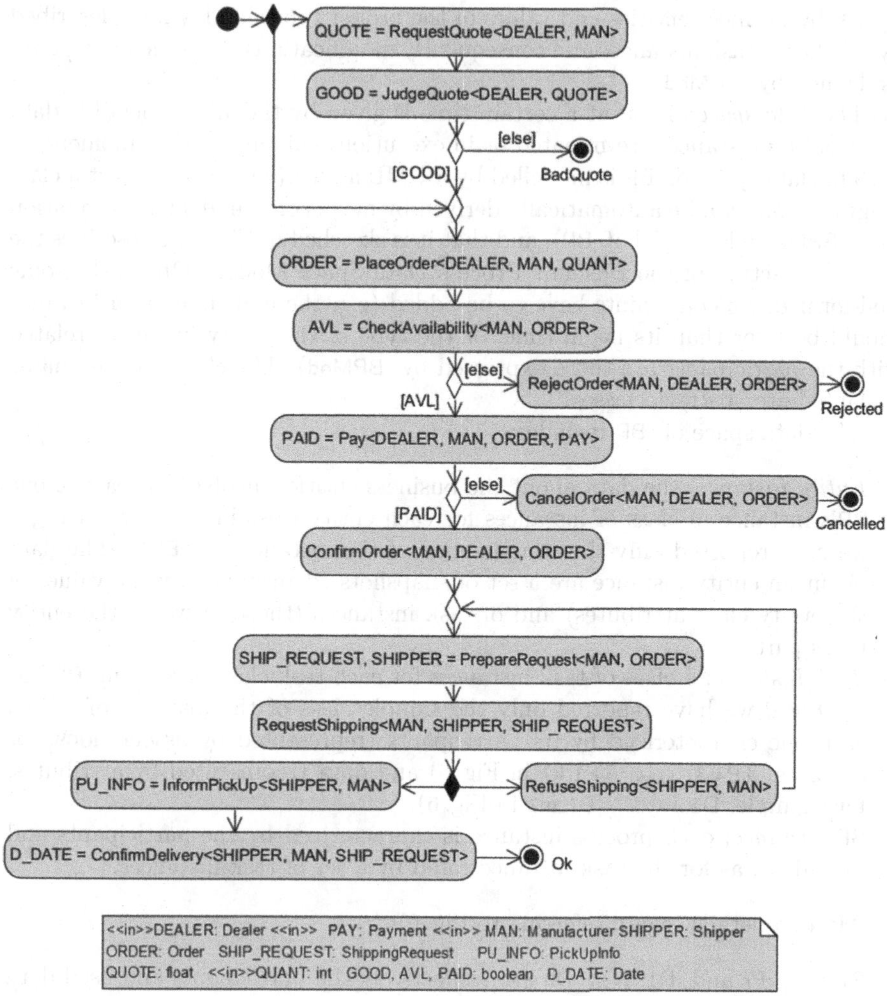

Fig. 5. Business process Buying model: behaviour plus participants and used data list

4 Business Process Data Space

A business process model, as the one presented in Sect. 3, is in some sense a template for the many possible process executions, since it describes how the process works, precisely defining who is acting, which actions are performed and over what. A business process execution is named *(business) process instance*. Thus, for each business process several instances can exist, that will be executed at different times as well as simultaneously.

Let BP be a business process whose precise model is BPMod. A BP's *instance* is determined by instantiating all the process participants and data marked by

≪in≫ by business entities and values of the proper types, and will be described by the flow of task instances and consequently modifications on participants/data as defined by BPMod.

The *data space* of BP at a certain time is given by the all the possible data about all its instances (terminated or in execution) existing at that moment.

The data space of BP is modelled by a UML model (consisting of just a class diagram) that can be automatically derived by means of a model transformation from BPMod (the model of BP), and that it is sketched in Fig. 6 (it describes the generic structure of the Business Process Data Space Model). Obviously, some well-formedness constraints have to be added (e.g. the end time of an instance should be later than its begin time, or the type of the entity instances related with the participants are those expressed by BPMod). The classes whose name is slanted are abstract classes.

The data space of BP includes:

- *Entity Instance*: the data about the business entities involved at least in one BP's instance, a class of instances for each entity class in BPMod (in Fig. 6 we have reported only the sample class of the instances of EC1). The data about an entity instance are a set of snapshots (determined by the values of the entity class attributes) and of task instances (those in which the entity takes part).
- *Task Instance*: a class of task instances for each task class present in BPMod (in Fig. 6 we have reported only the sample class of the instance of TC1), each one characterized by its participants (represented by associations, for example TP1_1, ..., TP1_k1 in Fig. 6) and data (represented by attributes, for example D1_1, ..., D1_m1 in Fig. 6).
- BP *Instance*: each process instance is characterized by the participants and used data, as for the task instances, and by a set of task instances.

More in details (again referring to Fig. 6):

- P1, ..., Pr and D1, ..., Dh are respectively the participants and used data of BP.
- EC1 (with attributes A1_1, ..., A1_n1), ... are the entity classes in the static view.
- TC1 (whose participants and used data are TP1_1, ..., TP1_k1 and D1_1, ..., D1_m1 respectively), ... are the task classes part of the task view.

All the instance info part of the process data space are enriched with a unique identity, and two time stamps, precisely the begin and the end of each process/task/business entity (end time is optional since the instances may be still running), whereas the entity snapshots are annotated with the time are taken.

Once produced the model of the data of the business process to enhance, the method requires to perform a dimensional analysis of it, that requires to elicit and state conditions on the minimum/maximum number of the various kinds of instances part of the process data space along the time. The dimensional analysis

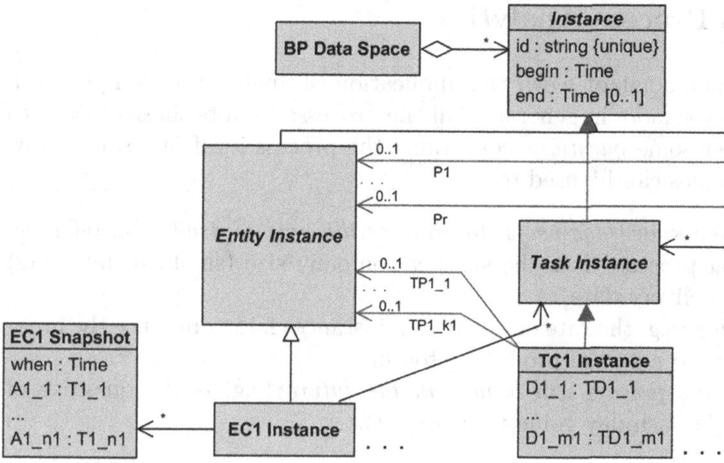

Fig. 6. Generic business process data space model structure

will be useful to understand whether the cardinality of the collected process data is so high to require big data techniques or not, and to decide which techniques to use to perform the data analysis.

Considering a hypothetical business process Buying, and assuming the following business community, the result of the dimensional analysis is:

Instances	Estimation
Buying instances	≤ 15.000 created each day for up to 10 years
Manufacturer instances	≤ 100
Shipper instances	≤ 10.000
Dealer instances	≤ 25.000
Payment instances	4
business object classes instances	3 × the number of the Buying instances

Notice that the workers and the systems instances are neither created nor destroyed by the Buying process, and thus their number may be assumed constant; the 4 payment systems are Visa, Mastercard, Bancomat and PostPay, and each process instance at most creates three business objects (i.e. order, shipping request, and pickup info).

So, we see that in this case the volume of the process data is not "big" (only 15.000 Buying instances per day), and so traditional storing and handling technologies may be used.

It is however easy to consider different processes, for instance concerning global e-commerce transactions, where the data space will be truly "big" (in the order of tens of billions of transactions/year).

5 Business Process Analytics

At a very abstract point of view, the application of analytics techniques to a business process (or more in general to all the processes of a business) means to be able to answer some *questions* concerning the process itself in a sound way. Analytics techniques can be used to:

- *discover hidden knowledge useful to improve the process itself* (e.g. referring to the Buying process, does the shipper company size (small/medium/big) influence the delivery date);
- *detect problems* (e.g. the rate of the Buying instances failing because the order is rejected due to a lack of product is too high);
- *forecast how the process will behave in the future* (e.g. is the quantity of product bought each day going to increase?).

To make the question elicitation a systematic activity, and to ground future work on supporting tools, such as a wizard guiding the elicitation, we give a conceptual model for the *questions* in Fig. 7.

A question should concern some *knowledge item* definable on the process data space, either *indicator*, i.e. a quantity computable on the process data space, or a *relationship*, i.e. a mapping between some quantities (at least one) and another one computable on the process data space. For example, the mean duration of the process instances, and the rate of female clients are indicators, whereas the number of items sold each day/month[3], the mapping between age and gender of the clients and the number of process instances in which they took part, and the mapping between zip code of the clients and the number of failed process instances are relationships.

To ensure that the found indicators/relationships are computable over the process data, they should be expressed by means of OCL expressions defined over the model of the BP data space, also enriched with auxiliary classes, operations,

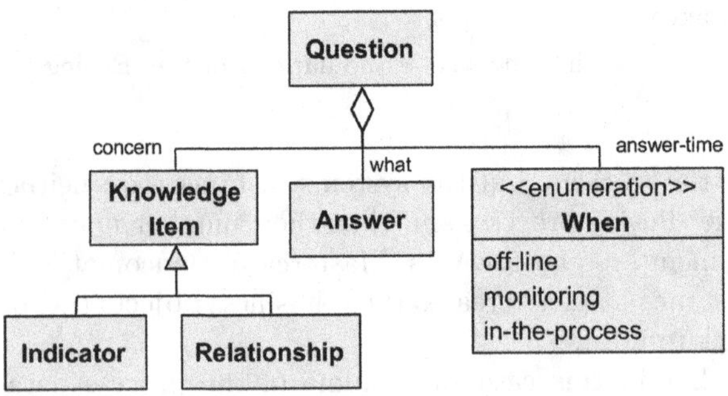

Fig. 7. Form of the questions

[3] Mapping between days/months and number of items.

and attributes. For example the duration of an instance may be modelled by means of a derived attribute Duration: Time of the class *Instance* defined by the OCL expression:

if not temination.isUndefined() then termination–begin else undefined.

The *answer* component of a question expresses what should be said about the knowledge item, e.g. in the case of an indicator: which is its value?, is its value larger than some specific value? whereas for a relationship the answer may either require to visualize such relationship, or to say whether the input values influence the output value (e.g., the gender and the age of the clients affect and how much the number of placed orders), or whether the available data allows to make some forecast on the evolution of the mapping.

Each question must also include the information on *when* its answer is needed, i.e. *off-line*, when it is needed to support the strategic decisions of the management (e.g. is true that the big size dealers have less failed orders for not being able to pay in time than the small size one?), *monitoring* when it is needed to generate some alarm while the process is running (the number of failed order during the current day is greater than 50%?), and *in-the-process* when it is needed to make some decision inside the process (e.g. to decide the quotation to propose depending on some analysis of the data on the past quotations followed or not by an order). The use of analytics techniques should allow to answer the above defined questions.

As shown in Fig. 1, the starting point of any application of analytics technique to a business process is to determine the relevant questions on the business process; we propose two different strategies to perform this activity: bottom-up (or data-driven) and top-down (or goal-driven), illustrated in the following subsections.

The Bottom up Strategy. The bottom-up strategy suggests to systematically look for the questions on the process data space, and then the analyst will have to select among them those relevant from the business point of view.

The method asks to look for the relevant indicators and relationships definable on the process data space, see Fig. 6, and then to build over them the interesting questions. The elements of the data space are essentially process, entity and task instances.

Trying to elicit the relevant indicators and relationships will lead also to a kind of inspection of the process, and possibly to modify it, and to discover that there are other relevant indicators/relationships that cannot be computed using the process data space, again this will lead to a modification of the process.

The Top-Down Strategy. In the case a preliminary set of questions is already available prepared by the stakeholders, we can also follow a different strategy. Usually the questions will be expressed informally, thus the work of the analyst should consist in trying to express them using indicators and relationships definable on the process data space. So all the terms appearing in the questions should be associated with indicators/relationships, and then each question should be accommodated in the schema of Fig. 7.

Examples of questions on the process Buying, found following our method, include: which are the manufacturers that cancel an order (their behaviour includes instances of Place Order immediately followed by Reject Order) with a percentage larger than 50%? Which is the rate of the dealers asking for a quotation before placing an order? Which is the rate of the dealers not placing an order after getting a quotation?

6 Conclusions

In this work, we have proposed a first step towards a holistic approach aimed at combining business process modelling and data-driven business process improvement. We briefly detailed its first steps (i.e. respectively creation of the Business Process Precise Model, of the Business Process Data Space and definition of the relevant questions).

As future work we plan to: (1) better refine the two strategies provided by our approach (i.e. "Bottom-up" and "Top-down") for determining the relevant questions on the business process expressed using the process data space, (2) investigate how integrating the existing analytic approaches in our method with the goal of providing answers the selected questions; (3) validate the applicability of our method on an industrial case study, and finally (4) derive a wizard tool that hints to the analyst one after the other all the possible knowledge items and the possible questions over them to make the procedure suggested by our method less cumbersome; moreover, since the process data space model is a UML model and a model of the questions can be also given, we plan to investigate the (semi-) automatic generation of the questions by means of model transformations.

References

1. Anderson, K.M.: Embrace the challenges: software engineering in a big data world. In: Proceedings of 1st IEEE/ACM International Workshop on Big Data Software Engineering, BIGDSE 2015, pp. 19–25. IEEE (2015)
2. Beheshti, S.-M.-R., Benatallah, B., Sakr, S., Grigori, D., Motahari-Nezhad, H.R., Barukh, M.C., Gater, A., Ryu, S.H.: Process Analytics. Springer, Cham (2016). doi:10.1007/978-3-319-25037-3
3. Casati, F., Castellanos, M., Dayal, U., Salazar, N.: A generic solution for warehousing business process data. In: Proceedings of 33rd International Conference on Very Large Data Bases, VLDB 2007, pp. 1128–1137. VLDB Endowment (2007)
4. Gamma, E., Helm, R., Johnson, R., Vlissides, J., Patterns, D.: Elements of Reusable Object-oriented Software. Addison-Wesley Longman Publishing Co. Inc., Boston (1995)
5. Object Management Group (OMG). Business Process Model and Notation (BPMN). http://www.omg.org/spec/BPMN/
6. Object Management Group (OMG). Unified Modeling Language (UML) Specification. http://www.omg.org/spec/UML/

7. Pourshahid, A., Richards, G., Amyot, D.: Toward a goal-oriented, business intelligence decision-making framework. In: Babin, G., Stanoevska-Slabeva, K., Kropf, P. (eds.) MCETECH 2011. LNBIP, vol. 78, pp. 100–115. Springer, Heidelberg (2011). doi:10.1007/978-3-642-20862-1_7
8. Reggio, G., Astesiano, E., Choppy, C.: A framework for defining and comparing modelling methods. In: De Nicola, R., Hennicker, R. (eds.) Software, Services, and Systems. LNCS, vol. 8950, pp. 377–408. Springer, Cham (2015). doi:10.1007/978-3-319-15545-6_23
9. Reggio, G., Leotta, M., Clerissi, D., Ricca, F.: Service-oriented domain and business process modelling. In: Proceedings of 32nd ACM/SIGAPP Symposium on Applied Computing, SAC 2017, pp. 751–758. ACM (2017). doi:10.1145/3019612.3019621
10. Reggio, G., Leotta, M., Ricca, F.: Who knows/uses what of the UML: a personal opinion survey. In: Dingel, J., Schulte, W., Ramos, I., Abrahão, S., Insfran, E. (eds.) MODELS 2014. LNCS, vol. 8767, pp. 149–165. Springer, Cham (2014). doi:10.1007/978-3-319-11653-2_10
11. Reggio, G., Leotta, M., Ricca, F., Astesiano, E.: Business process modelling: Five styles and a method to choose the most suitable one. In: Proceedings of 2nd International Workshop on Experiences and Empirical Studies in Software Modelling, EESSMod 2012, pp. 8:1–8:6. ACM (2012). doi:10.1145/2424563.2424574
12. Reggio, G., Leotta, M., Ricca, F., Clerissi, D.: What are the used UML diagram constructs? A document and tool analysis study covering activity and use case diagrams. In: Hammoudi, S., Pires, L.F., Filipe, J., Neves, R.C. (eds.) MODELSWARD 2014. CCIS, vol. 506, pp. 66–83. Springer, Cham (2015). doi:10.1007/978-3-319-25156-1_5
13. Stahl, T., Voelter, M., Czarnecki, K.: Development, Model-Driven Software: Technology, Engineering, Management. Wiley, Hoboken (2006)
14. van der Aalst, W.: Formalization and verification of event-driven process chains. Inf. Softw. Technol. **41**(10), 639–650 (1999)
15. Wikipedia. Event-driven process chain (EPC). https://en.wikipedia.org/wiki/Event-driven_process_chain
16. zur Mühlen, M., Shapiro, R.: Handbook on Business Process Management 2. In: vom Brocke, J., Rosemann, M. (eds.) Business Process Analytics. International Handbooks on Information Systems, pp. 137–157. Springer, Heidelberg (2010). doi:10.1007/978-3-642-01982-1_7

Traffic Flow Prediction with Improved SOPIO-SVR Algorithm

Xuejun Cheng[1,2], Lei Ren[1,2(✉)], Jin Cui[1,2], and Zhiqiang Zhang[1,2]

[1] School of Automation Science and Electrical Engineering, Beihang University, Beijing, China
lei_ren@126.com

[2] Engineering Research Center of Complex Product Advanced Manufacturing System, Ministry of Education, Beijing, China

Abstract. In urban public transport, the traffic flow prediction is a classical non-linear complicated optimization problem, which is very important for public transport system. With the rapid development of the big data, Smart card data of bus which is provided by millions of passengers traveling by bus across several days plays a more and more important role in our daily life. The issue that we address is whether the data mining algorithm and the intelligent optimization algorithm can be applied to forecast the traffic flow from big data of bus. In this paper, a novel algorithm which called mixed support vector regression with sub-space orthogonal pigeon-Inspired Optimization (SOPIO-MSVR) is used to predict the traffic flow and optimize the algorithm progress. Results show the SOPIO-MSVR algorithm outperforms other algorithms by a margin and is a competitive algorithm. And the research can make the significant contribution to the improvement of the transportation.

Keywords: Traffic flow prediction · SOPIO-MSVR · Classification model

1 Introduction

In public transportation area, advanced public transportation collection systems are applied to collect revenue. At the same time, they also generate huge amounts of data which is stored in the database. The data is very useful not only for individual travels but also for government agencies [1]. There are still many challenges using data for transportation analysis, such as a crucial need for data fusing approaches combining data with different features, structures and resolutions, data processing and mining techniques and a suite of schemes based on cyber and physical space data [2].

The public transportation card has become the preferred payment method of the city's transportation. The potential it holds focuses on these aspects: traffic route prediction [4], travel patterns mining [5], visual exploration of urban data [6], traffic flow prediction [7], passenger demand analysis [8] and a few of many examples based on its comprehensive categories and new applications. Traffic flow prediction is a universal problem that has aroused widespread attention. Although many models and algorithms have been applied to predict the traffic flow, simple traffic models and results somewhat don't meet the requirements.

L. Zhang et al. (Eds.): Monterey Workshop 2016, LNCS 10228, pp. 184–197, 2017.
DOI: 10.1007/978-3-319-61994-1_17

The booming demand for big data provides new methods of traffic flow. We hope to utilize more suitable models and more efficient algorithms by means of such rich amount of algorithms. The approaches to traffic flow prediction now are divided into three categories: parametric methods, nonparametric methods and simulations. Parametric methods consist of time-series models and Kalman filtering models, etc. The time-series models mainly indicate significant ARIMA (0,1,1) [9] and its improved models such as KARIMA [10], ARIMAX [11], SARIMA [12] models. These models have requests of estimation about a large number of parameters in multivariate space [13].

Because of stochastic and nonlinear traffic flow data, the research focuses more on nonparametric methods. The nonparametric methods consist of nonparametric regressions, Neural networks and support vector machine, etc. Davis *et al.* presented KNN methods for short-term traffic flow prediction [14]. Sun used a Bayesian network to forecast traffic flow [15]. And an example in supervised weighting-online learning algorithm was presented in [16] for prediction. Optimized neural networks combining with genetic approach was applied by Vlahogianni [16] to predict traffic flow under typical and untypical conditions. Zhong *et al.* put forward Hybrid models which they called designed regression and time delay neural network models [17]. A computational intelligence-based approach in the article [18] performed well on the effect of target values. Simulation approaches need to develop new tools to predict traffic flows.

Many research on the comparison of pros and cons about flow prediction models have been made. Chen *et al.* contrast the ARMA, ARIMA, SARIMA, SVR, Bayesian network, ANN, K-Nearest Neighbor, Naïve models, and pointed out different models are suitable for different time periods of the day [19]. Lippi et al. proposed that improved SVR models performed well than SARIMA models during the most congested periods [20]. Hinsbergen et al. did experiments with parametric and nonparametric models and results indicated that not one of the methods can be considered the best method in any situation [21]. More reviews can be found in [22–25].

SVM models are a type of machine learning models that can be utilized to predict the values in different fields and have effect on the accuracy of prediction [26, 27]. Due to intrinsic multi-input nature, SVM is favored among the multivariate or time-spatial models. Although SVM has drawn public attention from the research community around the world, some studies such as optimal design still deserve to be discovered and supplemented [28]. Nonparametric SVM algorithms had difficulty on parameters selection. And how to prevent local convergence when adjusting parameter is significant to some degree. Biological inspired algorithms are the valuable solution on complex optimization problems and local convergence problems. Pigeon inspired optimization was first proposed by Duan et al. and is a novel swarm intelligence algorithm on the basis of the movement of the flock of pigeons [29], the algorithm is used for Image restoration [30], three-dimensional path planning [31], Target Assignment [32], model prediction control [33]. The parameters according to pigeon inspired optimization (PIO) technology was used correctly for traffic flow prediction about travel logs (big data) of Guangzhou to serve as an input of the kernel optimal parameters in the SVM training. And comparative algorithms are conducted to present the relative dominance of the new algorithm. Solving the prediction problem need the better mathematic model and also better algorithm model.

In this paper, we solve the following problems, which are implicitly related:

(1) Can we improve the performance of the algorithm model and heighten precision of prediction using modified algorithm model?
(2) How should we deal with big data and do feature extraction by the tools such as SQL, Highcharts?

To answer these questions, we first introduce the algorithm model which called SOPIO-MSVM, PSO-SVM, DT-SVM, GA-SVM, ARMA. Next, we process the original data and research on the variation ruler during different time horizons. Finally, we evaluate the performance of different mathematic models and algorithm models and select the best mathematic model and algorithm model.

The structure of this paper is organized as follows. Section 1 introduces the research status of the short-term traffic flow prediction. Section 2 presents the basic method - SOPIO-SVM algorithm for traffic flow forecasting. Section 3 shows the experimental results with real data to verify the performance of the algorithm. Concluding remarks and future research opportunities are described in Sect. 4.

2 Theory of the Mathematic Model and New Algorithm Model

Principle of Basic PIO

The pigeons can find their ways back home via three methods: (1) The earth's magnetic field. (2) The sun. (3) The landmark. And using above tools, they can select the best strategies and reach the destination through the optimal route. A novel algorithm called PIO was put forward by imitating and studying the homing pigeon's behavior. There are two important operators in the algorithm: one is map and compass operator which is used to adjust the direction based on the magnetic field and the sun, and the other is landmark operator which is defined according to the quantitative values of the landmark (Fig. 2).

Map and Compass Operator

In the map and compass operator, Variate X_i is the pigeon i position, Variate V_i is the pigeon i velocity and D is the dimension of the search space about the pigeon i. Variance X_g denotes the current global best position which could be obtained by comparing all the positions among all the pigeons. Variance R denotes the extent to which the velocity on next generation will vary with the former generation and is called the map and compass factor [28, 29].

The relationship between the parameters shows in Eqs. (1)–(2)

$$V_i(t) = V_i(t-1) \cdot e^{-Rt} + rand \cdot (X_g - X_i(t-1)) \tag{1}$$

$$X_i(t) = X_i(t-1) + V_i(t) \tag{2}$$

Fig. 1. The map and compass operator

Fig. 2. The landmark operator

Landmark Operator

In the landmark operator, we let $X_c(t)$ denote the center of pigeon's position, $X_i(t)$ denotes the position of pigeon I at the t th iteration and $X_c(t)$ denotes the center position at the t th iteration. We present the strategy that half of these pigeons which are badly-behaved will be discarded and other pigeons which are unfamiliar the landmarks in the remaining pigeons will go after the nearest pigeons in the circle. In our definition, we use the formula (3)–(5) to state the behavior of the pigeons.

$$N_P(t) = \frac{N_P(t-1)}{2} \tag{3}$$

$$X_c(t) = \frac{\sum X_i(t) \cdot fitness(X_i(t))}{N_P \sum fitness(X_i(t))} \tag{4}$$

$$X_i(t) = X_i(t-1) + rand \cdot (X_c(t) - X_i(t-1)) \tag{5}$$

where *fitness* is the quality of the pigeon individual. For the minimum optimization problems, we can choose $fitness(X_i(t)) = \frac{1}{f(X_i(t)) + \varepsilon}$ for maximum optimization problems [28].

Proposed Pigeon Inspiration Algorithm

Sub-space Division Orthogonal Design

The orthogonalization design can ensure population distribution within the feasible, and also can solve the problem of too much complexity. Let $L_M(H^n)$ be an orthogonal array of n factors and H levels, where L denotes a Latin square, H^n is the full size of the orthogonal array, and M is the number of combinations of levels. $L_M(H^n)$ is a matrix of numbers arranged in M rows and n columns, where each row represents a combination of levels, and each column represents a specific factor that can be changed [34].

The basic orthogonal design of space $[l_1, u_1]$ about parameter a is presented in Table 1.

The scope of parameters about SVM is wide, so M is larger. It is obvious that more representative initial population which means that a higher value M is better. But M is limited by n and H. The sub-space division orthogonal design is adopted to solve the problem. The sub-space division orthogonal design steps is as follows:

Table 1. Basic orthogonal design

Step1) Select the smallest J fulfilling $(H^J-1)/(H-1)\geq n$
Step2) if $(H^J-1)/(H-1)=n$, then $n'=n$ else $n'=(H^J-1)/(H-1)$
Step3) execute algorithm shown in table 1 to construct the orthogonal array $L_M(H^{n'})$, which $M=H^{n'}$
Step4: Delete the last $n'-n$ columns of $L_M(H^{n'})$ to obtain $L_M(H^n)$

(1) The feasible solution space $[l,u]$ is divided into S subspaces $[l_1,u_1]$, $[l_2,u_2]$, ……, $[l_s,u_s]$;
(2) Use orthogonal design showed in Table 1 to produce M individuals, and select best S_{size} bodies in every subspace $[l_i,u_i](i=1,2,3\ldots s)$.
(3) Choose the best S bodies from the $S\times S_{size}$ [35].

Mixed Support Vector Machine

Support Vector Machine were put forward by Vladimir Vapnik and have been a statistical learning technique for regression and classification problems. The basic target of SVR is adopted a function which is shown as Eq. (6) to get predicted results $f(x)$ by pre-determined input x

$$f(x)=\sum_{i=1}^{n} w\phi(x)+b \tag{6}$$

where w and b are the two parameters of SVR, which need to be optimized to fit the training dataset. $\phi(x)$ is the nonlinear mapping about x to meet the requirement that the relationship of $\phi(x)$ and y is linear when the relationship of x and y is nonlinear.

The goal of *SVR* is to minimize the expected risk R_{emp} which is defined in (7)–(8)

$$R_{emp}=\frac{1}{n}\sum\nolimits_{i=1}^{n} L_\varepsilon(y_i,f(x_i)) \tag{7}$$

$$L_\varepsilon(y_i,f(x_i))=\begin{cases}0, if|y-f(x)|\leq\varepsilon\\ |y-f(x)|-\varepsilon, otherwise\end{cases} \tag{8}$$

where L_ε is called ε -insensitive loss function by Vapnik.

By introducing Lagrange multipliers and converting the optimization problem into the problem, the function in (6) can be transformed into the following form:

$$
\begin{aligned}
&f(x) = \sum\nolimits_{i=1}^{n} (a_i^* - a_i)K(x_i, x) + b \\
&s.t.\ 0 \le a_i^* \le C, 0 \le a_i \le C
\end{aligned}
\tag{9}
$$

where a_i^*, a_i are the Lagrange multipliers that can be got by solving the dual problem and $K(x_i, x_j)$ is the kernel function that equals the inner product of $\phi(x_i)$ and $\phi(x_j)$ [36].

The effects of the SVR algorithm model are strongly dependent on the SVM hyperparameters: the regularization factor C, the hyperparameter ε that defines the ε – *insensitive* tube, σ that represents the kernel parameter about the RBF kernel. ζ, d that represents the kernel parameter about the PLOY kernel. From [33], we can see that PLOY kernel has better extrapolation abilities higher orders of degrees for good interpolation, but the RBF kernel has good interpolation abilities and fails to provide longer range extrapolation. Using mixtures of kernels can ensure having both good interpolation and extrapolation abilities. The basic convex combination of the two kernels K_{POLY} [37].

And K_{RBF} can be computed as (11):

$$K_{mix} = \rho K_{RBF} + (1 - \rho)K_{PLOY} \tag{10}$$

Different kernels functions are described as follows:

The RBF function K_{RBF} is presented in (12)

$$k(x_i, x_j) = \exp\left[-\frac{|x_i - x_j|^2}{2\sigma^2}\right] \tag{11}$$

The polynomial kernel K_{PLOY} is presented in (13)

$$k(x_i, x_j) = (x_i \cdot x_j + \xi)^b \tag{12}$$

where σ, ξ and b are the parameters of description about the kernel's behavior.

The fitness of the new SOPIO-SVM is defined as:

$$RMSE = \sqrt{\frac{\sum_{i=1}^{n} (\hat{X}(k) - X(k))^2}{n}} \tag{13}$$

where $\hat{X}(k)$ is the prediction value and $X(k)$ is the real value.

The SVR-based model has the smaller performance criterion than other models that the reason is the SVR-based model can solve the traffic flow prediction problem with the nonlinearity and wave property than some model. Thus, employing the SVR model to build models about the traffic flow forecasting is appropriate.

SOPIO-SVM Algorithm

The calculation process of the new SOPIO-SVM is in Fig. 1.

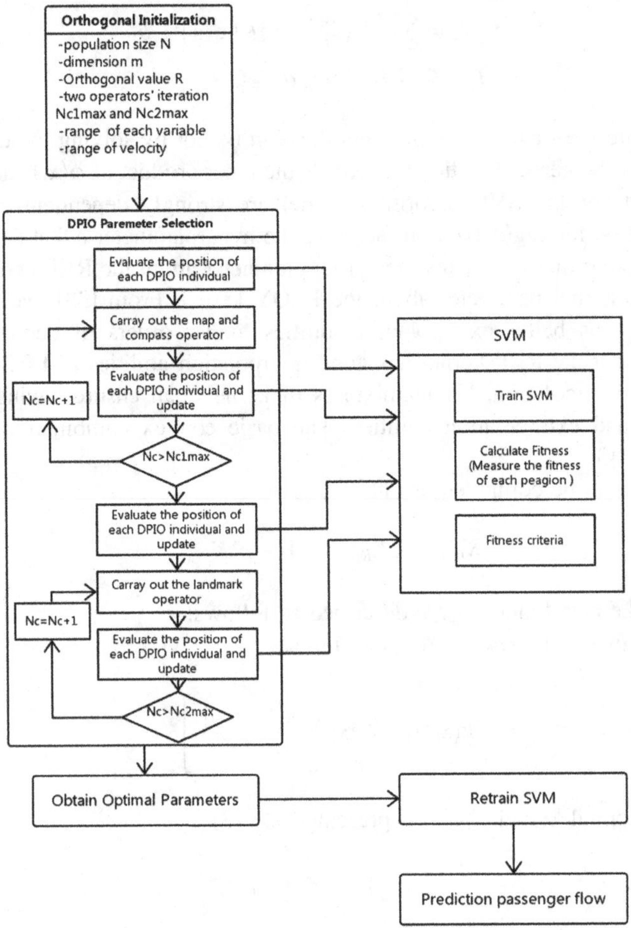

Fig. 3. Procedure of SOPIO-MSVR for traffic flow prediction

The detailed procedure of SOPIO-SVM for traffic flow prediction showing in Fig. 3 is described as follows:

Step 1: Set the parameters of the SOPIO algorithm model which include the dimension M and the range for values on every parameter like the input parameter $C, \varepsilon, \sigma, \xi, d$ of the mixed SVR, the population size N, the Map and compass operator iteration Nc1max, the landmark operator iteration Nc2-max, Compass operator iteration factor R and the number of orthogonalization space M, the factor of every orthogonalization space H.

Step 2: Generate an initial array according to the five parameters of the mixed SVR. And we choose that divided the array of the parameter into 5 sub-space. In every sub-space, we set M = 10 and then realize the orthogonal design. Finally, we choose the best values as the initial population.

Step 3: Operate the map and compass operator. Calculate the velocity and update the position of each pigeon according to Eqs. (1)–(2). And the fitness is defined as the output of the MSVR. Put the initial population into MSVR to find the fitness of each pigeon and record the new best value. If Nc > Nc1max, go to step 5.

Step 4: If Nc < Nc1max, renew the count of iteration with Nc = Nc + 1 and return to Step 3.

Step 5: Execute the landmark operator. Calculate the fitness of each pigeon and rank the pigeons based on their fitness values. Half of the pigeons whose fitness values are worse will be abandoned. The other half is valuable for find the best pigeon. To expel influence of these better pigeon, we choose to continue to search between the range of activities about the half pigeons. So we find the center of the left half of the pigeons according to (3)–(4) as the temporary destination. The Remaining Pigeons will fly to the intermediate destination by adjusting their flying direction according to (5).

Step 6: Rank the pigeons according to their new updated fitness values and find the best value. If Nc > Nc2max, go to Step 10. Otherwise, renew the count of iteration with Nc = Nc + 1 and go to Step 6, next the number remaining pigeon are one-fourth the initial number of the pigeon. With the method, the number of the remaining pigeon is $\frac{1}{2^n}$ $(n = 1, 2, 3\ldots)$ of the initial number of the pigeon.

Step 7: Stop SOPIO and train SVM with the optimal parameters.

Step 8: Predict the flow of passengers and output the result. By analyzing the error, we find the best algorithm model and mathematic model.

3 Experiments

Data Description

Compared with data from other industries, there are a few features on bus IC card data: a lot of dirty data, obvious nonlinear trend on traffic flow in weekends, workdays and holidays, difference with the significance of geographical position, road structure and weather. The row data collected is on the weekdays of the last five months of the year 2014 in Guangzhou, Guangdong province. The everyday traffic data is from 10 am to 12 pm.

Index of Performance

By analyzing the mathematical statistics theory, this paper concludes three characteristic indexes as the criterions to appraise the performance of the mathematic and improved algorithm which are measures of the deviation between actual and predicted values. Root Mean Square Error (RMSE) and Mean Square Error which evaluate the absolute error and Mean relative error (MRE) which is the performance criteria of the relative error. The smaller values of these of these indexes, the more accurate are the result of the traffic flow prediction. The calculation formulas of these indexes are shown as Eqs. (14)–(16)

$$RMSE = \sqrt{\left[\frac{1}{n}\sum_{i=1}^{n}(|m_i - \hat{m}_i|)^2\right]} \quad (14)$$

$$MAE = \frac{1}{n}\sum_{i=1}^{n}\left|m_i - \hat{m}_i\right| \quad (15)$$

$$MRE = \frac{1}{n}\sum_{i=1}^{n}\frac{\left|m_i - \hat{m}_i\right|}{m_i} \quad (16)$$

where $\hat{m}_i$ is the predicted value of the traffic flow, and m_i is the experimented value of the Traffic flow. n represents the total number of the traffic data.

Experimental Environment
Original data volume has reached 4.5 G and we store data in a Mysql database. Data statistics have been carried out in SQL programming language. The visualization chart is conducted with Highcharts in Chrome Chrome. Numerical experiments and proposed algorithm have been implemented in Matlab programming language with a 1.8 GHz Core (TM) 4 CPU personal computer (PC) and 8.0 G memory under Microsoft Window7. We adopt the static forecasting method to prevent the deviation propagating forward, which means that the forecasting value of the traffic flow at $t + 1$ will use the real value at t instead of the forecasting value at t.

Results
The algorithm model needs to be compared with other algorithm models to show its good performance. But previous research focuses on less on the data handling techniques and have different data structures and data features. It is impossible to have a direct comparison on the results. Therefore, this paper uses the sample data operating on the existing methods. Figure 3 presents the output of the algorithm aiming at the former three models for the traffic flow prediction of the route 10 and also it has a comparison on the model predicted effect from the three characteristic indexes RMSE, MAE, MRE. Table show all the three error indexes: RMSE, MAE, MRE, can be used independently to evaluate a prediction model. To test the superiority of the SOPIO MSVM, PSO-SVM, BP Neural Network, GD-SVM, GA-SVM, PIO-SVM, ARMA algorithm is also apply to evaluate the advantages and disadvantages of these algorithms. In building these six modes, the *MSE* (Mean Squared Error) is used as the fitness function for these six algorithms. To reduce the influence of the parameter setting, the parameters of the PSO, DT, GA, SOPIO which are applied to optimize the parameters of the MSVR model should be treated as the same criteria, excepting the parameter is required to be determined specially.

The range of five parameters in the MSVR model are set as $C \in [0.01, 100]$, $\varepsilon \in [0.01, 1], \sigma \in [0.01, 1], \zeta \in [0.01, 10], d \in [0.01, 1]$. The population size *pop_size* is 30, The crossover validation fold is 5. The maximum iterations are defined as 300. Considering the randomness of the intelligent optimization algorithm, the former six algorithms are adopted to optimize the parameters of the mixed support vector machine for 10 times random, the prediction results are described and the best fitness is shown as Fig. 4 based on last 100 h's test data.

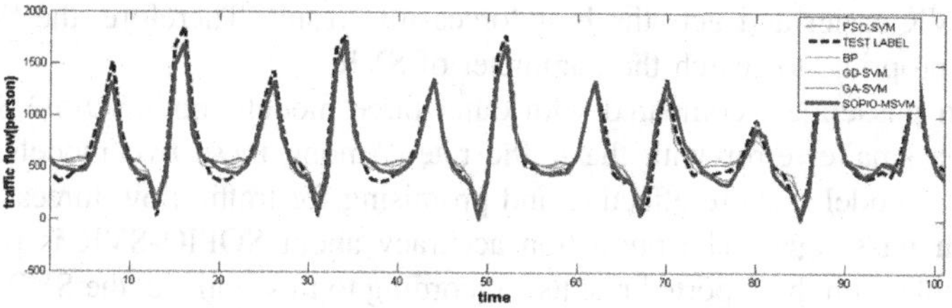

(a)

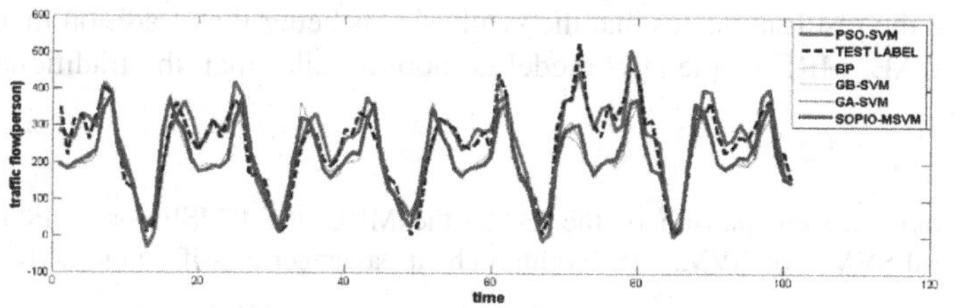

(b)

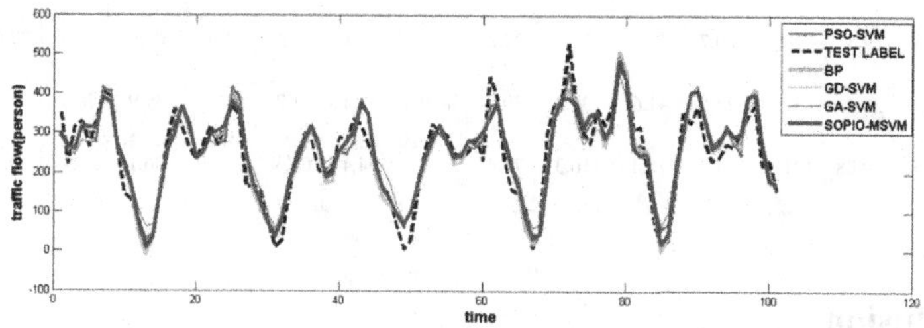

(c)

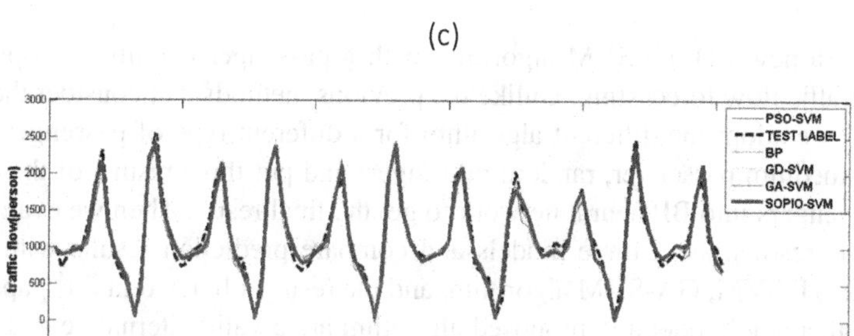

(d)

Fig. 4. Traffic flow prediction (a) Regular passenger. (b) Medium passenger. (c) Random passenger. (d) All passenger

From Table we can see that:

(1) **Regular passenger:** The performance of the SOPIO-SVR algorithm model are better than other four algorithms on the same condition. Also, it shows that the parameters resulting from PIO algorithm model make the parameter searching about SVR easier and gets the best forecasting result. Therefore, the SOPIO is more appropriate to search the parameter of SVR.
(2) **Medium passenger:** compared with other three models, both SOPIO-SVR and BP has a smaller error with the traffic rate. Among these two models, the BP algorithm model is more effective and promising for traffic flow forecasting.
(3) **Random passenger:** The prediction accuracy about SOPIO-SVR is promising comparable with the reported results. According to this statistic, the SVR with the mixed kernel is the best model for estimating the traffic flow.

The all traffic flow put the three passenger's traffic flow as an input of the BP neural network. And the result indicates that the synthesize is better than tradition model. And the RMSE, MAE, MRE of the new model is more Smaller than the traditional model (Table 2).

Table 2. Performance comparison of the MAE, the MRE, the RMSE for SOPIO-MSVM, PSO-SVM, Grid-SVM, GA-SVM, BP algorithm about passenger classification model

Task	SOPIO-MSVM			PSO-SVM			Grid-SVM			GA-SVM			BP		
	MAE	MRE	RMSE	MAE	MRE	RMSE	MAE	MRE	RMSE	MAE	MRE	RMSE	MAE	MRE	RMSE
Regular passenger	63.8	15.79	87.5	84.7	40.6	108.1	99.4	52.2	113.8	90.4	41.7	114.1	81.1	35.1	103.4
Medium passenger	21.5	29.5	28.7	20.7	27.7	28.7	22.2	56.0	27.1	22.0	31.9	27.9	27.3	32.6	36.8
Random passenger	25.9	30.4	37.4	27.5	41.6	36.2	30.6	44.0	38.4	31.2	54.6	39.9	28.6	33.2	38.2
Synthesize passenger	89.5	9.88	121.9	84.8	16.4	116.3	71.4	21.8	94.4	63.3	8.89	96.1	76.1	10.1	101.1

4 Conclusion

We propose a new SOPIO-SVM algorithm with a passenger classification prediction model for traffic flow forecasting. Unlike the previous methods that consider the overall traffic flow, we adopt the different algorithm for a different type of passenger (regular passenger, medium passenger, random passenger) and put three results of the different type of passengers into BP neural network to get the final result. Then we evaluated the effect on the results about three models and compare prediction results with the BP, PSO-SVM. GT-SVM, GA-SVM algorithm, and the results obtained in this paper reveal that the mathematic model and proposed algorithm are a valid alternative and superior to other mathematic models and algorithms under some circumstances.

For future work, it would be useful to search more appropriate methods to classify the passenger into different types and more appropriate parameter combination for SVR model. Also, we would try to apply the mathematic model and algorithm on different traffic data sets to validate the good or bad.

To sum up the conclusions we conducted as follows:

(1) Through the comparison with other the usual algorithms, the propose SOPIO-MSVR algorithm model is confirmed to have good performance on the traffic flow prediction.
(2) To find a proper pigeon inspired optimization for mixed support vector regression, the paper proposed sub-space division orthogonal design strategies to initialize the parameters as the basic PIO algorithm input which we called SOPIO-MSVM algorithm.

Acknowledgments. The research is supported by the NSFC (National Science Foundation of China) Projects (No. 61572057) in China, the National High-Tech Research and Development Plan of China under Grant No. 2015AA042101.

References

1. Pelletier, M.P., Trépanier, M., Morency, C.: Smart card data use in public transit: a literature review. Transp. Res. Part C: Emerging Technol. **19**(4), 557–568 (2011)
2. Zheng, X., Chen, W., Wang, P., et al.: Big data for social transportation. IEEE Trans. Intell. Transp. Syst. **17**(3), 620–630 (2016)
3. Min, Y.H., Ko, S.J., Kim, K.M., et al.: Mining missing train logs from Smart Card data. Transp. Res. Part C: Emerging Technol. **63**, 170–181 (2016)
4. Dimond, M., Smith, G., Goulding, J.: Improving route prediction through user journey detection. In: Proceedings of the 21st ACM SIGSPATIAL International Conference on Advances in Geographic Information Systems, pp. 476–479. ACM (2013)
5. Ma, X., Wu, Y.J., Wang, Y., et al.: Mining smart card data for transit riders' travel patterns. Transp. Res. Part C: Emerging Technol. **36**, 1–12 (2013)
6. Ferreira, N., Poco, J., Vo, H.T., et al.: Visual exploration of big spatio-temporal urban data: a study of New York city taxi trips. IEEE Trans. Vis. Comput. Graph. **19**(12), 2149–2158 (2013)
7. Jin, F., Sun, S.: Neural network multitask learning for traffic flow forecasting. In: 2008 IEEE International Joint Conference on Neural Networks (IEEE World Congress on Computational Intelligence), pp. 1897–1901. IEEE (2008)
8. Ma, Z., Xing, J., Mesbah, M., et al.: Predicting short-term bus passenger demand using a pattern hybrid approach. Transp. Res. Part C: Emerging Technol. **39**, 148–163 (2014)
9. Levin, M., Tsao, Y.-D.: On forecasting freeway occupancies and volumes. Transp. Res. Rec. **773**, 47–49 (1980)
10. van der Voort, M., Dougherty, M., Watson, S.: Combining Kohonen maps with ARIMA time series models to forecast traffic flow. Transp. Res. C Emerging Technol. **4**(5), 307–318 (1996)
11. Williams, B.M.: Multivariate vehicular traffic flow prediction—evaluation of ARIMAX modeling. Transp. Res. Rec. **1776**, 194–200 (2001)
12. Williams, B.M., Hoel, L.A.: Modeling and forecasting vehicular traffic flow as a seasonal ARIMA process: theoretical basis and empirical results. J. Transp. Eng. **129**(6), 664–672 (2003)
13. Ghosh, B., Basu, B., O'Mahony, M.: Multivariate short-term traffic flow forecasting using time-series analysis. IEEE Trans. Intell. Transp. Syst. **10**(2), 246–254 (2009)

14. Davis, G.A., Nihan, N.L.: Nonparametric regression and short-term reeway traffic forecasting. J. Transp. Eng. **117**(2), 178–188 (1991)
15. Sun, S., Zhang, C., Guoqiang, Y.: A Bayesian network approach to traffic flow forecasting. IEEE Intell. Transp. Syst. Mag. **7**(1), 124–132 (2006)
16. Jeong, Y.S., Byon, Y.J., Castro-Neto, M.M., Easa, S.M.: Supervised weighting-online learning algorithm for short-term traffic flow prediction. IEEE Trans. Intell. Transp. Syst. **14**(4), 1700–1707 (2013)
17. Zhong, M., Sharma, S., Lingras, P.: Short-term traffic prediction on different types of roads with genetically designed regression and time delay neural network models. J. Comput. Civil Eng. **19**(1), 94–103 (2005)
18. Zargari, S.A., Siabil, S.Z., Alavi, A.H., Gandomi, A.H.: A computational intelligence-based approach for short-term traffic flow prediction. Expert Syst. **29**(2), 124–142 (2012)
19. Chen, C., Wang, Y., Li, L., Hu, J., Zhang, Z.: The retrieval of intra-day trend and its influence on traffic prediction. Transp. Res. C Emerging Technol. **22**, 103–118 (2012)
20. Lippi, M., Bertini, M., Frasconi, P.: Short-term traffic flow forecasting: an experimental comparison of time-series analysis and supervised Dlearning. IEEE Trans. Intell. Transp. Syst. **14**(2), 871–882 (2013)
21. Van Hinsbergen, C.P., Van Lint, J.W., Sanders, F.M.: Short term traffic prediction models. Presented at the ITS World Congress, Beijing, China (2007)
22. Karlaftis, M.G., Vlahogianni, E.I.: Statistical methods versus neural networks in transportation research: differences, similarities and some insights. Transp. Res. Part C: Emerging Technol. **19**(3), 387–399 (2011)
23. Huang, W., Song, G., Hong, H., et al.: Deep architecture for traffic flow prediction: deep belief networks with multitask learning. IEEE Trans. Intell. Transp. Syst. **15**(5), 2191–2201 (2014)
24. Castro-Neto, M., Jeong, Y.-S., Jeong, M.-K., Han, L.D.: Online-SVR for short-term traffic flow prediction under typical and atypical traffic conditions. Expert Syst. Appl. **36**(3), 6164–6173 (2009)
25. Sun, S.: Traffic flow forecasting based on multitask ensemble learning. In: Proceedings of the 1st ACM/SIGEVO Summit Genetic Evolutionary Computation, pp. 961–964 (2009)
26. Cortes, C., Vapnik, V.: Support-vector networks. Mach. Learn. **20**(3), 273–297 (1995)
27. Meyer, D., Wien, F.H.T.: Support vector machines. The Interface to libsvm in package e1071 (2015)
28. Nieto, P.J.G., Garcia-Gonzalo, E., Lasheras, F.S., et al.: Hybrid PSO–SVM-based method for forecasting of the remaining useful life for aircraft engines and evaluation of its reliability. Reliab. Eng. Syst. Saf. **138**, 219–231 (2015)
29. Duan, H., Qiao, P.: Pigeon-inspired optimization: a new swarm intelligence optimizer for air robot path planning. Int. J. Intell. Comput. Cybern. **7**(1), 24–37 (2014)
30. Duan, H., Wang, X.: Echo state networks with orthogonal pigeon-inspired optimization for image restoration. IEEE Trans. Neural Netw. Learn. Syst. **27**, 2413–2425 (2016). doi:10.1109/TNNLS.2015.2479117
31. Zhang, B., Duan, H.: Three-dimensional path planning for uninhabited combat aerial vehicle based on predator-prey pigeon-inspired optimization in dynamic environment. IEEE/ACM Trans. Comput. Biol. Bioinform. **14**, 97–107 (2016). doi:10.1109/TCBB.2015.2443789
32. Li, C., Duan, H.: Target detection approach for UAVs via improved pigeon-inspired optimization and edge potential function. Aerosp. Sci. Technol. **39**, 352–360 (2014)
33. Dou, R., Duan, H.: Pigeon inspired optimization approach to model prediction control for unmanned air vehicle. Aircr. Eng. Aerosp. Technol. **88**(1), 108–116 (2016)
34. Wang, Y., Liu, H., Cai, Z., et al.: An orthogonal design based constrained evolutionary optimization algorithm. Eng. Optim. **39**(6), 715–736 (2007)

35. Li, M.W., Han, D.F., Wang, W.: Vessel traffic flow forecasting by RSVR with chaotic cloud simulated annealing genetic algorithm and KPCA. Neurocomputing **157**, 243–255 (2015)
36. Zhang, Y., Zhang, Y., Haghani, A.: A hybrid short-term traffic flow forecasting method based on spectral analysis and statistical volatility model. Transp. Res. Part C: Emerging Technol. **43**, 65–78 (2014)
37. Smits, G.F., Jordaan, E.M.: Improved SVM regression using mixtures of kernels. In: Proceedings of the 2002 International Joint Conference on Neural Networks, IJCNN 2002, vol. 3, pp. 2785–2790. IEEE (2002)

Workshop Multi-source Information IntelliSense Method Based on IPv6 Intelligent Terminal

Chao Yin[1], Zhengbing Pan[1], Xiaobin Li[2](✉), and Liang Li[3]

[1] State Key Laboratory of Mechanical Transmission, Chongqing University, Chongqing, China

[2] School of Economics and Business Administration, Chongqing University, Chongqing, China
xiaobin_lee@cqu.edu.cn

[3] Chongqing HITECH Information-Based Manufacturing Productivity Promotion Center Co. Ltd., Chongqing, China

Abstract. Aiming at currently problems that workshop information is multi-source heterogeneous, isolated and inefficient to interaction, the paper proposes a Workshop Multi-source Information IntelliSense method based on IPv6 Intelligent Terminal, and IPv6 Intelligent Terminal is taken as center, IPv6 protocol as the unified communications protocol of workshop, downward integrate Wireless Sensor Networks(WSN) to realize multi-source information IntelliSense and upward realize real-time, efficient interaction with PC. The method-related key technologies are studied, including implementation technology of plant-level IPv6 Intelligent Terminal and XML-based intelligent analysis and adaptation of workshop multi-source information. Finally, the effectiveness and practicality of the method are verified in a manufacturing plant.

Keywords: IPv6 · Intelligent terminal · Workshop multi-source information · IntelliSense

1 Introduction

Nowadays, Discrete manufacturing plant information is multi-source heterogeneous, isolated and, which results in the fact that efficient and real-time acquisition of workshop information is difficult, Exactly, the maturity of intelligent Terminal technology and the development of IPv6 in industry provide a solution.

At present, the domestic and foreign scholars have conducted some research on multi-source information acquisition and perception and many important research results are obtained. Wireless data acquisition technology of products production based on RFID has been studied, and product data acquisition system based on RFID has been design by C# programming [1]. It has been proved when RFID read-write device collect data in a label, precision rate of collected raw data flow is only 60–70% [2]. It has been concluded that there were four ways of data fusion which is centralized mode, distributed, hybrid and feedback mode [3, 4]. It has been studied that commonly there were

L. Zhang et al. (Eds.): Monterey Workshop 2016, LNCS 10228, pp. 198–208, 2017.
DOI: 10.1007/978-3-319-61994-1_18

two ways that data fusion within clusters and routing algorithms of data transmission between clusters for wireless sensor network data fusion method [5, 6]. Multithreaded synchronization technology and database aided design program have been used to get on-site real-time data collection at the scene of workshop [7]. The process model of production business and information flow model in discrete manufacturing enterprise workshop have been built [8], which also has studied the data collection methods of working condition, quality, material and tooling information in the process of production at discrete manufacturing plant; A template-based information collection method has been proposed, which realizes object-oriented approach to classified modeling of workshop information [9]. A design of IntelliSense system based on LOT architecture has been proposed, the system, which is a WSN based on ZigBee protocol, combines the embedded Linux, GPRS and Internet technology on ARM9 development platform to realize multi-source information transmission and interaction [10].

From what has been discussed above, domestic and foreign scholars have done many research on IntelliSense and collection of multi-source information, however research on applying IPv6 technology to workshop IntelliSense and collection of multi-source information is rare. Therefore, combines with existing research results, the paper proposes a Workshop Multi-source Information IntelliSense method based on IPv6 Intelligent Terminal, studied realization ideas of the method, the overall framework and key technologies including implementation technology of plant-level IPv6 Intelligent Terminal and XML-based intelligent analysis and adaptation of workshop multi-source information, and verified the effectiveness and practicality of the method in a manufacturing plant.

2 Workshop Multi-source Information IntelliSense Method Based on IPv6 Intelligent Terminal

2.1 Workshop Multi-source Information Attributes and Features

Production manufacturing process is a dynamic system with emerging and changing information, which causes the complexity of workshop multi-source information, as shown in Fig. 1.

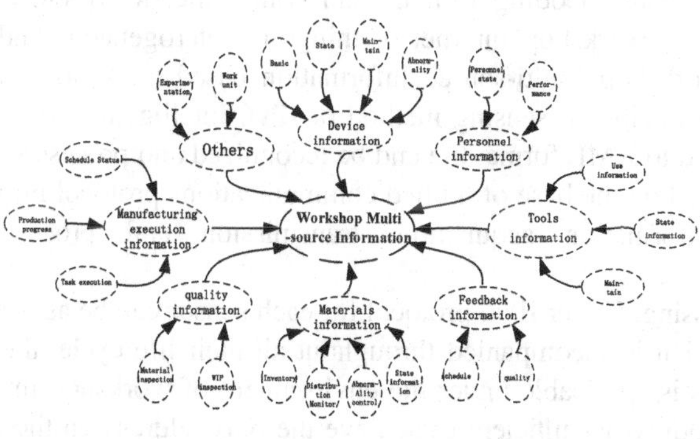

Fig. 1. Workshop Multi-source Information attributes and features.

According to the above Workshop Multi-source Information concept model analysis, we conclude that Workshop Multi-source Information is characterized in multi-source heterogeneity, indeterminacy, real-time change, Complexity, indeterminacy and integration, so the traditional Workshop Multi-source Information collection method is facing enormous challenges, manufacturers need a high efficiency, low power consumption, high real-time information processing and sensing systems, to meet market demand of agile manufacturing.

2.2 Implementation Idea

Currently, under the circumstances of lower IPv6 support rate of Intelligent Terminal equipment and the primary stage application of plant-level TCP/IP protocol, a gradual principle is needed to realize the industrial application of IPv6 Intelligent Terminal. By using dual stack technology, tunneling mechanism and protocol conversion technology to realize the coexistence and transformation of workshop level between IPv4 and IPv6.

Thus the implementation idea of the multi-source information intelligent sensing method based on IPv6 Intelligent Terminal is as follows: firstly using various types of sensors to manage WSN, each of which is equipped with an independent IP, and optimize WSN routing algorithms and data fusion algorithm, then the underlying multi-source information conversed by IPv6 router protocol and integrated process can be perceived by IPv6 Intelligent Terminal integrated wireless transceiver module, and be conversed to XML documents by XML configuration module, then be visually displayed, finally, Workers handheld terminals to make appropriate judgments and decisions for all kinds of information and do real-time interact with PC management side MES/ERP. Relevant process information will be uploaded wirelessly via the terminal or upper machine-position management side to a central server and be stored, thus reducing manufacturing costs, improve the efficiency and reliability of the plant information exchange, shortening the manufacturing cycle. This method implementation framework is shown in Fig. 2.

Compared with the traditional shop information acquisition method, the method has the following characteristics and advantages:

(1) Harmonized data encoding formats and communication protocols. Underlying information of workshop Internet of things is heterogeneous and complex correlation, Workshop Multi-source Information based on Workshop Multi-source Information intelligent sensing method of IPv6 Intelligent Terminal will be uniformly coded to XML format file and be recognized and processed, be transmitted and interacted on the base of unified communications protocol information. It can improve information acquisition, transmission and processing efficiency information.
(2) Easy addressing. Under IPv6 protocol for each sensor can be assigned a unique IP address, which is accompanied throughout all their life cycle, the entire production process is applicable under the environment of workshop internet of things, and IPv6 address is sufficient to achieve the only address on the entire network.

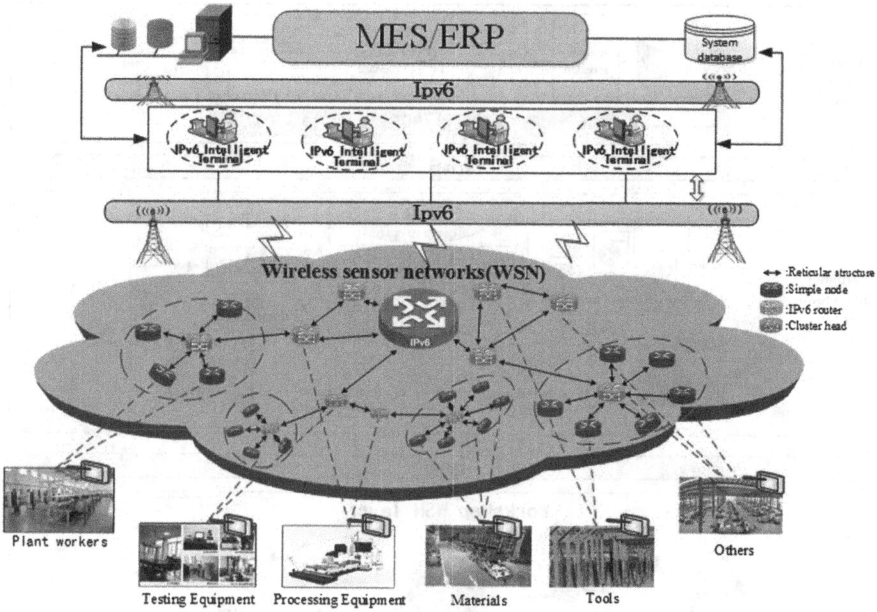

Fig. 2. Implement idea of the method.

(3) Efficient, fast and real-time interactive information. IPv6 Intelligent Terminal sets digital workshop production process flow card, quality test card, abnormal disposal card and electronic technology card of production process in one, it can realizes the functions– real-time collection of workshop internet of things bottom information, real-time control of production process, and real-time interaction of material quality equipment and other information.

(4) High security. WSN based on IPv6 protocol is securer, IPv6 network layer can achieve the functions of data denial of service attacks, against replay attacks, preventing passive or active data eavesdropping, and data theft attack. Therefore, it greatly enhances the security of wireless network workshop.

2.3 Overall Structure

To implement the method, we study the multi-source information intelligent sensing system based on IPv6 Intelligent Terminal. System architecture shown in Fig. 3:

The architecture includes information environment layer, IntelliSense layer, terminal interaction layer and management layer. Specifically described below:

(1) Environment layer: the layer consists of RFID reader, various types of sensors and monitoring equipment, including equipment information, material information, and so on multi-source information;

(2) IntelliSense layer: the layer makes up of WSN sensor nodes, which realize efficient data gathering between nodes and preliminary integration process by improving LEACH-c routing algorithms and data fusion algorithm;

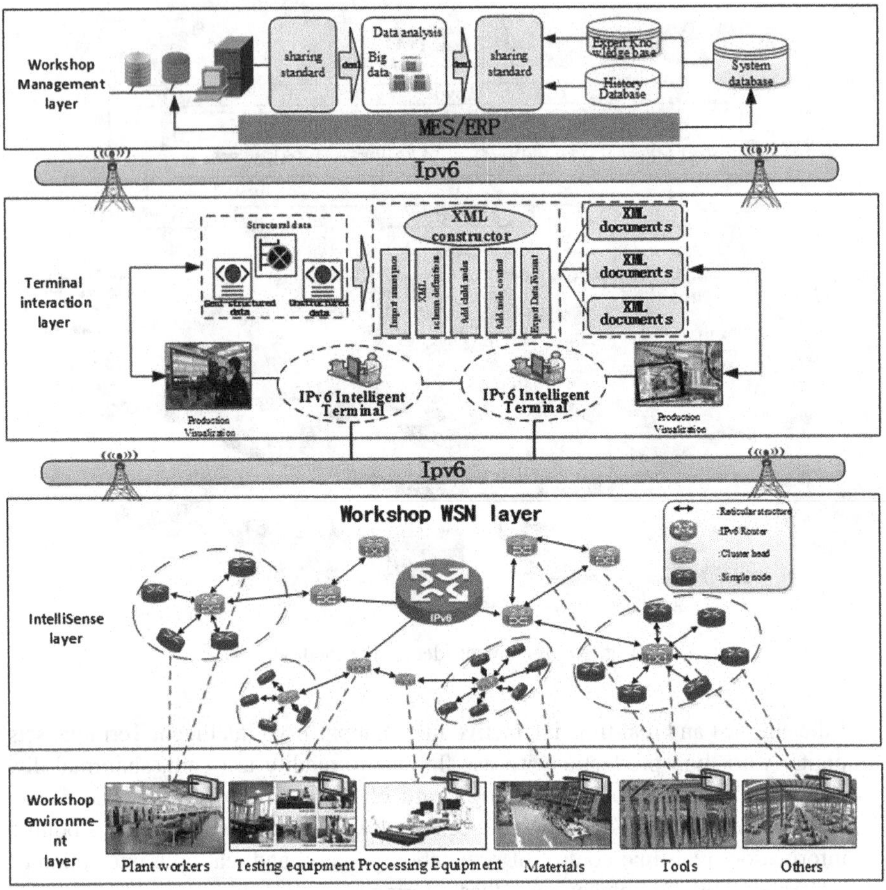

Fig. 3. Overall structure of the method.

(3) Terminal interaction layer: the layer's operation process: workers handheld IPv6 Intelligent Terminal obtaining information from industrial robot and NC equipment, and so on multi-source information. After extracting the original signal, the structure, semi- structure, non-structural data will be processed into exportable and visible XML document through integration of XML structure module;

(4) Management layer: PC side realizes data processing function of information modeling, template instantiation, the establishment of information sharing standards and data analysis etc. Finally realizes efficient information interoperability between the underlying multi-source information, production management systems, shop managers.

3 Key Technology Research

3.1 Plan-Level IPv6 Intelligent Terminal Implementation Technology

The proposed IPv6 Intelligent Terminal is an integration equipment of software and hardware, composed by plate device level, SoC devices, internal bus, processor, memory, information adapter and so on module, which can realize IntelliSense of Workshop Multi-source Information based on IPv6 protocol, real-time monitoring of manufacturing process, dynamic optimization of production process and equipment maintenance. Advantages of the terminal are as follows:

(1) Independent terminal, obtaining information exchange with the plane management system through wireless communication;
(2) Fast response, short response time, stable work, high confidentiality of information;
(3) Low-power consumption, and can work in harsh environment in the workshop.

• Design of Software and hardware structure of plant-level IPv6 Intelligent Terminal

Based on IPv6 communication protocol, workshop Intelligent Terminal provides rich data interface such as serial bus interface, Ethernet interface, communication conversion interface and man-machine interface in which man-machine interface is composed of LCD module and keyboard module [10]. Based on RFID and wireless transceiver module, the terminal is integrated XML information adapter to adapt to the workshop networking environment, and safe Workshop Multi-source Information acquisition and interactive. The hardware structure is as follows in Fig. 4:

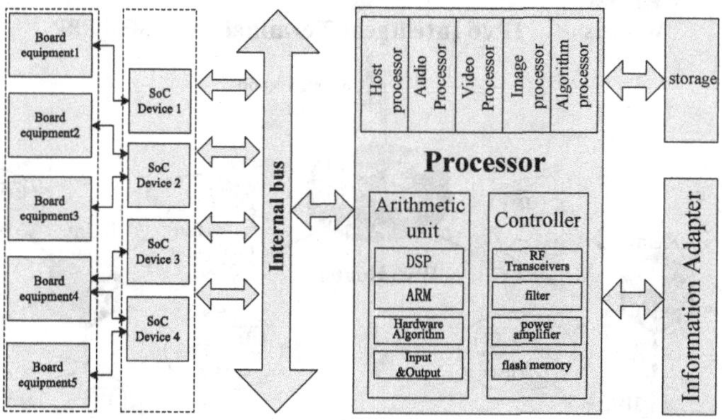

Fig. 4. Hardware structure of plant-level IPv6 Intelligent Terminal

Based on the above hardware architecture, the workshop level IPv6 Intelligent Terminal application software system is developed by java development tools. Software system structure is constituted by the operating system, middleware, application platform and security components. The management platform and Intelligent Terminal use B/S architecture; the network layer and transport layer use IPv4/IPv6 protocol. The interactive terminal provides users access to the browser to access the web server resources to achieve information sharing and interaction.

- The integration of workshop IPv6 Intelligent Terminal and sensor

Based on ZigBee and wireless network communication protocol, traditional Intelligent Terminal can obtain the information interaction between shop floor information acquisition and computer management, which only is used in a short distance and not suitable for high complexity network. In this paper, based on workshop class Intelligent Terminal with IPV6 protocol for the whole network unified communication protocol, the IPv6 technology has multiple advantages to solve the above problems. When the sensor network nodes, which extensive layout in workshop processing equipment, testing equipment and materials, gather real-time multi-source information of workshop, the information is transported to the IPv6 Route - integrated gateway module to complete conversion between the routing protocol and IPv6 protocol-through routing protocol and then the processed information, which is a uniform data format, is transmitted to IPv6 Intelligent Terminal through wireless network to obtain the function of network node information capture and perception of the underlying sensor of terminal and the result is transmitted to first seat management. The integration schematic of shop floor IPv6 Intelligent Terminal and the underlying sensor is shown in Fig. 5:

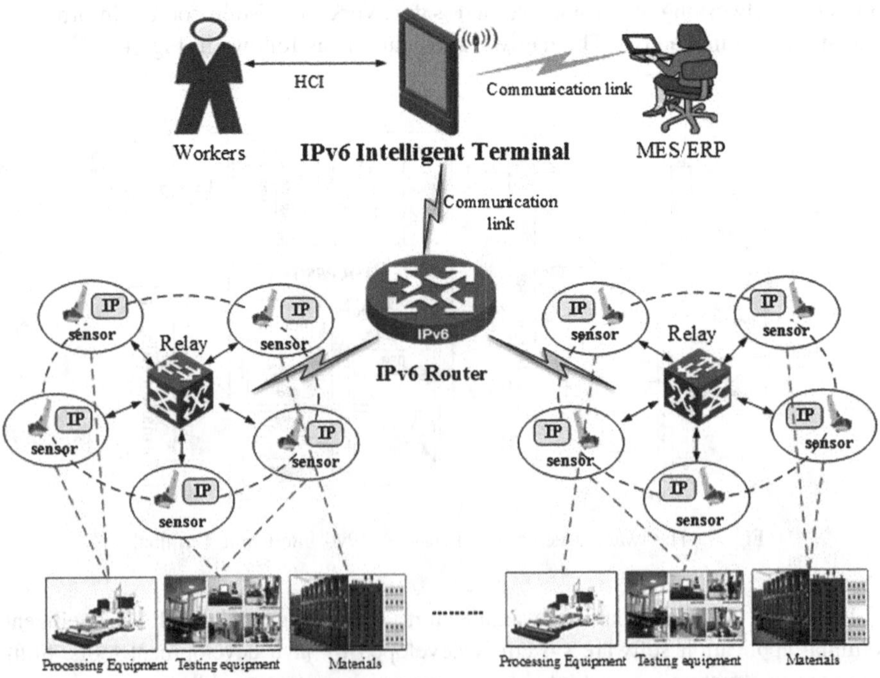

Fig. 5. Integration frame of workshop IPv6 Intelligent Terminal and sensor

3.2 Intelligent Analysis and Adaptation Technology of Workshop Multi-source Information Based on XML

According to the requirements of the B2MML specification, based on XML technology, defines the analytical model in workshop multi-source information. the model implements an information analytical management service function for workshop multi-source information, including processing information analysis, process information analysis, the quality of information analysis and inventory information analysis and so on. The implementation scheme as shown in figure X, based on SOAP transmission protocol, the system defines an integrated service model and a configurable implementation environment based on parser, implemented based on the information parser pluggable integration in workshop multi-source information; The Workshop Multi-source Information collected by the system include: processing information, quality information, process information, stock information is subscribed to the template library. In a configurable analytic environment, the system template library makes subscription information automatically sort into the appropriate module, and through the SOAP parser for intelligent parsing the incoming information. Analytical data via the SOAP into intelligent adapter conduct intelligent information matching with workshop application service. After SOAP information interaction based on event-driven, the matching results are stored in the workshop of multi-source information database, and, through soap subscription and publishing system feedback information, they are used to improve the product structure design, process design, production resource scheduling of production task. The information transmission of whole intelligent parsing and matching process is reversible.

Workshop production data has the characteristics of real-time and massive, the post-processing information of intelligent parsed is intelligent matching database of system information. By using SOA and modular, Adapter model based on digital production is proposed and designed in this paper to realize intelligent adaptation of multi-source information in workshop, which supports for intelligent data analysis, extraction and optimization. The adapter model includes progress information adapter model, quality information adapter model, process parameter adapter model and process information adapter model, et al. Figure 6 is structure diagram of the adapter which supports the multi-source information intelligent processing. After the system sends a request for automatic or manual application, the adapter database was transmitted into processing data adapter model and processed. The adapter model can realize service function management, secure transmission management, message monitoring distribution, algorithm management, event management, connection management, et al. Based on the types and characteristics of information source, adapter information source access device intelligently matches and links source data and MES system application services through the algorithm model, thus realizing intelligent adaptation management of multi-source information in workshop.

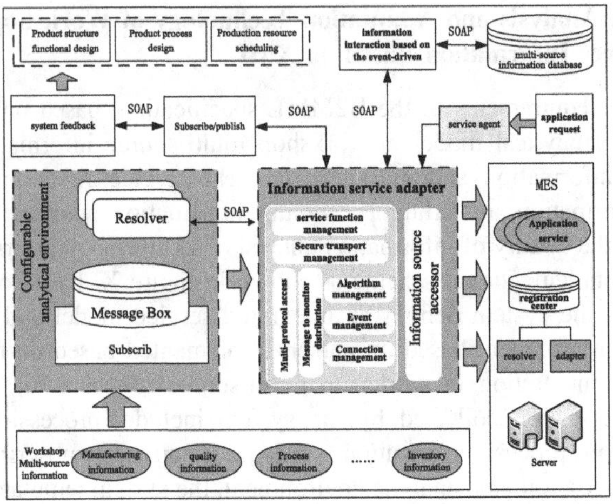

Fig. 6. Intelligent analysis and adaptation technology of Workshop Multi-source Information based on XML

4 Preliminary Experiments

Based on the above findings preliminary studies, our group carried out design and development of the original configurable information collection system, having built Workshop Multi-source Information IntelliSense method prototype system based on IPv6 Intelligent Terminal, which were deployed at a machine shop in Chongqing University Institute of manufacturing engineering, and completed the preliminary application verification of the method mentioned. As shown in Fig. 7. In the following papers, experimental verification process is discussed through multi-source information IntelliSense of machine shop clutch production process.

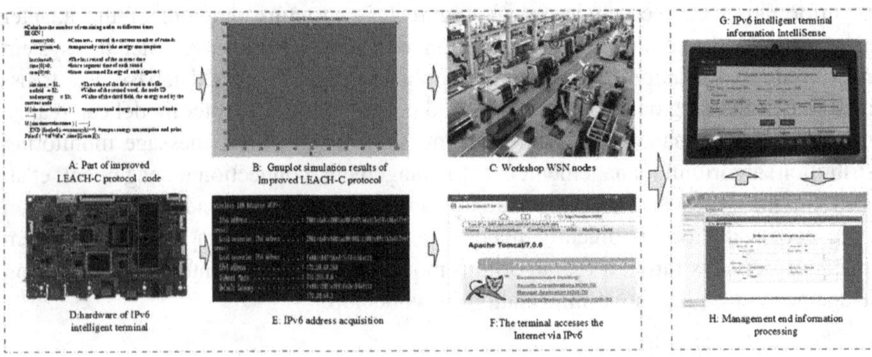

Fig. 7. Experimental verification process legends

(1) WSN optimization. Because of characteristics in the workshop such us highly-discrete equipment, intensive staff, dynamically changed processing tasks, based on an improved LEACH-C routing algorithm, we chose Jiangsu Link sensor to arranged a large number of sensor network nodes in the shop floor processing equipment, special tools, test equipment, and other materials, forming the underlying WSN, as shown in Fig. 7 (A: routing algorithm MATLAB code, B: the algorithm Simulation results, C: WSN nodes);
(2) Application of IPv6 Intelligent Terminal. Plant-level IPv6 terminal access via IPv6 support required proficiency test, our group improved Shenzhou PCpad to Plant-level IPv6 Intelligent Terminal prototype (IntelliPCpad). The test environment: Layer 3 Switch that supports IPv4/IPv6 dual protocol connects to CNGI/CSTNET network and publish the IPv6 prefix advertisements, Then, the IPv6 router connects to layer 3 Switch and connects to the IPv6 network through IPv6 transparent transmission. Later, IntelliPCpad opens Wi-Fi to connect IPv6/ipv4 network, as shown in Fig. 7 (D: hardware of IPv6 Intelligent Terminal, E: IPv6 address acquisition, F: The terminal access the Internet via IPv6);
(3) Multi-source Information access by IPv6 Intelligent Terminal and interaction between IPv6 Intelligent Terminal and management end. Describe IntelliPCpad information acquisition and processing as well as IntelliPCpad interaction with MES by IntelliSense Clutch production process material information, process information, as shown in Fig. 7 (G: IPv6 Intelligent Terminal information IntelliSense H: Management end information processing).

Through the above test, our group initially realized multi-source information IntelliSense and adaptation of clutch production process in IPv6 environment. Preliminarily test the validity of the method proposed, which also provides some technical support for the workshop production management of IPv6 environment.

5 Conclusions and Future Work

A Workshop Multi-source Information IntelliSense method based on IPv6 Intelligent Terminal is proposed, besides, we study technology roadmap, implementation idea and overall architecture of the method and key technologies including the implementation technique of IPv6 at workshop level and intelligent parsing and adaptation of multi-source information. The case given preliminarily validates the validity and practicality of proposed method. Groundbreaking works of the paper are as follows:

(1) The plant-level IPv6 Intelligent Terminal is designed and applied to manufacturing workshop successfully. The ability of information acquisition and management in workshop is improved rapidly by varieties of advantages of IPv6 Intelligent Terminals, such as portability, low power consumption, high response speed, stable work, information confidentiality and so on.
(2) A series of problems such as information is multi-source heterogeneous, isolated, inefficient in current workshop are solved by the method mentioned above which is based on XML specification language and IPv6 protocol.

To improve the method, our group will be focused on WSN security and maintenance policies based on IPv6, workshop production monitor and control system of workshop, which are all.

Acknowledgment. This work was supported by the National High-Tech. R&D Program, China. (No. 2015AA043801), and the Science and Technology Program of Guangdong Province (No. 2015A010103022).

References

1. Rongsong, H., Lilan, L., Tao, Y.: Research on a RFID-based wireless acquisition technology for production state data. Mod. Manuf. Eng. **1**(7), 113–117 (2012)
2. He, L., Zhang, Z., Tan, Y., et al.: An efficient data cleaning algorithm based on attributes selection. In: 2011 6th International Conference on Computer Sciences and Convergence Information Technology (ICCIT), pp. 375–379. IEEE (2011)
3. Zhang, J., Yan, Q., Zhai, L.: Multi-source remote sensing data fusion: status and trends. Int. J. Image Data Fusion **1**(1), 5–24 (2010)
4. Krishna, M.B., Vashishta, N.: Energy Efficient Data Aggregation Techniques in Wireless Sensor Networks. In: 2013 5th International Conference on IEEE Computational Intelligence and Communication Networks (CICN), pp. 160–165 (2013)
5. Wu, Y., Li, X.Y., Liu, Y.H., et al.: Energy-efficient wake-up scheduling for data collection and aggregation. IEEE Trans. Parallel Distrib. Syst. **21**(2), 275–287 (2010)
6. Yue, J., Zhang, W., Xiao, W., et al.:A novel cluster-based data fusion algorithm for wireless sensor networks. In: 2011 7th International Conference on Wireless Communications, Networking and Mobile Computing (WiCOM), pp. 1–5. IEEE (2011)
7. Luo, G., Liu, H., Jiang, Z.: The research and design of the real time data acquisition system based on RFID. Manuf. Autom. **37**(11), 135–140 (2015)
8. Jiwei, L., Schuan, Y.C.: Information Acquisition and Methods Reseach of MES in Production Process in Discrete Manufacturing Workshop. ChongQing University (2011)
9. Hai, T., Tao, H., Lin, B., et al.: Design of an intelligence system based on Internet of things. Exp. Technol. Manag. **30**(7), 103–108 (2013)
10. Yue, W., Li, X.: Research on technical architecture model of mobile intelligent terminal. Mod. Sci. Technol. Telecommun. **6**(6), 13–23 (2013)

Author Index

Astesiano, Egidio 168

Bi, Xiaoqiang 99

Cheng, Xuejun 184
Cui, Jin 184
Cui, Yapeng 122

Dai, Yun 55
Dou, Lei 99
Du, Yi 11, 37

Feng, Yu 139
Fu, Jianhui 55

Hu, Yanjuan 131
Huang, Biqing 139
Huang, Xiaoting 99
Huang, Yan 77

Jia, Zhiping 43
Ju, Lei 43

Kim, Jae Kwon 3

Laili, Yuanjun 155
Lee, Jong Sik 3
Lee, Kang Sun 3
Leotta, Maurizio 168
Li, Feng 43
Li, Jianhui 11
Li, Liang 111, 198
Li, Xiao-bin 66, 111, 198
Li, Xin 99
Li, Yanfeng 77
Liu, Huan 25
Liu, Jiayi 25
Liu, Jie 155
Lyu, Fei 37

Ma, Cuixia 77

Pan, Zhengbing 198
Pham, Duc Truong 25, 87

Qiao, Lihong 122
Qie, Yifan 122
Qin, Jian 99
Qiu, Lei 66
Qu, Haitao 99

Reggio, Gianna 168
Ren, Lei 11, 37, 184
Ren, Luquan 131
Ricca, Filippo 168

Sheng, Victor S. 155

Wang, Chunhui 43
Wang, Dongsheng 55
Wang, Shi 55
Wang, Weiming 55
Wang, Yao 131
Wu, Qianhui 139

Xu, Wenjun 25, 87

Yang, Yun 111
Yin, Chao 66, 111, 198
Yu, Chongsheng 99

Zhang, Lin 87, 155
Zhang, Yan 77
Zhang, Yu 99
Zhang, Zhiqiang 184
Zhao, Hongwei 131
Zhao, Yuanyuan 87
Zhong, Xin 87
Zhou, Ti 77
Zhou, Yuanchun 11
Zhou, Zude 25, 87

Printed in the United States
By Bookmasters